Marxist Introductions

General Editor
Steven Lukes

Marxism and International Relations

V. KUBÁLKOVÁ AND A. A. CRUICKSHANK

Oxford   New York
OXFORD UNIVERSITY PRESS
1989

Oxford University Press, Walton Street, Oxford OX2 6DP

Oxford New York Toronto
Delhi Bombay Calcutta Madras Karachi
Petaling Jaya Singapore Hong Kong Tokyo
Nairobi Dar es Salaam Cape Town
Melbourne Auckland

and associated companies in
Berlin Ibadan

Oxford is a trade mark of Oxford University Press

First published 1985 by Oxford University Press
First issued (with a new Preface, Postscript, and
Bibliographical Supplement) as an Oxford University Press paperback 1989

British Library Cataloguing in Publication Data
Kubálková, V. (Vendulka)
Marxism and international relations –
(Marxist introductions)
1. Foreign relations. Marxist theories
I. Title   II. Series
327.1'01
ISBN 0–19–282615–8

Library of Congress Cataloging in Publication Data
Kubálková, V.
Marxism and international relations / V. Kubálková and A. A. Cruickshank.
   p.   cm.
''First published in 1985 by Oxford University Press''—T.p. verso.
Bibliography: p.   Includes index.
1. Communism and international relations.   I. Cruickshank, A. A.
II. Title.
HX550.I5K79   1989   327—dc19   88–32214
ISBN 0–19–282615–8

Printed in Great Britain by
Richard Clay Ltd.
Bungay, Suffolk

For our daughter Maruska (Mishi)

Acknowledgements

Our thanks go to Professor P. A. Reynolds, the Vice-Chancellor of the University of Lancaster who made most helpful detailed comments on many chapters of this manuscript as well as for the years of his friendship and support. Professor Hedley Bull of Balliol College, Oxford was to a large extent responsible for our undertaking the project in the first place. He, too, very kindly read the manuscript and helped considerably in the final conception of the book. Leon Moo, the research assistant, prepared the map and generally rendered most valuable and painstaking service in all matters to do with the completion of the manuscript. His assistance was particularly valuable in the tracking down of literally hundreds of articles and books that had to be studied in the writing of the book.

The views expressed, and of course any mistakes are ours and we are fully responsible for them.

Cleveland Point, 1984

Preface to the Paperback Edition

The new Postscript to the paperback edition (pp. 249–62) unfortunately allows only a sketching of the changes to 'Marxism and International Relations' that have taken place since the writing of the book around 1983. A hundred years after Marx's death 'Marxism and International Relations' has suddenly become a legitimate, even fashionable subject of academic enquiry. Indeed the Western, essentially Anglo-American, discipline of International Relations now boasts its own, long overdue, Marxist left wing. Where in Chapter 10 in which we covered theories of imperialism, of dependency, of World System, or of Cold War, these had to be culled from *outwith* the discipline, there now has to be added the work of 'Marxist Professors of International Relations' such as American Richard Ashley, Canadian R. W. Cox, and British John Maclean to name only three.

The reasons for *Marxism's* entry in the eighties into the field of International Relations are not easy to discern. Certainly its 'migration' from continental Europe to English-speaking countries generally recognized as the most backward in Marxist culture but the most advanced in International Relations studies, is quite in conformity with Marxism's traditional migratory habits. In its new home Perry Anderson's claim that Marxism as a critical theory has experienced an 'unprecedented ascent' (Anderson, 1983, 19, 24, 30[1]) would appear to be borne out by the extent to which it has provided the inspiration for a new Marxist 'critical approach' to International Relations studies.

The academic rise of critical theory evidently took place against the backdrop of developments in International Relations themselves, developments that affected Marxist thinking on International Relations not only in the West but world-wide. Mounting political, military, economic, and ecological problems across the globe have forced those Marxists previously inclined to underestimate the conceptual and political importance of International Relations to

---

[1] See also M. Burawoy, 'Introduction: The Resurgency of Marxism in American Sociology', *American Journal of Sociology*, Vol. 88, Supplement 1982, S5 ff.; R. Aronson, 'Historical Materialism, Answer to Marxism's Crisis', *New Left Review* 152, July–August, 1985, 76; B. Ollman and E. Vernoff (eds.), *The Left Academy: Marxist Scholarship on American Campuses*, New York, 1982, 137.

rethink these attitudes, and that in particular to the notion of peace.

In Table 1 (pp. 254–5) in an addendum to Chapter 10 we show the range of sources on which the Western critical Marxist approach draws and we attempt to delineate the major themes so far pursued by its protagonists. As an addendum to Chapter 3 we outline the main points of Soviet 'New Thinking' that were adopted in 1986 at the 27th CPSU Congress as the Soviets' new state ideology, and we refer to the modifications to International Relations of 1987–8 made in the Chinese Three World Theory as an addendum to Chapter 4. The stress in Soviet 'New Thinking' on the importance of International Law and International Organization should be read as a supplement to Chapter 8. In light of these developments, Chapter 9 on Gramsci would now seem to claim a place at centre stage, for not only do some of the most promising theoretical avenues in the critical International Relations approach open with an application of his conceptualizations, but Soviet 'New Thinking' itself can in our view lend itself to interpretation through Gramsci's concepts as a strategy of Gramscian anti-hegemony. 'New Thinking' then becomes a product of the nascent anti-nuclear 'historical bloc' in the formation of which a weakening Soviet superpower would seek to assert an intellectual ascendancy.

There is of course the argument that no addenda to the book is necessary: simply put, that International Relations, assumed to be 'intractable' to Marxists, did in the end defy them. And its equally simplistic conclusions: first, Soviet Marxism-Leninism (assuming that ever to have been Marxism) in order to make any sense of contemporary International Relations was obliged to draw so extensively on non-Marxist sources that 'New Thinking' is Marxism *no longer*. And second, the assertion of having '*transcended*' Marxism that most 'Marxist Professors of International Relations' offer in support of their claim to have ceased to be Marxist.

It is within the context of the book that has as a main purpose an accounting of the many interwoven strands of Marxist approaches to International Relations in the last hundred years that any such argument that implies a sudden demise of Marxism seems far-fetched.

Graduate School of International Studies
University of Miami, Florida, 1988

Contents

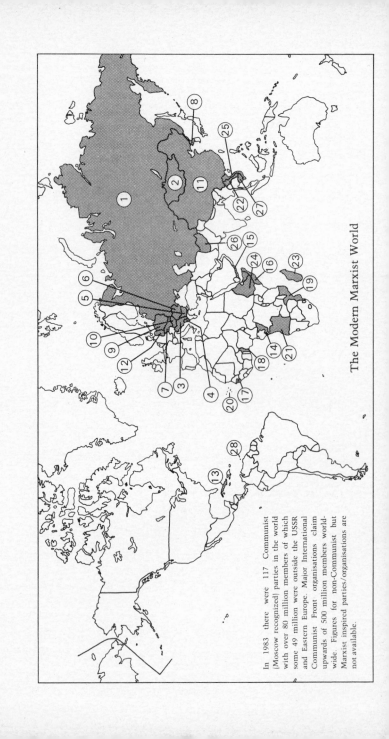

The Modern Marxist World

In 1983 there were 117 Communist [Moscow recognized] parties in the world with over 80 million members of which some 49 million were outside the USSR and Eastern Europe. Major International Communist Front organisations claim upwards of 500 million members world-wide. Figures for non-Communist but Marxist inspired parties/organisations are not available.

	Country	Est. Date of Marxist Regime
1	Union of Soviet Socialist Republics	1917, 25 October
2	Mongolian People's Republic	1924, 26 November
3	Federal Republic of Yugoslavia	1945, 29 November
4	People's Republic of Albania	1946, 11 January
5	Bulgarian People's Republic	1947, 4 December
6	Romanian People's Republic	1947, 30 December
7	Czechoslovak People's Republic	1948, 25 February
8	Democratic People's Republic of Korea	1948, 9 September
9	Polish People's Republic	1948, 14 December
10	Hungarian People's Republic	1949, 18 August
11	People's Republic of China	1949, 1 October
12	German Democratic Republic	1949, 7 October
13	Republic of Cuba	1959, 2 January
14	The Republic of the Congo	1963, 15 August
15	People's Republic of South Yemen	1967, 30 November
16	Somali Democratic Republic	1970, 20 October
17	Republic of Guinea-Bissau	

	Country	Est. Date of Marxist Regime
18	Republic of Dahomey (Benin)	1974, 30 November
19	People's Republic of Mozambique	1975, 25 June
20	Republic of Cape Verde	1975, 5 July
21	People's Republic of Angola	1975, 11 November
22	Lao People's Democratic Republic	1975, 2 December
23	Malagasy Republic (Madagascar)	1975, 30 December
24	Socialist Ethiopia	1976, 20 April
25	Socialist Republic of Vietnam (Earlier: Democratic Republic of Vietnam)	1976, 2 July
26	Democratic Republic of Afghanistan	1945, 2 September
27	People's Republic of Kampuchea (Earlier: Royal Government of National Union of Kampuchea)	1978, 27 April 1979, 7 January
28	People's Revolutionary Government of Grenada	1975, 17 April 1979, 13 March (until its overthrow in October 1983)

1 Introduction

Marxism and international relations, as topics, do not blend easily. The discipline of International Relations[1] is frank in its recognition of the fact, and Martin Wight, for one, makes his point unequivocally: 'Neither Marx, Lenin, nor Stalin made any systematic contribution to international theory; Lenin's *Imperialism* comes nearest to such a thing and this has little to say about international politics.' He goes further, averring that these Marxist revolutionary political theories attempt 'to reconstitute that older political phenomenon, a universal church of true believers', which makes 'the realm of the diplomatic system and sovereign states and international law . . . necessarily irrelevant, transitory, trivial, and doomed to pass away'. Wight continues; 'the absence of Marxist international theory has a wider importance than making it difficult to recommend reading to an undergraduate . . . It creates obscurity, so fruitful to the Communists themselves . . . so that only an expert sovietologist can usefully discuss what Lenin really said (and where) . . . and how this doctrine has been revised. . . .' (Wight, 1966, 25).

So it is that whilst we find, as the three philosophical traditions of International Relations studies, the Hobbesian (realist), the Grotian (internationalist), and the Kantian (universalist) (Bull, 1977), there is no Marxian nor Marxist. The implications are clear. It means that the ideas that generated and set in motion the international political movements and fashioned the Marxist/Communist states (movements and states that together are estimated to have affected in various ways half of mankind), in so far as they can be seen to constitute theories of international relations, should be styled

[1] Throughout this book we shall try to distinguish between International Relations as a discipline and international relations in the real world by the use of capitals and lower case respectively. Rather than becoming embroiled in definitional argument concerning the precise content of International Relations as subject we will use as a point of reference only those of the many perspectives and concerns of Western studies of International Relations which we outline on pp. 18–24.

not Marxist but Kantian—Kantian tradition being closest and the one into which Marxism can be made most easily to fit. In fairness to International Relations analysts, however, there is another side to the story. R. N. Berki in a seminal article on the subject (Berki, 1971) points out that intellectually international relations may be intractable for Marxism, and indeed, despite both the discipline of International Relations and that of Marxism being by definition 'internationalist', international relations can be made to fit into the Marxist intellectual structures only with difficulty.

The problem is probably not as simple as Wight would have it when he concludes that Marxism or Communism is a 'theory of domestic society . . . [which] has been tugged about and cut about to cover a much wider range of political circumstances than it was designed for' (Wight, 1966, 25). In the following introductory comments we shall try to elaborate and explain some of the truly incredible divergencies between Marxism and International Relations. In the process we introduce the distinction between the Marxism of political movements and states—that is to say in its role as political ideology—on the one hand, and 'academic', largely Western, Marxism on the other. There follows an attempt to locate international relations first within the Marxist intellectual structure and, second, within the context of the Western social sciences. Finally, we seek to place Marxism within the three philosophical traditions of the discipline of International Relations.

International relations, 'Communism' and Marxism

Mostly joined now only in their use of the same Marxist parlance, Marxists across the globe and spanning decades have ceased long ago to bruit the same message. To a large extent 'true' Marxism exists now only in the eye of the beholder and the approach that we intend to adopt, namely to consider to be Marxist anyone who believes himself so entitled, may be expected to kindle ire in the eye of many an individual beholder. Our approach derives from our belief that Marxism will no more 'go away' (through perhaps neglect on the part of International Relations specialists) than will international communism or other arguable Marxist variants cease to claim to be Marxist (by dint, for example, of the force of Western Marxist debate).

We are of course aware that to many Western Marxists Engels, Lenin, Stalin, Mao, Tito, and the two communist giant states are no longer Marxist; that their inclusion (particularly in the case of Stalinism) in Kolakowski's trilogy (Kolakowski, 1981), for example, arouses an emotional response in some Marxists (Miliband, 1981, Kolakowski, 1981a). Indeed, for a non-Marxist or lapsed Marxist it is difficult to estimate the relative seriousness of 'sin' (degree of 'revisionism') and its effect on the integrity of Marxism. Which indeed is the more culpable: the escape from practice on the part of many Western Marxists when in their new found university homes they became isolated from socialist movements; or the escape from theory on the part of such political movements as went too far in the subordination of their Marxism to the pursuit of (world) political goals? Marxism of these two varieties, in their enormous theoretical and practical political range, constitutes in our view one of the most potent forces known to history. Our purpose here is not to pronounce on the respective merits and integrity of the variants but to focus on their combined erosive effect on international relations—and in turn on the effect of the realities of international relations on their respective doctrines.

Whilst such comment as we have so far made as to the *theoretical* difficulties that international relations present for Marxism apply equally to Marxists of every hue, political movements inspired by Marxism did not find it difficult to accommodate international relations *in practice*, so international relations turns out to be yet another area in which Marx's predictions were to prove incorrect. In recognizing the error of Marx's expectation that class struggle already in that century would absorb nationalism and eclipse international system as the main element(s) of world politics, we have to remember that the nineteenth-century development that led to this particular error was one in which tensions, injustices, and social and political turmoil stemmed mainly from internal as opposed to external contradictions of capital. The situation has since reversed itself—it now would appear that peace and the survival of nations can be seen even in theory to be prior to traditional Marxist (domestic) concerns.

As we have implied, it would seem that on international relations Marxists after Marx have become sharply divided—along lines that coincide to a large extent on the one hand with 'applied' (Communist) political movements and, on the other, with the theoretical (Western Marxist) variety. The Marxist-based political movements—with perhaps the sole exception of the Trotskyists—have come to participate in, and even to embrace, much of the framework that they were to be instrumental in eclipsing, such as state, sovereignty, nationalism, international law, diplomacy, international organizations, and war. Their theories of international relations are studded with concepts that to Marx would appear contradictions in terms: socialism in one country, socialist state, all-people state, right of national self-determination, socialist international law, peaceful coexistence of states with different socio-economic systems (in Soviet theory), nation-class (Li Ta-chao and Mao), peaceful coexistence (Chinese and Yugoslav), 'fraternal diplomacy' (of the Eurocommunists), the nationalisms (of all), socialist 'non-alignment' (Yugoslav and Cuban), 'fraternal aid', or 'struggle against counter-revolution or revisionism' (as code words for acts of aggression and wars amongst socialist states). Needless to say, to Marx the suggestion of mutual accommodation of two sets of irreconcilable principles, namely those on which the states-system rests and those that the international communist movement was to adopt, would have seemed little short of madness! Nor did the Western Marxists, though mainly located in those parts of the world where Marxist revolutions failed, escape the effects of international relations. Far distanced from political militancy and bereft of any international horizon it was in fact not only their theory which 'gradually contracted into national compartments' (Anderson, 1976, 69), but with it the whole universe as, like Marx a century earlier, many Western Marxists continued (and continue) to construe their 'problematics' as domestic theory.

Thus in real terms the impact on Marxism of the existence both of nation(s) and of international system has been considerable. The characteristic feature of most Marxist political movements has been a fierce nationalism and consequent emotional attachment to states and relations among them, with the notion of world society implied in Marx's rejection of divisions into classes and states quietly shelved. In contrast, a characteristic of many Western Marxists has been their introspective state-centrism and neglect, if not disdain for international relations. Thus, with a number of exceptions (such as the world-system and dependency approaches which in their placement of emphasis on the world as a whole over its parts under-scores, however differently, international relations), most Marxists have become ensnared in one way or another in those areas most neglected in their theory: nationalism (cf. Nairn, 1975, 1977) and international relations.

International relations within the context of Marxism

Marxism is not only a messianic political ideology but also a comprehensive intellectual structure encompassing in one broad sweep virtually all of the themes of the social sciences of the Western 'bourgeois' variety. Its very comprehensiveness helps to explain why Marxism ceased in the West to be of the (all-encompassing) classical Marxist variety. After all, University chairs are occupied by specialists in only one area (of economics, sociology, anthropology, philosophy, etc): Karl Marx (for one) could have occupied chairs in all of these 'bourgeois' disciplines. It is inherent in Marxism, in other words, that as a result of its enormous range and complexity it invites reductionism: it is only that variety of Marxism espoused by political movements and in need of a comprehensive concrete ideology that still deploys Marxism in a synthetic fashion. If, then, there are 'parts' to Marxism, might we ask which are those that may be left out without compromising the remainder, to leave us with a doctrine that has ceased to be Marxist?

Marxism in our view can be made to fall into several planes of thought and values that bear with different degrees of generality and centrality on the system. Either these can be isolated and taken out of context or parts may be substituted from other philosophical systems. Together with the proclivity typical of Marxian ideas to lend themselves to conflicting or contradictory interpretations the process of dismemberment continues until only certain parts appear to be 'compulsory' and others 'optional'. Along, say, four such planes it has become not uncommon for Marxists to confine themselves to focusing explicit attention on three or even only two such levels.

On the most general level, plane 1, and ethically the core of Marxism (but not quite the sufficient element) is a moral outrage, a protest against Western-style industrialism and one or other of its putative effects. *Within* the state Marxists point to various types of oppression, inequality, dehumanization, and degradation that are derivatives of class oppression. *Externally* Marxists may refer to various forms of national subjugation such as that of colonial or semi-colonial states. Of course other philosophical systems, without being Marxist, share such distaste, but Marxists base theirs on recognizably distinct Marxist grounds, joining, for example, in the designation of capitalism as the culprit—albeit whilst differing on the precise definition either of capitalism or of method by which to contrive its termination. Which leads us to the next plane, 2. Characteristically Marxists base their moral outrage (plane 1) again on distinctive Marxist grounds, and specifically on those assumptions about man and society and on the derivative belief in the attainability of communism as a discrete type of social organization. For the first time in history man's full development is conceived possible wherein the causes of moral outrage cease to obtain. Belief in the possibility of communism derives from the perceived nature of humanity and communism constitutes history's moral climax. It would appear that without this belief the logic of Marxist theory is seriously impaired, and yet with hardly a murmur the Frankfurt School (for example) gave up the idea of communism. Such were the School's presentiments and preoccupations with the negative aspects of capitalism and its effect on man's alienation that his destination—the culmination of his development—was left unexplored or admitted to be unknown (with communism a highly unlikely contender).

The difference between level (or plane) 1 and plane 2 is to be seen in terms of degree of 'compulsoriness': where plane 1 is mandatory, plane 2, surprisingly, is not. Lacking also in compulsoriness is plane 3, except in so far as the inclusion of either plane 2 or plane 3 (or both) is to the Western Marxist credo mandatory. Plane 3 differs from planes 1 and 2 in the level of specificity. Whereas both planes 1 and 2 added something new to the formula, plane 3 is revelatory—of the mechanisms by whose instrumentality the realization of human fulfilment will materialize. This is achieved through reference to a version of historical materialism with or without use of (again a version of) dialectical materialism/dialectical method. Historical materialism, the characteristic Marxist theory or philosophy of history is a belief in historical process developing in distinct stages that are characterized by the mode of production appropriate to that particular stage, from primitive communism, through phased stages (the exact sequence has given rise to heated debate) of qualitatively different social formations, based on the prevalence of one dominating mode of production. The dialectical method in its broadest sense suggests that everything is in constant flux, with movement and change in a positive direction, each stage of development as consistent with dialectical method creating the means and conditions under which that stage will be transcended. Communism is thus seen to emerge directly or at least ultimately from capitalism. Plane 4 is contributed by the (modern 'bourgeois') Western social sciences. Here are located those concrete historical, economic, and political analyses carried out within the disciplinary purlieus appropriate to such academic departments as economics, development studies, sociology, anthropology, etc.; these areas connected in various ways and at different points to plane 1, 2, and/or 3. Were it not for certain powerful inhibiting factors, to which we shall turn later, the place into which International Relations fits would be here. Political movements and official ideologies encompass planes 1, 2, and 3, but typically most Western Marxists and Third World Marxists would select plane 1 as compulsory, with areas of levels 2 or 3 optional, and study these within the context of Western academic disciplines. Where, specifically, in Marxism is the subject of international relations broached?

There are essentially two such locations. The first and most obvious sees international relations as an integral part of that section of Marxism described since Plekhanov as historical materialism. Historical materialism *comprehends* international relations in so far as that body of ideas claims to be a comprehensive theory or philosophy of history. There, in the account of the story of class struggle as it evolved throughout history, international relations occupy a place whose highs and lows in the historical record depend on their approximation to the class struggle and the major class formations, as, for example, in theories of imperialism where groups of states become 'protagonists of class struggle' and when international relations thus become of central importance—*central* to Marxism. It is, however, always to be remarked that only certain categories of international relations might be so regarded. It is never international relations *per se*, and never international relations as a general or universal category, that figure prominently. Marxists directly connected to political movements tend to incorporate historical materialism into their discourse—whilst conversely those unconnected to political movements may disregard historical materialism. There are at least two reasons for this: first, for political movements Marxism performs the additional (sometimes the sole) role of an ideology, offering as comprehensive as possible an account of the particular society's past, present, and future. The second reason is that from the account of that society, as provided by a version of historical materialism, a revolutionary strategy—a characteristic of 'applied' Marxism—can be evolved. The difference between Marxist political movements may well lie only in their idiosyncrasies of design in their revolutionary strategy reflecting their own particular (national) circumstances, based, however, on somebody else's simplified version of historical materialism. It can then be concluded that all political movements going by the name of Marxist may boast a brand of historical materialism from which the shadowy outline of a theory of international relations of greater or lesser substance may be seen to emerge.

In the second place there is the contribution to an understanding of international relations even by those Marxists who treat historical materialism as an 'optional' part. The contribution here may be either negligible or, indirectly, very significant. An indirect contribution to *methodology* offered by, among others, Lukács and, more particularly, by Althusser, led, for example, to a re-thinking of the relations of 'totality' or 'structure' to the constituent parts. Althusser's structuralism, as a method, encouraged the growth of a number of social studies areas either adjoining 'international relations' or which incorporated them indirectly in their concerns. Furthermore, the diffusion of structuralist ideas, as Bottomore has pointed out (Bottomore, 1981, 12) has been responsible for an important shift of emphasis in recent Marxist thinking towards the analysis of *modes of production*—leading not only to the revival of Marxist political economy but to the popularity of a number of specific fields.

Important conclusions regarding international relations may be derived from the following fields: studies of development and underdevelopment; studies of the historical development of the capitalist economy (the study of world-system in particular); studies of social formations of kinship and the social relations of production of social classes, of state, of culture, and of ideology. International Relations is not specifically one of these growth areas, but most of the others impinge on international relations which unquestionably constitute an important aspect of social formations and of modes of production. There are of course other areas relevant to international relations that involve no necessary debt to French structuralism. These include such studies as those dealing with international legal philosophy, nations, and nationalism, while those dealing with Marxist historiography would subsume a 'theory' of international relations in the minds of the writers before any sense at all could be made of their subjects. But in the future development of Marxism international relations might yet assume a more prestigious Marxist form and status if the trend among French Marxists in particular proceeds further towards 'looking outside the conventional confines of the disciplines and outside the conventional literature' (cf. Seddon, 1978, vii). The attempt to establish a *general theory of modes of production and their combination* must inevitably give to international relations an important role.

Why is it that international relations as a subject is *not* one of those Marxist 'growth areas', and what prompts Marxists to relegate the subject to the status of a casual by-product of other seemingly unrelated 'problematics' rather than carving the area out in bold relief? By turning now to Western studies of International Relations and their relation to other Western social studies we hope to discover clues to suggest the answer.

The academic discipline of International Relations in the West and Marxism

Introduced as an academic discipline only early in this century International Relations is the youngest of the Western social sciences. As such it has developed largely in the English-speaking countries of the West, but its literature has included contributions also by French, German, and Scandinavian authors. The subject has its own hierophants, reference to whose pronouncements has been used to delimit the parameters of 'debates' on vital issues. There have been in fact a number of 'great debates' but there remains still a number of important as yet unresolved issues concerning matters of content and methodology. In terms of the former there has been brought into question in the last few decades, by such authors as Burton, Nye, Keohane, Rosenau, and many others, such hitherto sacrosanct perspectives as that of 'inter-state' (generally regarded as synonymous with international), and there have evolved, as possible relevant alternative factors to the understanding of the contemporary world, such concepts as national liberation movements, class alliances, multinational companies, and other transnational bodies. State-centrism, however, remains the animus. The confusion arising from the lack of a common methodology persists and the emphasis shifts continually from a tendency towards the methods of current affairs/modern history at one extreme to those of the philosophy of man and society in search of elements of 'world society', the 'ordering' of that society, and justice, at the other extreme. In terms of methodology it has been argued (Little, 1980, 1) that in fact the problems of International Relations stem from a mixed parentage and the handicap of two (philosophy and history) antithetical methodologies visited upon the offspring, where other social sciences (and history itself) seceded at different times from the same parent (philosophy). Thus, whilst there is a perfectly respectable Marxist tradition in anthropology, sociology, and economics, International Relations in this regard goes begging.

Little, in search of an explanation of the seeming anomaly, points out that historians pursue their researches into the past relatively unshackled by preconceived notions; they are not as a rule guided by any prior notions of historical pattern or form such as, for example, ideas of progress, epochs, stages, etc. Philosophers in contrast search for, and are guided by, the unchanging aspects of human experience (Little, ibid. 1). That is not to say of course that for historians events are random, not subject to cause (cf. Caporaso, 1980, 621). They tend to study the 'constant flow of events precipitated by human interaction and attempt to explain the relationship between the events using narrative account' (Little, 1980, 1). Marxism whose historical materialism is always, by definition, a 'philosophy of history' is therefore methodologically significantly different in its starting point to that of International Relations. For Marxism, history is not formless, it not only boasts a definite structure but (Marxism claims) there are discoverable laws of motion to describe and explain these structures. The patterns identified by Marxists are a combination of the idea of stages (based on the assumption of qualitative differences in relations across time and periods) combined with the idea of progress— an idea central to nineteenth-century sociology and meaning a change in a constant direction normatively approved (Caporaso, 1980, 621). Thus, methodologically speaking, the main objectives of mainstream International Relations and of Marxism are, so to speak, on different wave lengths and operate at cross purposes. The discipline of International Relations is, in the main, influenced by the historical tradition to regard the past as 'cut out of one cloth' without such discontinuities as those represented by the qualitatively different stages of Marxism. International Relations none the less find a certain uniformity elsewhere: indeed where change in abundance is to be found— in events, sequences and personalities—this phenomenal diversity is reduced to unity at a theoretical level. Despite the descriptive variety this leads not only to a readiness to compare historical cases but also to a proclivity to theorize and generalize both about international events and about *states* across time and space in a fashion Marxism would never allow. Throughout the course of the discipline's short history all of the various schools of International Relations, despite the wide-ranging disagreements of traditionalist, behaviouralist, and others, have shared the propensity to make *general propositions about international relations*. Marxists could make such (general) propositions only within the context of historical epochs and of social formations identified by the same (dominant) mode of economic production. Furthermore, Marxists would make such propositions only with the proviso that there is no such general category as 'state'—state, says Poulantzas, is only a 'regional' concept. And, we might add, states are invariably only what we would call class-states. Unless the class nature of the state is established (and the way in which this is established differs with Marxists from school to school) the level of abstraction of state—and hence also of international relations—is for the Marxist, all Marxists, too speculative. Thus for Marxists there would never be a 'theory of international relations' but at best a 'sociology of international relations'—to reflect the derivative nature of states as actors.

To this extent, then, the discipline of International Relations is too abstract and as far as Marxism is concerned goes too far. But so too do Marxists reach too far—and in no less important a regard. Marxism as a philosophy of history claims to recognize forms and patterns in the unfolding pages of history, and claims also the ability to project these (recurring) patterns into the future and so to predict the future course of events, at least in broad outline. Nor do they (Marxists) draw the line here, since Marxism ascribes to revolutionary forces an active part in the unfolding of an (objectively given) future. Such an epistemological position is far beyond any acceptable limit of most theories of knowledge of the various International Relations sub-schools. It has been suggested that the distance in this regard between International Relations and Marxism has political[2] roots, derived from the fact that International Relations developed their initial impetus after World War I in the two status quo countries, the United Kingdom and United States, where, furthermore, Marxist scholarship was 'notoriously impoverished' (Bottomore, 1981, 2). Marxism's association is with the have-nots, the irredentists, the

[2] A German, E. Krippendorff, dealing uncharacteristically (for a Marxist) with the establishment of the 'bourgeois' discipline of International Relations goes so far as to suggest that its inception was in fact designed to 'structurally obstruct' the dissemination of revolutionary insights provided by Marxism. It would have been a contradiction of the very purpose (stabilizing *bourgeois* society) for which this 'university discipline has been created' if it was to be admitted that war was the product of the rivalry between capitalistically producing societies, and that later wars could be avoided by simply superseding the capitalist mode of production. (Krippendorff, 1982, 27.)

dissatisfied, and the dispossessed, who may feel they have nothing to lose and are thus ready for a commitment to change.

Marxism and the three philosophical traditions of International Relations studies

The complex relation between Marxism and International Relations thus appears to spring from a mix of methodological, epistemological, and political roots. The total rejection of the state-centrist model by Marxist theory leads to a direct challenge to much of the base of existing Western studies on International Relations (Thorndike, 1978, 56). Whilst Marxism adapted quite happily in practice to international relations, in theory the two appear still incompatible. Let us look now at the three philosophical traditions of International Relations with a view to making clearer the tenuous relation to them of Marxism. We draw for our account of the traditions from Hedley Bull's formulations in *Anarchical Society*.

First, the *Hobbesian* tradition describes international relations as a state of war of all against all, each state pitted against every other. International relations represent in this view a scenario of pure conflict between states where the interest of each mutually excludes the interests of the others. War is the most typical activity, and peace merely describes only a time of recuperation from the previous war and a preparation for the next. Within this 'immoral' framework anything goes, the only acceptable rules being ones of prudence or expediency. Thus agreements may be kept if it is expedient to keep them: they may be broken if it is not.

Second, in the *Kantian* or universalist tradition, the dominant theme is only apparently the relationships amongst states, but is really the relationship among all men in the community of mankind. This relationship, even if not actually in existence, is conceived to exist in potential, and when it does come into being will sweep the system of states into limbo. Within the community of mankind the interests of all men are identical. Conflicts of interest exist only on a superficial or transient level among dominant groupings of states. The particular international activity which in sum most typifies international activity is the horizontal conflict of ideology that cuts across

state boundaries and divides human society into two camps—
the trustees of the immanent community of mankind and those
who stand in its way. And thus there are moral imperatives in
the field of international relations, actions of states enjoining
not coexistence and co-operation but the overthrow of the
system of states and its replacement by a cosmopolitan society.
The community of mankind is not only the central reality in
international politics in the sense that the forces able to bring
it into being are present, but is also the end or object of the
highest moral endeavour, so rules that sustain coexistence and
social intercourse among states should be ignored if the imperatives of this higher morality require it. Between the elect and
the damned, the liberators and the oppressed, the question of
mutual acceptance of rights to sovereignty or independence does
not exist.

Third, the *Grotian*, or internationalist tradition stands
between the Hobbesian and the Kantian. As against the former
it holds that states are limited in their conflicts by common rules
and institutions. Against the latter the Grotian approach accepts
states and the Hobbesian premiss that they rather than
individual human beings are the primary reality in international
politics. The working of international politics involves both
conflict and co-operation. States are bound not only by rules of
prudence and expediency but also by the imperatives of morality
and law. These imperatives enjoin not the overthrow of the
system of states and its replacement by a universal community
of mankind but rather coexistence and co-operation amongst
states.

As we have remarked earlier the fitting of Marxism into these
three traditions is not easy: a situation, incidentally, that reflects
on Marxism as much as on the discipline of International
Relations or, alternatively, on the delineation of each of these
three traditions. One might of course argue that Marxism is a
simple subtype of the Kantian paradigm. The argument is correct
in part. Kant, after all, was one of the important intellectual
influences on Marx, and Marx certainly shares his negative
attitude towards states and the belief in the necessity of their
demise. The two show also a proclivity to regard the
achievement of the essentially harmonious (to Marx,
Communist) society as a moral goal from which derives the

flexible/amoral nature of the rules for the conduct of states to apply in the meantime. Nobody put into more effective practice than the Marxists (and Lenin, the supreme exponent), the dictum that the end justifies the means!

There are other affinities. For example the Marxist view that international conflict is simply an extension of class conflict that will disappear with revolutionary victory can be taken as an example of an essentially Kantian approach. There is too the approach to war which, with Kant, all Marxists invariably present as 'unjust'—unless they themselves take part, in which event the war becomes 'holy'.

But in discussing the Kantian-Marxian relationship we are in fact re-enacting the protracted debates amongst Marxists themselves where, in the view of Kautsky, Mehring, and Plekhanov, the similarity between Kant and Marx is only skin-deep. Particularly in such debates on this subject around the turn of the century, and on the centenary of Kant's death in 1904, these Marxists attacked those of their contemporaries (Vörlander, Weltmann, etc.) who styled themselves Kantian or neo-Kantian Marxists. By elevating Kantian influence and thereby hazarding the whole Marxist tradition in especially its ahistorical approach, individualism, and assumption of free will, they threatened the basic integrity of that (Marxist) tradition. The neo-Kantian Marxists, rather than being revolutionary, were of a radical democratic or reformist orientation, seizing as they did on the universalist aspect of Marxism but blurring at one and the same time socialism's class content.

It would appear, therefore, that Marx does not go the whole distance with Kant and as a matter of fact seems in many ways to straddle (albeit with some difficulty) both the Kantian and Hobbesian traditions. Only the Grotian tradition (certainly to Marx) is totally antithetical. The connection to Hobbes, however superficial, is just as close as is the Kantian, and in fact conflict is to Marx, if anything, even more intense and more polarized than it is to Hobbes, since it cannot be protracted beyond capitalism's dying stage. But in the identification of the source of such conflict Marx removes himself from the Hobbesian tradition into a dimension all his own wherein the classes and class struggle/conflict takes pre-eminence over the role allocated to them in the Hobbesian and Kantian traditions.

Conflict to Marx derives not from human nature and from states as derivatives of man's nature but from economic causes, and, finally, the concept of universal harmony is only a harmony that derives from the removal of class differences and does not encompass other aspects of human nature.

Thus there is to be located between the Hobbesian and Kantian paradigms not only the Grotian but also the Marxist—although there is, involved in the locating, a different understanding of 'between'. The major feature of the Marxian view, the one that separates it sharply from both that of Hobbes and of Kant, is that having invested the 'borrowed' (if proprietorial claims are taken to be settled!) elements with class content, there is the obvious reluctance to talk about international relations at all. And so, the identification of only three traditions could be defended on the grounds that Marxists (and particularly Marx himself) would not want his name to be taken in vain *vis-à-vis* approaches to the study of international relations!

On the other hand, objection could be taken to such a subordination of Marxism to Kantian tradition even though Marxism would find itself there in company with such auspicious forerunners as Islam or Christianity. Part of our purpose in this book is to show that no matter how awkwardly it relates to international relations, Marxism, one of the most powerful forces in this century, should be seen to constitute a tradition all of its own, even if that tradition has ambivalence as its major feature—and evinces a certain discomfort in the presence of international relations.

There are indeed problems in pinpointing the elements of a Marxist tradition. First of all most Marxists cherish *two* pictures of international relations: there is the distantly perceived Marxist goal of a world society possessed of no class or state differences, and there is the interim 'transitional' model in which more appropriate (even state-centrist) expedients had to be incorporated in their definitional frameworks. Among those approaches 'of convenience' we will look in subsequent chapters at Leninism and its contemporaries, Stalinism and the later Soviet, East European, Chinese, Yugoslav, Vietnamese, and Cuban Neo-Marxist, as well as Western. These transitory, 'working' approaches to international relations very often differ materially from one another to the point where if they were called upon to form a separate tradition, their shared features would amount only to those of the broadest and most vague! The shared features of a Marxist tradition if such were to be identified would include:

1. A rejection of a possibility of an analysis segregating 'economic' and 'political' and insistence instead on using *the method of political economy.*
2. That means to them that it is never states but class formations (variously defined and identified) considered to be the main analytical units, and class struggle (in various forms) is the motive force in world politics enacted through the agency of international relations. *The substance of international relations in other words is inter-class relations.*
3. The foreign policy of a state and the nature of the states-system itself can then be seen to be determined either by the domestic class structure of state(s) (as for example the Soviet and her bloc's approaches as well as those of some Western Marxists) or by the globally—as opposed to domestically— defined class conflict (the PRC), or, shaped by the demands and dynamic of the world-system as a whole (dependency and world-system approaches). For the first approach the findings of sociology and comparative politics become an important prerequisite for further analysis, whilst for the second and the third a study of sociology or political economy of the world as a whole becomes mandatory. All of these approaches share the conviction of course that *the ruling classes in whose hands rest the powerful state machines are concretely based on and react to the basic imperatives of production—either domestically or worldwide defined.*
4. *The states-system is usually fragmented along the lines of the main class formations* with types or categories of international relations to correspond, and guided by separate rules. Mixes of Hobbesian, Kantian, and even Grotian features are not uncommon in individual types coexisting in the resultant models of 'revolutionary transition' of international relations.
5. Within the context of political economy a tendency is not uncommon (particularly amongst Western Marxists) *to allocate to the 'political' aspect (and states-system with it)*

a more significant place. That tendency may be only marginal but can go as far as the jettisoning of economic determinism and approximating (non-Marxist) studies of International Relations.

The introduction of more specific factors would irrevocably disunite the field of Marxists covered in this book. If, for example, 'imperialism' were to be taken as the main motive force of history, as Thorndike suggested (Thorndike, 1978), the immediate and least of the consequences would on these grounds alone be to discard as non-Marxist not only the Soviet approach but also, for example, the theory of 'exterminism'.

The major themes in brief

In the following Chapters we try as far as possible to superimpose the perspectives and concerns of Western studies of International Relations on the various Marxist streams. The placement of stress within the study of International Relations may vary from that put on simple inter-state relations to one embracing a much wider study of world politics so as to comprehend actors other than states (such as international, subnational, and transnational organizations). A characteristic feature of Marxists is of course the emphasis on the role of class as a subnational or transnational entity acting internationally through the medium of state. The perceived degree of integration amongst states (and other actors) in the International Relations discipline may range from a simple parallel coexistence of states to the more usual situation in which the degree of contact and interaction between states is such that other states bulk as important factors in the state's calculations. This pattern is usually referred to in International Relations studies as the *states-system* or *international system*. We shall argue that although most Marxists have in their theoretical schemes, implied or asserted, the phenomenon of 'external function' of state as an elementary step in the study of international relations, the difficulties actually begin in the theoretical explanation of the states-system. For states within a states-system are not simply reacting externally to domestic economic dictates but also to the actions of other states. The simple substructure-superstructure approach to each state in a states-system thus fragmented in other words runs into difficulties; these are succinctly summarized by a Romanian Professor Sylviu Brucan.

We shall have to recognize that on the international level even the role played by the mode of production is different from that in society. Indeed, we cannot apply Marx's theory regarding the relationship between base and superstructure in national settings to the international arena where there is neither a base nor a superstructure as a unitary whole as long as production relations function within national economies. Therefore the relationship between the two works vertically within national societies and not horizontally from one nation to another. Thus radical changes in the base of a particular country . . . do not directly affect the superstructure of other (including neighbouring) nations (Brucan, 1976, 11).

For indeed the inevitable question poses itself, whether 'classes behave differently depending on national size and wealth' (ibid. 18), or in other words is the class relation modified by its national site and by that state's membership in the states-system? Such problems are central to the Marxist philosophy of international law and their intractability is borne out by the failure of generations of Marxist international lawyers (Korovin, Pashukanis, Kozhevnikov, Tunkin to name a few) to explain in class terms the nature of one (shared) system of international law in a fragmented states-system (Chapter 8).

Except for its duration for the briefest of periods, Marx (Chapter 2) wholly rejected the idea of a states-system as a form of political structure of the world, and instead clearly favoured what is referred to in the literature of International Relations as *world society*. World society, in one of its meanings, is a society detached from the perspective of state and referring to an *integrated* world-wide human society having values and institutions in common. Whilst world society in some usages of the term may still have the states-system in its make-up, Marx refused categorically to recognize any possibility of a capitalist world economy (characterized by world-wide production and exchange) developing in tandem with the states-system. The world's political superstructure (to use a term now unpopular with Western Marxists), or states-system, corresponded in Marx's view to the early stages in the development of capitalism, and since he anticipated imminent

economic changes *within* states (revolutions) that would
result in the abolition of states, his conviction was that a world
society of socialism and communism would create a radically
different organizational—no longer political—form ('political'
for Marx being coterminous with a society based on classes).

The first post-Marxian generation of Marxists, acutely aware
that these Marxist predictions had somehow gone awry, tried
in various ways to resolve the dilemma of the world economy,
as they now call it, and its atavistic superstructural reflection,
the system of states (Chapter 3). To Bukharin, for example, the
world economy adjusts to the states-system and states become
a 'territorial expression of economic life' and a part of the
relations of production. International relations are based on the
economic relations of large chunks of capital based on national
sites and using the states' political facilities. But the awareness
of the importance of nations and nationalism, categories
neglected or misunderstood by Marx, as an important reinforcing
agency of the states-system, led some of these Marxists to see
also the states-system (or aspects of it) in a different light. Marx's
unquestioning interpretation of nations (and states) as closely
related to economic substructural impulses becomes modified
in varying degrees. Thus the plurality of nations as cultural
entities predating (and also post-dating) classes in the view of
some (cf. Bauer) is regarded as a desirable feature of future
communist society. Other (revisionist) Marxists such as Eduard
Bernstein, in explaining international relations, discard the
economic impulse altogether.

As we have already remarked there seem essentially to be two
alternative Marxist approaches to international relations
according to the selection of the factor of which international
relations (derivative as they always are in Marxism) is a
function: either domestically or globally defined class conflict.
In the first view the states-system is seen to be seriously (socio-
economically) fragmented into types of states and types of
relations. This, for example, is the Soviet approach (Chapter 4).
However, Soviet doctrine concedes that the states-system is in
fact an *international society* (defined in Western literature on
International Relations usually as having shared interests and
values reflected in common institutions), and indeed the Soviet
concept of 'peaceful coexistence' is predicated on the

understanding that the world is such an international society, holding the shared value of 'peace' as the sole alternative to nuclear annihilation, and devising various institutions for its achievement. But at the same time Soviet theorists insist that such an international society is in fact split down the middle into coexisting socio-economic systems, that is into global social formations based on antithetical modes of production and distribution. In the Soviet reading, what Marx designated as 'stages' in historical materialism 'overlap' in time, and it is considered advisable that this transitory temporal overlap is survived peacefully—and with as much co-operation as possible from a moribund capitalism—by the socialist replacement. The socialist states in Soviet theory are in fact already more than a mere international society, transiting as they are towards the world society. It is argued that the relations of communist states are grounded on a different, superior foundation (socialist internationalism) armed with a superior new socialist international law (Chapter 8), new types of international organizations, and new types of mutual relationships (Chapter 6). The socialist socio-economic system effects the 'transit' by deepening its integration, enlarging itself by co-option of the states of the Third World (Chapter 7), and thus is enabled to transcend ordinary international relations.

Chinese Marxism (Chapter 5) since the Sino-Soviet rift has abandoned the Soviet view of coinciding capitalist and socialist social formations as overlapping historical stages, and has rejected with it the centre-piece of that interpretation, namely the Soviet version of 'peaceful coexistence'. With it also went the axiom that the external behaviour of states is a function of the domestic class structure of a society. As with all other Marxist movements that won over states, the Chinese, too, use Marxism on behalf not of classes but of nations and for the rationalization of their advancement within the hierarchy of the states-system. We argue (Chapter 6) that approaches to international relations of Marxist regimes are in fact a function of their placement within the states-system with Marxism providing a supplementary instrument in their scramble for preferment within the system (as in the Yugoslav and Cuban commitment to the leadership of the non-aligned movement, and the balancing act of Tito and Ho between East and West). The

Marxist regimes in fact resist the Soviet encroachment not so much in Marxist terms but, paradoxically, by reference to the institutions and the language of international relations.

The Chinese approach seems to restore the early Chinese Marxism of Li Ta-chao and is a further attempt to couch state-centrism and nationalism in Marxist terms. They portray the world as one unit based on a world economy, they identify its major contradiction, and they group and regroup states (into three worlds) not in respect of the states' domestic class structures and mode of production but in relation to the global contradiction. Both approaches (Soviet and Chinese) exalt nationalism: Soviet nationalism is boosted by the USSR's portrayal as a superior class formation, whilst the Chinese true to the Li Ta-chao tradition portray the Chinese nation as the 'oppressed' pole of the global class struggle.

The Western Marxists and neo-Marxists we refer to (Chapter 10) as 'Marxists: the Professors' and distinguish them from 'Marxists: the Diplomats' (Chapters 4–7) on the grounds that they have no vested interest in the international system. They can therefore argue that the locus of class struggle is still within domestic society and play down the international relations aspect. We attempt to reconstruct what their rendition of the 'external function of state' would be as a rudimentary approach to international relations. But the neglect can no longer be construed as a general Western and Third World Marxist attitude to the international dimension. Methodologically armed with the theories of Lukács, Gramsci (Chapter 9), and particularly of Althusser, many of them, implicitly or explicitly, try again to reconcile the states-system with the world economy. The dependency approach with its initial concern for the problem of Third World 'underdevelopment', represents a variant of international relations theory for *inter alia* it focuses on relationships of two types of states: the globally oppressed (Periphery) states, and the globally oppressing (Centre or core) states. The world-system approach of Wallerstein and of many of his followers views the world holistically with one (capitalist) world economy and one system of states. The hierarchy existing within the states-system corresponds to the states' location in one of three spheres of the world—core, periphery, and semi-periphery—with the states' behaviour having (as in the Chinese approach) little to do with their domestic class structure and everything to do with their positions within the one system. A full circle, returned to Marx one might argue, since the holism of this approach makes the world into one unit, and one world economy, and for superstructure not just one state but several. The world-system approach thus transcends the international system or international society thinking and in this deterministic context (the determinism based on the needs of the system rather than the orthodox Marxist economic determinism) the story of Marxist international relations becomes radically altered. For international relations have now almost become treated as internal relations within one world system. However, a new wave of Marxist attempts that seek to restore the importance of international relations would seem to be in the making. In the early 1980s, as a result of significant international events (the escalation in the nuclear arms race, the birth of world-wide peace movements), an omission of long standing on the part of the Marxists, namely neglect of the Cold War and the East-West conflict, appears at last to be in the process of being corrected.

Thus we are left with a broad choice of answers. The politically-oriented Marxist diplomats' theories afford often greater insight into their own behaviour in the states-system than into the workings of the states-system. Of all the Marxist approaches it would seem to be the ones prepared to compromise and to regard international relations as a 'see-saw of class and nation' factors (Brucan) or that see the state (as Skocpol puts it) 'fundamentally Janus-faced', with dual anchorage in class-divided socio-economic structures and an international system of states, which offer the most potentially rewarding (but for Marxists most exacting) directions for the construction of further theoretical explanations.

Throughout the book we try to discover not only how Marxists can handle international relations in general and the East – West and North – South conflict in particular, but also whether Marxism in the hands of Marxist states or movements can be seen to have brought change to international relations in contributing to these major conflict areas. We also examine (Chapter 7) the extent to which international law and organizations are undergoing change under Marxist influences, as well as the possibility that there is taking place the erosion of crucial features of the international system. A recurrent observation, and in our view an obstacle to the Marxist understanding of world politics, is to do with the perceived ambivalence and multitude of interpretations that Marxists throughout the world place upon the Soviet Union's foreign policies. Among 'Marxist sovietologists' there continues to be wide disagreement as to the nature of the Soviet Union as a social formation, let alone her role in international relations as a simple or Marxist superpower. Nor does there appear to be even broad consensus reached as to that superpower's advance (deliberately or fortuitously is of little consequence) on the goals of international socialism by 'inadvertently' preparing from within the states-system for the system's transcendence. Implied in these chapters is the view that the relationship between Marxism and international relations, uneasy though it might always have been, has had its effect on both.

Part I

Until the October Revolution

2 Marx and Engels

It is not at all surprising that international relations did not particularly interest the two founders of Marxism. Both Marx (1818–83) and Engels (1820–95) were born in the decade following the convening of the Congress of Vienna, as a result of which not only was sweeping political change brought to post-Napoleonic Europe, but the machinery was created for the regulation of international relations 'in concert'. In the lifetime of both Marx and Engels, therefore, and throughout the nineteenth century until the final breakdown of the 'bliss' in 1914, the international situation was on 'its best behaviour', so what has been called in retrospect 'classical international politics' and 'classical Marxism' historically coincide—with unfortunate methodological effect on Marxism.

This classical period for international politics and a 'balance of power' system operated by the Concert of Europe has been sufficiently recorded elsewhere. It is enough to say here that the system was immeasurably different from that into which it developed a century later: then the system had been relatively small (confined to Europe), with most of the world's territory and populations held as colonies, politically dependent on the metropolises of which they were a part. The international system was then operated by a small circle of European states roughly equal in size and strength, and ruled by élite groups of often interrelated aristocratic dynasties. The realization of a broad popular democratic involvement was still the distant dream of a few and nationalism was still in the early stages of development. In this period of classical international politics an international status quo had met with no serious challenge. Alliances were flexible, free as they were of permanent or profound ideological differences. Particularly in a situation in which the military capabilities of potential adversaries were relatively stable—and measurable to within fairly exact tolerances—war could still be regarded as the continuation of a diplomacy dedicated to the regulation and maintenance of the power balance.

Neither Marx nor Engels lived long enough to witness the onset of imperialism which was to become for the next generation of Marxists a summary description of an unequal type of relations between states and a characteristic of the development of capitalism after Marx and Engels. The great areas of inequality, anomaly, and tension in Marx's time were still to be found within the territorial confines of individual states. In fact, to Marx, capitalism was not yet a global mode of production but remained still a closed and homogeneous economy with no room within the theory for any difference in economic conditions between different countries (Brewer, 1980, 28). Hence capitalism had not yet experienced the need to subordinate the noncapitalist hinterland (or periphery). If the opportunity for expansion into the periphery presented itself, full advantage would of course be taken, but no matter how brutal in its impact, capitalism was none the less seen to perform a positive role in these areas with its processes of industrialization deemed progressive and beneficial. Class struggle, in other words, already to the Marxists the motive force of history, had yet to break out of its territorial bonds and make an entrance upon the international stage.

The (European) international political structure was in essence a more or less faithful reflection of the economic substance of capitalism, in Europe displaying as main features competition and anarchy. In these circumstances international relations remained similarly rudimentary, casual, and unobtrusive. Although Marx and Engels wrote international relations into the programme of their future research, the subject was well down on the list, and, as in the case of a number of other areas, was not completed—indeed in this case hardly broached. In a situation where the dynamic of capitalism and that of the international system were completely unconnected, Marx and Engels misread the future course of both: and particularly was this true of their reading of the international system. The dynamic of capitalism appeared to Marx and Engels to be heading irrevocably towards the absorption of the international system taking with it a nascent nationalism. In their reading, a burgeoning class struggle through a sequence of virtually simultaneous revolutions *within* all advanced European capitalist states was to replace both the international system and nationalism as the main elements of *world* (now no longer *international*) society. As it turned out none of these predictions was confirmed by the march of events. The international system and nationalism flourished and, it became increasingly clear, had a long way to run. The references relating to this 'dying' political category are fragmentary, and the glimpses we catch of international relations are fleeting. Marx's guess that the transitory stage would be of negligibly short duration is now out by over a century.

Marxian 'Misconceptions'

Quite clearly, then, certain typical Marxist misconceptions about international relations are attributable to the dynamic of both capitalism and that of the international system in the nineteenth century. There seems to have been something of a short circuit at some point between 'domestic' and 'universal' global levels resulting from Marx's premature expectations regarding the demise of the international level. In other words a paradoxical situation arises when Marx and Engels incline to a conceptualization of the world as one unit of capitalism, whilst the homogeneity of nineteenth-century capitalism seemed to allow the application of their major theories on a states level, as domestic theories. From a philosophical standpoint man and society are their main concern and here too Marx in particular was inclined to take the world as a unit. His economic analysis in *Das Kapital* for example was tied to no national context in particular: it is the analysis of the *abstract* and *pure* capitalist mode of production that took up much of his attention. And so we have Marxism as by definition a universalist doctrine, committed by the concept of international class struggle to the notion of world society; and yet its main categories inhabit a domestic society, the despised states. Whilst perhaps in Marx's case not without a certain theoretical plausibility, this is lacking in the case of those of his successors who fail to make the necessary theoretical adjustment.

Related to the paradox is the failure to produce an adequate theory of state, and particularly of nation. States, nations, and countries are often used interchangeably and are seen to have in common only the idea of their being mere surface projections of the basic conflict between classes. 'The state is only a transitional institution which is used in the struggle, in the revolution, to hold down one's adversaries by force, it is pure nonsense to talk of a free people's state' (Marx, Letter to A. Bebel, 1968, 335). States are only secondary units, their importance deriving from the primary analytical unit of classes (defined as occupying opposed positions within the society), and from the fact of their engagement in an unceasing struggle. States, then, are a mere epiphenomenon of classes, and the assumption that states act also externally to defend the interest of the strongest class follows. Although spelled out for the first time by Lenin, the proposition, and its axiomatic nature, is implied by Marx who finds a capitalist state's foreign policy to be a function of its domestic (class) structure.

Western Marxists in particular have criticized Marx on the grounds of his leaving behind an incomplete or imperfect theory of state—criticism, as we have observed, that might equally be made in regard to nation. Luporini's explanation of this curious theoretical gap is persuasive: to the effect that Marx failed to integrate two conceptual pairs, on the one hand structure and superstructure in the analysis of the mode of production in *Capital*; and, on the other, the state/civil society in the historical and political analyses (that is to say at the level of social formation). Thus the second pair always remains descriptive and analytically unrelated to the first, and that, argues Luporini, is why the question of state as well as of nation remains unresolved (see Mouffe, 1979, 9).

The theoretical weakness is particularly obvious in a nation where the possible connecting link between state and class is extremely strained. As Bloom (Bloom, 1941, 58 ff.) has shown, the meeting-point between class and nation was found in the conclusion that in any historical period there was always one class whose advantage coincided with the 'national interest', the latter ultimately reducible to the interest of society (in the improvement and better exploitation of the means of production). 'A national class' described the phenomenon of the proletariat raising itself to the position of a 'national class, constituting itself as the nation'. Until that point, however, the proletariat 'in England as in France, in America as in Germany . . . was stripped of every trace of national character' (Marx and Engels, 1969a, 58). To Marx and Engels, therefore, who by no means counted as theoreticians of nationalities or nations, the bases on which rests the concept of race remain obscure. 'Race is itself an economic factor' (Marx and Engels, 1934, 517): and so too, it would seem, is nation, judging from the denial of the validity of other evidence—such as common language, culture, or territory (Kubálková and Cruickshank, 1980, 43). Although the question of nations and nationalism was addressed more seriously with advancing years, national boundaries were seen always as being eroded by the capitalist system as 'national onesidedness and narrowness' came increasingly into collision or obstructed the path of development of the capitalist mode of production.

International relations

The interest of Marx and Engels in international relations is essentially on two interrelated levels, the first being analytically prior to the second, and with the relationship between the two similarly theoretically incomplete along the lines suggested by Luporini. The first of these levels was world politics, and the second (current) international relations. But the difference between them is much more than semantic. World politics, for which classes and class struggle provide the driving force, supply that framework within which Marx and Engels based their grand social and economic theory of society (historical materialism). Though fitting uneasily into the framework, international relations as part of the existing political organization of capitalist society inevitably became part of that context. Particularly in their later years, however, both Marx and Engels paid increasing attention to the more concrete level of 'current affairs', becoming aware, one suspects, that the historical flow of actual events could thwart their theoretical designs. Either these same international relations might not after all lend themselves to a speedy enough absorption into the projected universal world society or could otherwise complicate the transition.

It is not always appreciated that Engels alone published more on military and diplomatic matters (taking up altogether over

2,000 closely spaced pages of the German edition of his works)
than on any other subject (Gallie, 1978, 67). Over a period of
years he regularly subscribed articles to British and American
publications on current issues. He found time also to undertake
a detailed study of the strategies of various military men and
writers such as Clausewitz, and to write a running analysis of
the American civil war. As Professor Gallie has pointed out
Engels was probably the most perceptive military critic of the
nineteenth century, and because of his and Marx's broader
theoretical framework was capable of 'sweeping interpretations
and assessments on every major diplomatic and military move
on European chessboards' (ibid.). Although such findings have
not been theoretically integrated with those of historical
materialism nevertheless the two levels are not in serious
contradiction. Despite being argued over these 2,000 pages, the
rules of international relations that emerge are, however,
relatively simple and easy to follow since they refer to the
purportedly brief period to elapse before, during, and after the
revolutionary transformation and before the final demise of
international relations. Marx and Engels give more than a hint
of the nascent *types* of international relations that were to
characterize the writings of many later Marxists. Because state
is a component part of a social formation which is in turn based
on one prevalent mode of production, it follows that the state
is an instrument of the strongest class(es) and that externally,
in the general run of intercourse with other (capitalist) states,
it will act to protect these same capitalist interests. The nature
of foreign policy in other words will depend on the mode of production extant in that society. In these circumstances Marx and
Engels refuse to be unduly impressed by the achievements of
any individual statesman, and their focus on class determination
of foreign policy is never blurred either by individual
achievement or by such other considerations (geographic, for
instance) as may be taken seriously by other approaches: 'it is
still true that man proposes and God (that is, the extraneous
force of the capitalist mode of production) disposes'. How, he
wonders, could Napoleon possibly have 'swept away the feudal
system'—the only authority allowed an individual in a certain
place at a certain time is no more than the enactment of what
is historically 'necessary' (Engels, 1943, 347).

This highly ambivalent relation between the subjective and objective in history, in, that is to say, the scope allowed for the assertion of man's will within the context of economic determinism, is in fact the very core of Marxism—the hinge, in other words, of the relation between social existence, with its various component parts, and social consciousness. *Social existence* would appear to consist of biological and geographical factors, and most importantly of the *social substructure, or base*, comprising the dialectically related forces and relations of production. All ideas, philosophy, art, religion, politics, and also state, are part of the *social superstructure*. For our purposes it is significant that such obviously substructural phenomena as classes (rather than such superstructural epiphenomena as states) are important. The 'high-sounding dramas of princes', to which Marx and Engels were by no means oblivious, are a reflection, a mere surface projection, of more important conflicts taking place at another level.

Since there existed in Marx's time essentially only two modes of production, namely capitalist and pre-capitalist, it is their observations on these that are most revealing. The revolutionary transformation from capitalism to socialism, regarded by both Marx and Engels as imminent, was also to be abrupt in its passage and in one fell swoop to embrace all, or most, advanced capitalist countries. Thus there was no thought of the possibility of a *coexistence* between capitalist states and those socialist states in which the revolution had already been successful; although it did cross their minds that a period of coexistence might prevail between socialist 'states' and the pre-capitalist areas. Equally perplexing was the important question of the nature of relations amongst the victorious socialist states, between the 'communes' (or 'Gemeinwesen'). These were terms coined by Marx to indicate the replacement by these classless societies of states as instruments of class rule.

It is perhaps an appropriate point at which to take stock of the possible types of relations arrived at by Marx and Engels. These seem to us to fall into broad categories:

1. Relations amongst capitalist states.
2. The (ruled out) possibility of coexistence of socialist and capitalist states.

3. Relations of capitalist states to pre-capitalist social formations.
4. Relations of socialist countries to pre-capitalist formations.
5. Relations amongst future socialist countries.

1   *Relations amongst capitalist states*

The rules governing these relations are, according to Marx, quite simple: The bourgeoisie fights not only the classes within its own state but also internationally, i.e. 'the bourgeoisies of foreign countries. The international relations of capitalist countries are always a result of foreign policies in pursuit of criminal designs, playing upon national prejudices and squandering in piratical wars the people's blood and treasure.' (Marx, *The Civil War in France*, 1968, 260.)

The only possibility of the bourgoisie being able even temporarily to overcome its fragmentation lies in those instances when, bonded together by a common fear, it unites against its 'worst enemy', the international proletariat. Marx claims repeatedly, as for example in the *Communist Manifesto*, that the proletariat is uncompromisingly international; its allegiances are to the proletariat in a global sense and not to the states in which they happen to have been born. The proletariat has no country, *ergo* proletarians of all countries can be expected to unite. Professor Ulam is clearly in error when he claims in his definitive work on Soviet foreign policy (Ulam, 1974) that from the *Manifesto* one can infer by analogy that this cohesion similarly applies to the bourgeoisie to the extent that to Marx and Engels 'capitalism is internally conflict producing but externally, in the international arena peace making'. For the fact that 'The bourgeoisie . . . is already linked up in brotherhood against it [the international proletariat] with the bourgeois of all other countries—and Herr Bismarck's international policy of conspiracy' (*Critique of the Gotha Programme*, Marx and Engels, 1968, 323) does not remove the fact that short of the unifying influence of the fear of a (united) international proletariat the inter-capitalist relations are always based on conflict, in a state of constant battle. Wars are a regular feature of capitalist, international relations periodically replacing limited diplomatic attempts to resolve the conflict peacefully. Wars are strongly denounced by Marx and Engels, and their life-span is linked to that of capitalism. Gallie draws to our attention Engels's prescient anticipation of the apocalyptic destructive capacity of military technology realized a century later (Gallie, 1978).

The apprehension was not however translated into the theory. So long as capitalism is with us, so for that length of time will wars be waged. The connection of wars with capitalist or other exploitative modes of production is not, however, absolute, for, as Engels concedes, wars existed on the inter-tribal level long before the emergence of classes or states. Whilst the inter-capitalist wars are seen to be obviously unjust, Marx and Engels recognize the possibility of the just war, as fought for example between the enslaved and the slave-master and consequently as a legitimate instrument in the impending revolutions.

On none of these issues are Marx and Engels particularly innovative. Their analysis, with some small modification to international relations, would fit quite comfortably into a Hobbesian/Machiavellian power realist paradigm. The modification, we need hardly add, would mainly be to allow the accommodation of Marxism's more specific materialistic explanation (more, that is, than that normally adduced by the power realists) as to the state's aggressiveness in its pursuit of power. For Hobbes and Machiavelli the power drive derives simply from human nature, made manifest in the anarchy of an international system, which, with no 'world government' or other central source of authority to moderate it, renders the rough and tumble of the power-realist vision of the world an unlovely sight. To this, Marx and Engels add the economic dimension on which the power drive is based and by which it is defined. Thus *Das Kapital*, by virtue of being an anatomical text on the economic functioning of capitalist society, is also *inter alia* a revelation of the whys and wherefores of the international behaviour of capitalist states. In contrast to the Hobbesian or Machiavellian positions, for Marx not all men are necessarily 'bad', nor slave to some inherent power drive. To Marx, answering to such drives is a result of human alienation, and once the two principal causes of alienation (private property and division of labour) are removed, the inherent human potential to live harmoniously in a classless, stateless society will be realized. At that point Marx parts company with Hobbesian tradition to join the Kantian philosophical stream.

2   *The impossibility of coexistence between capitalist and socialist states*

In regard to such questions of strategy as the location of the first revolutionary outbreak and the methods to be used, the Marxist classics have almost invariably been proved incorrect by historical events. Both Marx and Engels are particularly adamant in regard to the necessarily global nature of the forth-coming revolutions, ruling out completely the possibility of any but a fleeting *coexistence* of capitalist states (that is to say those not as yet scoured by revolution) with the new socialist states. Trotsky in particular used this argument (as have Trotskyists since) against the integrity of the Soviet experience when he argued that because the Russian revolution remained isolated and unsupported by revolutions elsewhere that country could not but 'degenerate' to a limbo between socialism proper and capitalism, with its future absolutely dependent on further socialist revolutions. Since the theoretical possibility of a coexistence of capitalism and socialism is to Marx and Engels as absurd as the coexistence of night and day, and since we now live by the Marxian account in a state of perpetual 'twilight', some quotation from Marx and Engels in support of their conviction in this regard seems justified: 'Empirically, communism is only possible as the act of the dominant peoples "all at once" and simultaneously, which presupposes the universal development of productive forces and the world intercourse bound up with communism' (Marx and Engels, 1965, 46), or 'this is to be a universal revolution, and will, therefore, have the whole world as a field for operation' (Engels, 1963, 332 ff.). There are many more references to this particular feature regarding the dispersion of revolutionary force and momentum to the ends of the earth to show that the development was absolutely taken for granted. Revolution would be world-wide. Perhaps, admits Engels, 'it will start in all the civilised countries of the world, or at least in Great Britain, the United States, France and Germany, but at one and the same time. It will take a longer or shorter time in each of these countries, according to the degree of industrial development in the respective countries, and in doing so the rest of the world will be influenced so that their development towards the same revolution will be hastened. Every social reform remains a utopia until the proletarian revolution and the feudalistic counter-revolution measure swords in the world war' (loc. cit.).

3   Relations of capitalist states with pre-capitalist areas

As we have remarked, Marx and Engels did not believe that the capitalist mode of production was in urgent need of areas into which to expand. If, of course, such areas were to become available then obviously the capitalists would make the most of any opportunity of extracting profit from them. Marx is aware of the early connection of capitalist countries to these areas through the deployment of merchant capital[1] which, despite their inclusion in the world market, did not necessarily lead to the transformation of their societies. And yet as soon as industrial capital took hold, the capitalist conquest of these areas could proceed to play a progressive, though ruthless, role in promoting capitalist industrialization. The reason that capitalism developed first in Europe and was slow to penetrate Asia was to be found in the nature of the previous modes of production in these areas; European domination being the result and not the primary cause of this difference (Brewer, 1981, 60). It follows that capitalist states are not responsible for conditions of backwardness in these areas. Two further points might be made with reference to the shape and pace of capitalist development and subsequent relations. Since capitalism is developing evenly and is homogeneous (circumstances that explain the simultaneity of the anticipated revolutionary outbreaks) the theory does not provide for different levels of capitalist development (such as represented in neo-Marxist concepts of a capitalist centre and a capitalist periphery). Acknowledgement of such a differential in development would of course prepare the way for the recognition also of distinct types of (unequal) international relations.

Marx and Engels were convinced that capitalism, then confined exclusively to Europe and North America, should be studied *in situ*, for it was there that history would take its next

[1] *Merchant's or commercial* capital is that part of capital which takes over functions of buying and selling from *productive (or industrial)* capital. It performs a distinct, non-productive function which is common to all branches of industrial capital (Brewer, 1981, 38).

great leap. That the flavour of the whole theory is Eurocentrist in emphasis would seem to originate in a certain ignorance of non-European areas and not in any marked preference for Europe—or as a result of any particular racial or national prejudice. And indeed the special socio-economic formation prevalent in many of what have come to be referred to as to-day's Third World countries (such as India, China, Egypt, Meso-potamia, Persia, Arabia, Turkey, Tartary, Java, the Dutch East Indies, 'semi-Asiatic' Russia, etc.) did fail to fill the theoretical bill, and in many important respects failed even to exhibit the characteristics of any other (class) socio-economic formation. It is as an acknowledgement of his lack of knowledge and under-standing of these areas that Marx bracketed them as the *Asiatic mode of production*. Though still falling short of specific cate-gorization, he further described such countries as 'primitive', 'unchanging', 'barbarian', 'semi-barbarian', 'the East', 'nations of peasants', 'backward' (but beginning to develop modern economies—as in the case of Russia and Turkey). Typified in their purest form by no private ownership of land, system of village communes, or strong central government power, such societies he regarded as inherently stagnant: ones in which, thanks to the total absence of the two classes whose ten-sions were deemed to supply the revolutionary dynamic, the task of breaking out of their Asiatic mode of production without outside influence was hopeless. In these circum-stances, the capitalist conquest of the colonies clearly became the only way out and, for a Eurocentristic Marx, European colonialism had a positive role to perform. 'England has to fulfil a double mission in India, one destructive, the other regenerating—the annihilation of old Asiatic society in Asia' (Marx and Engels, 1972, 583–4). However inhuman the features of European colonialism, it was the only instrument to hand for the achievement of socialist victory in those areas. Ahead of theories of modernization and development Marx and Engels anticipated a certain 'diffusion' through which the capitalist states would assist the backward areas in 'catching up' and emulating European – capitalist standards. The capitalist impact on these backward countries is there-fore clearly positive though, as Kiernan has pointed out, Marx (unlike Lenin) would seem to imply that imperialism is a morbid excrescence on the face of capitalism rather than an integral part of its nature (Kiernan, 1974, 194).

4 *Relations of socialist countries to backward areas*

At this point, it will be recalled, Marx and Engels felt secure in the expectation that the installation of socialism on a world-wide basis would take place at any moment. In the case of the backward areas the stagnation/immiseration was an unarguable fact of life and of such degree that it would appear that the coexistence of socialism with other modes of production was contemplated. The question then to be faced was that of leadership: if the European proletariat were to assume power it must shoulder also the additional task of taking control of the colonies as well as fulfilling the function which the European capitalist colonialism would in that event have failed to perform (Letter to Kautsky, Marx, 1934, 399). There seemed little doubt that colonialism, whether operated by capitalists or the proletariat after the revolution in Europe, presented for these countries the only chance of breaking out of their intrinsically stagnant developmental backwater.

5 *Relations between socialist countries*

This category of relations would represent to Marx a conceptual *non sequitur* since it purports to describe relations between units (states) which in the Marxist framework will not exist as socialist, or, at best, in a pre-communist (socialist) state would refer to a complex of 'dictatorships of the proletariat' (in a domestic sense only) whose 'relations' would be as ephemeral in nature as would be the existence of such groups on the way to communism. Whether therefore in the present context there can be justified a discussion of intercourse that would be designed to secure the withering away of participant (proletarian) groups, and having as its purpose the hastening of the end of the 'relations' themselves, is questionable. Beyond that point, however, the picture becomes even more indistinct since Marx and Engels themselves say very little on the subject. Presumably, with the removal of capitalism, classes, and states, the 'Hobbesian' power drive would disappear and universal harmony would prevail. In fact the absolute unity of mankind as the essential ideal of marxism and its achievement seems to be predicated on the rejection of division into both classes and states. But this is where Marx's rejection of international relations as a post-revolutionary organizational arrangement might have been unrealistic, or conversely the continuing existence (impossible to do away with) of international relations might be seen for ever to thwart the achievement of the Marxian goal of the unity of mankind. Thus international relations, as Berki pointed out, are more relevant to Marxism than is usually understood, creating as they do what may be for Marxism possibly intractable problems.

Although Berki attempts to show that in terms of Marx's thought it may not make sense to speak of non-antagonistic diversity (Berki, 1971, 86) we refer to Marx himself for a tacit acceptance of the possibility of such non-antagonistic diversity in the future organization of mankind. Indeed he considered the eventuality to be unavoidable for, as Engels put it, 'Between one country and another, one province and another and even one locality and another there will always exist a *certain* inequality in the conditions of life, which it will be possible to reduce to a minimum but never entirely remove . . . ' (*Critique of the Gotha Programme*, Marx and Engels, 1968, 335–6.)' Alpine dwellers for example will always have different conditions of life from those of people living on plains'. And this is precisely the point: so long as separate entities (socialist 'states') continue to exist, unity inevitably means hegemony. In other words, although it may be true that the hypothetical future of a unified centralized Marxist community would no longer display the features of capitalism, neither would it have achieved the higher human freedom postulated by Marx. Nor, as we have observed, would the Marxian ideal be realized in the form of a community of independent nations, for in the latter case, though it may have come to represent freedom and progress over capitalism proper, it would remain a system still visibly bearing the stigmata of capitalism. In this regard Berki also argues that so long as there is a plurality of 'socialist states' it would mean by definition their being based on ownership by a group or part of a whole, which in turn, by logical extension, would mean in Marxist terms of reference that 'an economically integrated world still consisting of separate nations is, whatever the internal structure of these nations, *a capitalist world*' (Berki, 1971, 101). Berki is here setting aside what previously would have appeared to have been axiomatic, namely, international relations dependent on the domestic structure of states, to argue that international relations amongst these classless communities would forever remain capitalist and thus stand in the way of the achievement of the central ideal.

A short step from there leads us to the recognition of the possibility of conflict and war amongst such socialist communities—a likely enough contingency if we consider that Marx and Engels themselves failed to establish an absolute link between wars and class societies. From what sort of base might the rules of such 'new type international relations' grow if the classless nature of these societies would render the external protection of the 'national class interest' of these societies meaningless? Are we then returned to Hobbes, or to Grotius, or to Kant, having made, as far as International Relations is concerned, an unnecessary detour?

3 First Marxist Theories of Imperialism and of Nation

Barely three decades had passed since the death of Marx in 1883 and only two since that of Engels in 1895, and already international relations had attained a measure of respectability and had gained a place in Marxist theory denied them by Marx and Engels. The reason for this was neither a sudden change of Marxist heart nor the inspired 'discovery' of international relations. The newly-won esteem sprang rather from a turn in the development of capitalism which now for the first time gave to international relations the appearance of having some part to play. The more precise outline of this newly-assigned role is defined by any one of three approaches: first, the approach that sees international relations fitting into the categories associated with historical materialism (as for example in theories of imperialism and world-economy where international relations become part of the *relations of production*); second, the approach that views, at least in part, international relations—or specific aspects such as wars, nations, and so on— as an independent force. This second approach (typical of the Austro-Marxists for example) treats political and ideological factors not as mere reflections of economic forces, but regards the whole social process as a web of interwoven forces, economic *and* others (and nationalism above all). In the third approach international relations are seen as a force largely independent of economic forces. The Marxist credentials of such authors as the leading revisionist Eduard Bernstein become progressively unclear as they arrive at the conclusion that international relations simply cannot be fitted into the all-embracing mould of historical materialism.

In the most orthodox of these approaches, in terms of their placement within the bounds of historical materialism, international relations (still of no intrinsic interest in themselves) now, by virtue of their becoming a component part of world-economy, became a respectable category of political economy. The reason for the transformation lay once again in the Marxist misreading of future developments. We saw earlier that for Marx and Engels the main sites of the capitalist mode of production were *states*. Confirmation of this location in the Marxist analysis lent validity to Marxist theory as a theory of domestic society with secondary reference made to *horizontal* interactions amongst neighbouring 'sites', the horizontal (inter-state) dynamic thus becoming overshadowed by the crucial importance with which the *vertical* (class) relations within each state was endowed. It was into these state vessels (often used coterminously with nations) that the world class struggle was, as it were, decanted, and for Marx and Engels it was within these containers that the revolutionary explosions were sympathetically to ignite. In the course and in the aftermath of the ensuing eruptions international relations would be eclipsed as populations freed from the bondage of states joined together in one all-embracing 'world society'. Since classes would now have gone by the board, the new structure would be no longer political but instead would rely on economic and 'administrative' underpinnings and be characterized by a set of common values. In such a scenario international relations clearly had no part to play.

In the event, the process was frustrated by structural changes taking place in the capitalist mode of production, the most significant of which would appear to have been the transference of its operational locus from the state to the world at large. In the process of effecting this momentous shift, however, instead of bypassing the existing political structure of the international system, the capitalist mode of production was to adopt the international structure and *adjust* to that structure. The upshot has been the coincidence of the capitalist mode of production and the territorial organization of the world into nations and states.

Marxists went to considerable lengths to show that Marx and Engels had been aware of these processes at work, in however rudimentary a form, and had only failed to appreciate their intensity and potential. Up to a point the claim was valid. Marx and Engels had of course been aware of the internationalization of capital, but the trade in commodities that they had witnessed had now been supplemented by a dramatic increase in the export of capital. Marx and Engels, who had certainly also identified the causes of the drive to expansionism inherent in capitalism, did not live long enough either to see the fierce scramble for colonies or to appreciate the scale of the wars fought over them. As soon as the territorial parcelling-out was completed, any further expansionist inroads had to be made at the expense of the rival empire, and in this connection the intensity of the rivalry was at its highest between the ascending power, Germany, and the most extensive colonial ruler, Britain. Marxists were in agreement that war, and the coming world war, were connected with the development of capitalism and associated more particularly with such developments as the emergence of monopolies, the export of capital, and the intensification of inter-capitalist rivalry. There were differences of opinion in the Marxist analysis regarding the interconnection between the capitalist mode of production and international relations, and its functioning. There were greater variations of opinion on the charting of a new post-Marxian revolutionary strategy—the approach to nationalism and international relations in this regard becoming major stumbling-blocks.

With such notable exceptions as Karl Liebknecht, parliamentary Social Democrat contingents voted for war credits on the eve of World War I despite a Second International (1891–1914) resolution to the contrary. In the course of contentious debates on this issue the central conflict in Marxism between proletarian internationalism and nationalism (that is class loyalty and cohesion as opposed to concepts of nation and state) became painfully apparent. It seemed that in emulation of the capitalist mode of production the international socialist movement had taken on the old 'feudal' vestments of international relations—an attire which neither has since seen fit to discard. International relations has continued in theory to be a nebulous factor but in reality has proved an enormously powerful obstacle in the path of revolutionary strategies—whilst at the same time acting as (one of the) *instrument*(s) towards effecting the demise of the capitalist mode of production. As Lenin put it:

There is no doubt that the development is going *in the direction* of a single world trust that will swallow up all enterprises and all states without exception. But the development in this direction is proceeding under such stress, with such a tempo, with such contradictions, conflicts and convulsions—not only economical, but also *political*, *national*, etc., etc. [authors' italics]—that before a single world trust will be reached, before the respective national finance capitals will have formed a world union of 'ultra-imperialism', imperialism will inevitably explode, capitalism will turn into its opposite. (Lenin, 'Introduction' to N. Bukharin, 1966 14.)

The new generation of Marxist theories, which within the 'updated' context of historical materialism went about explaining also the nature of international relations, have come to be called classical theories of imperialism: 'classical' to convey the idea of more, many more, such theories to come—and to embrace particularly those purporting to explain the process of decolonization and the persisting iniquity of international inequalities. Since the 1960s an enormous body of Marxist literature has developed (see below, Chapter 10) that had both directed attention to classical theories of imperialism and also sought to use these as an intellectual springboard from which to launch Marxist renditions of present-day problems. There is no need here to duplicate the arguments of the contemporary literature dealing with Marxist theories of imperialism, but three interconnected areas which are either explicitly covered by or implied in the theories of imperialism are of relevance to our context: first, theories of imperialism as a generic category describing unequal relations between capitalist metropolises and colonies; second, theories of relations amongst imperialist states, that is, pertaining to imperialist rivalry or ultra-imperialism (the explication of conflict/co-operation and war being of course part and parcel of these two types of relations); and, third, theories of nation and nationalism, either taken as derivative from theories of imperialism or as separately contrived. The development along one or other of these lines in the areas mentioned may be found in the following: chronologically first, as far as theories of imperialism are concerned, was Rudolf Hilferding's *Finance Capitalism* (1910), followed by Rosa Luxemburg's *Accumulation of Capital* (1913), Bukharin's *Imperialism and World Economy* (1915), and Lenin's *Imperialism as the Highest Stage of Capitalism* (1916). This latter work quite undeservedly 'stealing the show' was in actual fact a quite straightforward synthesis and summary of the work of Lenin's colleagues.[1] In the penetration of its conclusions regarding the future course of imperialism Kautsky's *Ultra-imperialism* (1914) sets the author some distance apart from his Marxist fellows.

As far as theories of nation and nationalism were concerned, most of these authors were called upon to devise strategies in response to the 'nationality question' which became an increasingly vexatious political issue. Some of the theories in this connection were implied in theories of imperialism, and most notably among the others were those of the Austro-Marxists, taking as 'backdrop' the multinational Habsburg Empire. These latter-day writers constructed more evolved theories than any Marxist before or since, among them Otto Bauer's *The Nationalities Question and Social Democracy* (1907) and the works of Renner and Adler. Finally, there is Stalin's *Marxism and the National Question* of 1916.

The theoretical positions taken in these writings vary widely but despite being 'hopelessly divided' (Winslow, 1931, 732), Marxists of that generation as a group exhibit a distinct homogeneity. The binding agents are to be found in, for example, their truly international character, each having an intimate knowledge of the work of the others. All were actively engaged in political parties or as participants in the Second International. The academic (or 'professorial', as Rosa Luxemburg styled it) variety, of which Carl Grünberg and Antonio Labriola were forerunners, though its advent was still a little way off, has made up for lost time and has since come to monopolize the Marxist field in the Western world.

The new economic developments: world economy

Among the new developments remarked by Marx and Engels in embryonic form was the tendency to a falling rate of profit

[1] Lenin's famous five features of imperialism were: (1) the concentration of production and capital leading to the domination of the world economy by big monopolies, (2) the fusion of bank and industrial capital and the consequent rise of a financial oligarchy, (3) the especially important role attributed to the export of capital, (4) the division of the world among monopolistic leagues of international capitalists, (5) the completion of the territorial partitioning of the world among the great imperialist powers.

on capital. Non-Marxist economists had also recognized the tendency, and thus its causes were seen to range from under-consumption to (a cause offered by Marx) the growing organic composition of capital.[2] The resort to the export of capital and the associated drive for colonies was seen as a capitalist measure to offset the declining rate of profit. Other important processes related to these involved the growing concentration[3] and the centralization[4] of capital—processes which Marx had recognized but which were left to Rudolf Hilferding to elaborate for the new era. Cutthroat competition, seen as central to the functioning of capitalism, tended in due course to create monopolies, or joint stock companies which either completely 'swallowed up' or otherwise gained control over small firms. Capital, in other words, came increasingly to form itself into large chunks, hierarchically organized. In the course of this formative process, industrial and financial capital—still in Marx's time separate—merged into *finance* capital, in the hands of banks. Monopolies, also in an emergent situation, were not yet strong enough to control the world market and hence, in exchange for tariff walls erected by the state on their behalf, supported states in their expansionist policies.

The majority of writers mention most of these developments, but argue vigorously on matters of interpretation. The result is a number of idiosyncratic theoretical variations, the elaboration of which, beyond their relevance to International Relations, would be outside our present scope. All of the most important elements are given at least a mention in Rudolf Hilferding's work and many are also outlined in a book (1902) by a liberal radical writer, Hobson, in which he focuses particularly on the theory of export of capital as an attempt to offset the declining rate of profit on capital. Hobson's work deals also with certain domestic sociological effects, brought about by the operation of

[2] The rate of profit is $s/(c + v)$ (where s = surplus, c = capital laid out on equipment, i.e. constant capital, v = wages, i.e. variable capital). Class struggle keeps the s/v (rate of exploitation) constant whilst c/v (organic composition of capital) is growing and as a result the rate of profit $(s/(c + v) = (S/v)/(c/v + v/v))$ is declining.

[3] Concentration of capital—the growth of capital through the reinvestment of profits.

[4] Centralization of capital—the process of amalgamation of a plurality of capitalism into larger combinations.

these processes, among them the emergence of a 'labour aristocracy'.

The accuracy of Hilferding's description of the processes of 'internationalization' of capital was duly acknowledged by Bukharin and Lenin, but another side to the process had still to be appreciated. Internationalization, and the spread of capitalism into the world economy on the lines Hilferding suggested, would of itself have led to a world under the eventual control of several large capitalist transnational companies: a system which would not necessarily approximate, much less coincide with, the political territorial division of the world into states. In other words, Hilferding anticipated capitalism's development *outside* the sphere of international relations. Bukharin's contribution was to see the connection between this process (internationalization of capital) and a parallel process, the *nationalization* of capital. He grasps the fact that the existing international structure provides a *facility* fully recognized and exploited by the expanding capitalist companies. States, with their tariff walls and protectionism, offer attractive operational sites, that is to say a 'facility' into which may be channelled large 'chunks' of finance capital. The companies (and their capital) thus become *national* (not transnational or international). This convenience of siting themselves within the walls of nation-states meant also a corresponding strengthening of the state site in question.

Bukharin's pen draws a fascinating map of the world with places relocated to allow for the inclusion of both capitalism and international relations. Previously international relations had been based on the struggle between 'national' states, which is nothing but the struggle between the respective groups of the bourgeoisie. But now these 'national economic organisms . . . have long ceased being a secluded whole'. The 'map' reveals that the nature of international relations has changed: ' . . . they are only parts of a much larger sphere, namely *world economy*'. Just as once every individual enterprise was part of national economy so every one of these 'national economies' is included in the system of world economy. To Bukharin, then, the struggle between modern 'national economic bodies' is a 'struggle of various competing parts of the world economy'. Where previously competition had taken place first and foremost inside the national boundaries with only marginal competition on the level of the world as a whole, the relation has now been reversed. The competition, largely eliminated within states, is transferred to a world at large: now it is whole countries that are subject to absorption by others, not simply capitalist enterprises. 'Imperialist annexation is only a case of the general capitalist tendency towards centralisation of capital, a case of its centralisation on the maximum scale which corresponds to the competition of state capitalist trusts' (Bukharin, 1966, 119–20).

Thus the 'world economy' possesses every major feature that once characterized national economies. The world 'whole' replaces the national 'wholes' and international relations become internalized on a world scale. There are now social relations of production on a world scale and one world-wide international division of labour which results from two sets of factors: first, from the different natural conditions that prevail in different areas, and second, from the different levels of development attained in these areas. 'Important as the natural differences in the conditions of production may be, they recede more and more into the background compared with the differences that are the result of uneven development of productive forces in the various countries' (ibid. 20). It follows that the cleavage between town and country upon which such stress had been placed by Marx, whilst confined then to one country only, has become reproduced on a very much wider scale. Entire countries now appear reduced to 'town' scale (that is the industrialized countries), whilst the vast agrarian territories are seen as 'country' (ibid. 21). Furthermore, an international division of labour of this sort is an 'economic *prius* impossible to destroy. . . . Not economic self-sufficiency, but an intensification of International Relations . . . such is the road of future evolution' (ibid. 148). Like many of his contemporaries, Bukharin gets carried away by the emphasis placed on the nature of state. Writers before Bukharin had seen states as relatively independent entities, and although instrumental (through the medium of foreign policies) in articulating the interests of the strongest class(es), held aloof from the multitude of individual capital. Bukharin now postulates a virtual merger of state and (by finance capital united) capitalists, a merger epitomized in the expression 'state monopoly capitalism'. Here, then, nation-states assume considerable importance—as categories of political economy and component parts of the world economy. Bukharin explains in a footnote that he is concerned with only one of the two meanings conveyed by the term 'national': 'when we speak of "national" capital, "national" economy . . . we have in mind, here as elsewhere, not the element of nationality in the strict sense of the word but the *territorial conception of economic life*' (authors' italics). The concept of nation-state, and with it international relations, are of interest in so far and inasmuch as they are filled with economic content. It is, as we shall maintain, a position *not* characteristic of the Austro-Marxists who, when they too address themselves to the concepts of nation and state, do so with a like regard for that 'strict sense' disregarded by Bukharin.

In the Bukharin representation the world is thus a world of economic enterprises organized nationally. 'It follows that world capitalism, the world system of production, assumes in our times the following aspect: a few consolidated, organised economic bodies ("the great civilised powers") on the one hand, and a periphery of underdeveloped countries with a semi agrarian or agrarian system on the other' (ibid. 73–4). Thus there emerge types of (inter-capitalist) international relations between the 'towns' (to use Bukharin's imagery) and between capitalist countries and colonies. Thus also, what in Marx's time had been mere 'external' relations between homogeneous capitalist states and pre-capitalist social formations become types of international relations within the context of one (capitalist but hetero-geneous) economy: a first type that is operative amongst the individual 'towns' and a second between Bukharin's 'towns' and 'country'. The split that now separated these Marxists from Marx ran even deeper: the class struggle, previously contained within individual states, now spilled over into the world economy and the new adversaries in that struggle are no longer classes but states. States have become class-states to accord with the position they occupy *vis-à-vis* the global division of labour, and instead of oppressor and oppressed classes within states, we now have oppressor and oppressed states, representative of the global class conflict. Paying heed to Bukharin's repeated injunction that 'bourgeois science . . . does not understand that a basis for the classification of various "policies" must exist in the social economy out of which the "policies" arise' (ibid. 113), we proceed now to distinguish between (1) relations amongst imperialist states, and (2) relations between these imperialist states and colonies.

1.   The relations amongst imperialist states

The anarchy that is characteristic of the world's political structure, that of a world divided into legally sovereign states with no central source of authority, received an enormous boost when at national level an anarchic capitalist competitiveness was overtaken by the formation of cartels and relocated itself on the international level. The competitive nature of both capitalism *and* of international intercourse was in itself bad enough: in the eyes of many Marxist theorists of imperialism the effect of the two combined is profound. To Bukharin, as to Lenin, Hilferding, and Luxemburg, wars in these circumstances became inevitable, inescapable. Peaceful competition was impossible except in interim breathing-spells between wars. Militarism was necessary, calls for disarmament and neutralism ridiculous. Just as states had once upon a time been divided up into capitalist concerns, the world economy is now comprised of capitalist states, and whilst previously it was capitalist firms that would fall victim, to be swallowed up in the competitive process, the same fate could now the more readily befall states, since international relations legitimates and facilitates the use of force.

In a classical Marxist formulation Bukharin offers a most lucid explanation of the nature of conflict: he refers to the growing discord between the basis of social economy which is world-wide and the peculiar structure of society, in which the ruling class (the bourgeoisie) itself is split into 'national groups'. These 'national groups', with contradictory economic interests, are at one and the same time opposed to the 'world proletariat' in competition amongst themselves for the division of surplus value created on a world scale. International relations, the division of the world politically into states, have now in this reading become *a part of the relations of production*, and act as the proverbial Marxist 'fetters' standing as obstacles in the path of the world-wide forces of production. Conflict in such circumstances is inevitable: the tendency is to seek by way of bloody struggle rectification of this discrepancy through extension of the state frontiers—a rearrangement which bears within itself the seeds of ever more violent conflict (ibid. 106). Bukharin proceeds to amend Clausewitz: wars are not a mere continuation of politics by other means but an active 'continuation in space of a given mode of production. . . . Simply to define war, however, as a conquest is entirely insufficient, for the simple reason that in doing so we fail to indicate the main thing, namely, *what* production relations are strengthened or extended by the war, what basis is widened by a given ''policy of conquest'' ' (ibid. 113). It was a view shared fully by Lenin. There was no such thing as a general concept of 'aggression' and one could in fact surmise that 'aggression by a proletarian state' was a nonsensical proposition. In fact proletarian states—in that short period of coexistence—could be expected to attack capitalist states, for in those early stages no such thing as peaceful coexistence was contemplated. A future socialist state could not go wrong in its foreign policy: for history rallied to its side and progress was its watchword. The foundations of the (future) USSR's foreign policy were set.

Whilst agreeing on the analysis of the *nature* of war and more generally on conflict amongst capitalist states, the individual Marxist schools are divided as to the method of adjustment of the relations of production (including international relations) to the world-wide forces of production. Karl Kautsky (1854–1938), for one, saw the possibility of that adjustment being brought about by capitalism itself. In his theory of 'ultra-imperialism' (1914) he thought capitalism would go through an additional stage, which would see an aggrandizement of the policy of cartels into a foreign policy; this phase of ultra- or supra-imperialism involving the union of imperialists across the globe would bring to an end their struggles with one another. The notion, in other words, of a co-operative effort in the Grotian tradition enabling a joint exploitation of the world by internationally merged finance capital.

Lenin's *law of the uneven development of capitalism* effectively demolished the Kautsky thesis. Whereas Kautsky, following Marx, postulated the possibility of an *even* development of capitalism, Lenin totally rejected the idea: 'inter-imperialist' or 'ultra-imperialist' alliances, no matter what form they might take, whether of one imperialist coalition against another, or of a general alliance embracing *all* the imperialist powers, are *inevitably* nothing more than a 'truce in periods between wars'. To Lenin, in other words, the tendency to war between rival capitalist countries is constant and inevitable.

2. *Relations between imperialist countries and colonies*

The same 'law of uneven capitalist development' when applied to the relationship between advanced and backward countries meant the possibility of the *reversal* of their relative positions. According to Lenin, a disparity existed between the development of productive forces, the accumulation of capital, the division of colonies, and the spheres of influence for finance capital, and thus, according to Lenin, colonies are relatively speaking more exploited; it is there, where capital is at its weakest, that the revolutionary outbreaks would be most likely to occur. Hobson's concept of a 'labour aristocracy' (or rather its negation in Lenin's case where the colonies generated the revolutionary impulses) is the mechanism by which is effected the transference of the revolution from these areas back to the advanced capitalist countries.

Hobson, Bukharin, and Lenin see eye to eye in so far as the labour élite of advanced countries may be invited to share in the extra profits (superprofits) that the exploitation is to yield and may as a consequence be deflected from their true revolutionary path. Pushing this line of reasoning beyond Hobson, Lenin and Bukharin believed that once the source of such superprofits (and with it the source of the labour leaders' corruption) was purged by revolutionary action, the labour leaders would 'come to their senses'. Receiving its initial impetus in the colonies, the revolutionary wave would develop to the point where it would roll over and engulf the advanced capitalist countries, and so the effect of imperialism on colonies is (as it was for Marx) ultimately positive. There is no suggestion of any permanent and irreversible damage being done to the colonial areas: their incorporation into the world capitalist economy and the unevenness of this development (the cause, it will be recalled, of the emergence of imperialism in the first place) involves simply a recharting of the route leading to the world-wide demise of capitalism.

Rosa Luxemburg's views on this subject diverged radically from, in particular, those held by Bukharin and Lenin. Although any number of Marxist economists were able to demolish her theory—specifically her revision and application of Marx's schemata of reproduction as set forth in Volume II of *Capital*—there is a closer affinity between many of her conclusions and those of present-day neo-Marxists. For these reasons, if for no other, Luxemburg's thoughts on the subject deserve a mention. By pushing Marx's notion of the concentration of capital to an (international) extreme she, in contrast to Lenin, sees in process the polarization of wealth between poor and rich nations—albeit her perception is of a temporary rather than a permanent development. In contrast to Lenin's envisaged possibility of a reversal of relative positions in the disequilibrated capitalist economy leading to fresh conflicts, Luxemburg saw a widening gap opening between the positions; and a gap which has been identified by her Marxist grandsons as a permanent feature of the capitalist economy. Her own position on the political spectrum is incidentally even further to the left than was Lenin's Left in the Second International—but differences of a still more fundamental nature distinguish Luxemburg's position from that of Lenin's faction.

In terms of the driving force behind capitalist expansion, Luxemburg sees survival as an additional motivation beyond the inherent capitalist drive for profits. Again, capitalism to Luxemburg is inherently incapable of autonomous existence: it absolutely requires areas not yet capitalist into which to expand. Those 'outside' areas to which she refers are those 'outside' the mode of production, that geographically speaking may lie either outside the capitalist states or within their perimeter. Capitalism as a dependent mode of production becomes self-destructive once it absorbs all of the non-capitalist areas: its demise is then assured and only a matter of time. Thus for Luxemburg the relation between the capitalist countries and the pre-capitalist colonies has much more of a life and death character than is seen to be the case by either Lenin or Bukharin. In the interim, while awaiting the fate that must follow the absorption of all of the 'outside' areas, 'catastrophes' in the shape of wars succeed one another and precipitate the end (Luxemburg, 1951, 446). Imperialism is thus a 'final stage' in the historical career of capitalism (ibid. 417). It is self-destructive in its progressive 'sterilisation' of its virgin lands and markets, and the relationship with colonies assumes thus a degree of urgency unknown even to Hobbes or Machiavelli as capitalist states engage in these areas in what is essentially a defensive struggle against their inevitable (capitalist) demise. It is an unavailing struggle, however, since the end is preordained. Essentially then, Luxemburg, far from seeing any possibility of capitalism's becoming a world economy, would have viewed such an eventuality as something of a logical impossibility: it was at that point also that capitalism would destroy itself.

In the course of promoting an analysis that attracted as much criticism as did that of Karl Kautsky, Luxemburg was the first-ever Marxist to escape the marked Eurocentristic inclination of all of her Marxist contemporaries. Although others travelled the same road in their elevation of non-European areas to prominent parts of their theories, Luxemburg was the first to push the study of the interrelationship between imperialism and its colonies to such original conclusions. One conclusion that she did not reach was the neo-Marxist postulate that the imperialist presence would have a lasting negative effect on the colonies. The reason for the omission is not hard to find: Luxemburg's theory of 'catastrophes' to describe the abbreviated future of capitalism did not allow any possibility of capitalism's remaining alive in the colonies long enough (let alone permanently) to damage the colonial areas to that extent. Luxemburg, aware that capitalism, on its way to inevitable extinction, could still in its death struggles put an end also to the whole of mankind, arrived at two conclusions, conclusions that were seemingly inconsistent with her theories. First, and in order to preempt such a fate for mankind, she urged the 'international working class to revolt against the rule of capital' (ibid. 419). As a second prophylactic against the ultimate catastrophe Luxemburg placed herself in the forefront of her generation's anti-war campaign. Her name is usually linked in this regard to that of Karl Liebknecht, her fellow member in the *Spartakusbund*. Although their careers (and their deaths at the hands of an assassin) followed a similar course, their pacifist attitudes derived from slightly different sources. Liebknecht's anti-militarist stance stemmed from his belief that the military, in the course of its history, had developed as a force in its *own right* and was no longer simply another means for the achievement of political ends: 'The history of militarism is firstly the history of the political, social-economic and above all, cultural tensions between states and nations; secondly it is the history of class struggles within single states and nations.'[5] Far from merely talking about anti-imperialism, Liebknecht, seeking to bolster his views with concrete action, found himself over the years in and out of prison as a political activist, and was eventually charged with high treason. Nevertheless, he contrived to expose a strong interlocking relationship between the state and the armaments industry, accusing the Krupp concern of having illicit access to the Ministry of War. In addition to such domestic links he proved the existence of co-ordinated activity between the international armaments industries, as for instance the Austrian and Belgian-based Krupp factories supplying arms to Russia (financed by French capital) despite the fact that Russian and French hostility was the reason advanced for increased military expenditure in Germany. Likewise those same British naval dockyards which were filling orders for warships for Britain had financial interests in other firms handling similar orders on behalf of Austria and Italy (Trotnow, 1975, 181).

Liebknecht and Luxemburg were among those Marxists most upset by the response of the socialist movement to the outbreak of World War I. According to the (1907) Stuttgart Congress of the Second International it had been decided, first, to oppose the outbreak of war altogether. If despite such efforts war were to break out, then it was resolved, second, to work for its speedy conclusion and in the meantime to use the economic and political crisis conditions introduced by the war for the mobilization of the people and the hastening of the overthrow of capitalism. In the event, however, these resolutions went by the board and Liebknecht's lone vote in the Reichstag against war credits turned into no more than a heroic gesture. Luxemburg herself put it well when she described the transformation of the 'proud old cry' of 'Working men of all countries, unite!' into 'Working men of all countries slit each

[5] K. Liebknecht *Militarismus und Antimilitarismus unter Besonderer Berücksichtigung der Internationalen Jugendbewegung*, Leipzig, 1907 (quoted in Trotnow, 1975, 43).

other's throats!' To her the war was a 'relapse into barbarism and contrary to general belief, an act of forsaking the fatherland, [for] the German people victory or defeat in this war is equally disastrous' (quoted in Carsten, 1974, 58–60).

Nations, nationalism

The lack of a theory of nation was a continuing source of embarrassment to classical Marxism and such notions as Engels's 'non-historical nations' did nothing to relieve the situation as before and during World War I, the nationalism both of the imperialists and of the working class continued to get in the way of the various Marxist expectations. In this regard several aspects of the 'national question' can be discerned. The first of those differences lay in the *theoretical explanation* of nations and nationalism, either by way of the concept of historical materialism or by reference to factors transcending historical materialism, and, second, the different *strategies* that were devised for the working-class movement by just about every Marxist, showed little or no regard to, or connection with, the theoretical explanation. In this latter context the spectrum ranged enormously from a total rejection of support for nationalism, as exemplified by Rosa Luxemburg's position, to Lenin's concept of national self-determination designed to capture nationalist movements and steer them into the Bolshevik orbit with a view to their eventual 'fusion'. Trotsky shared this view of Lenin's as sole precondition for 'peace between nations' as opposed to the 'peace of diplomats'. At the other end of the spectrum were, most notably, the Austro-Marxists who, acutely aware of the circumstances of the multinational Austro-Hungarian Empire, favoured the preservation of national autonomy within a multinational state. This solution was believed to have merit both in such a preservation for its own sake and because autonomy was deemed a *sine qua non* for the perpetuation of otherwise irreplaceable cultures (Löwy, 1976, 90).

It is the theoretical explanation of the phenomenon of nation rather than the different revolutionary strategies that interests us in the present context. Our selection of a few from a broad spectrum of theories is necessarily arbitrary.

Nationalism as cause or effect of 'uneven development' and of imperialism?

The explanation of nationalism is implied as a corollary of Lenin's law of uneven development of capitalism. Capitalism did not permeate evenly the target areas but, striking at a differential rate within these areas (as across the spectrum of the regions involved) meant the inevitable establishment of a varied-conflict pattern of exploiter – exploited. In those regions, therefore, nationalism became a defensive response with feedback to a region prior in the developmental chain which in its turn developed a more self-conscious, more assertive 'great power' nationalism. The connection is implied in most economic theories of imperialism and made explicit in the writings of such as Stalin and Sultan-Galiev. This interpretation simply connects the emergence of two types of nationalism with the unevenness of capitalist development. The first impulse comes ('properly') from the economic substructure but their reactive interplay assumes an autonomous dynamic of its own (independently of the substructural basis). So powerfully influential might nationalism become that the continuing international conflict, and in fact national identity itself , may be seen to overshadow the class conflict. International relations are thus vested with economic and (only indirectly) with class content. Nationalism as such, and as a foundation of the international system, may thus be regarded as an *effect* of the development of the capitalist mode of production and of its separate social formations.

The dividing line is not always clear between this approach and that which takes nationalism to be a *contributing* factor in the development of imperialism. In such a case nationalism might be seen to act as a more or less independent force—a force and an action that are often difficult to explain in Marxist terms. The classical statement of this latter position is made by Hilferding (1910, quoted in Bukharin, 1966, 109).

With a steady and clear eye does it [finance capital] view the Babylonian confusion of peoples, and above all of them it sees its own nation. The latter is real; it lives in a powerful state, which keeps increasing its power and grandeur, and which devotes all its forces to making them greater. In this way, the interests of the individual are subjugated to the interests of the whole—a condition without which no social ideology can live; a nation and a state that are hostile to the people are tied into one whole, and the national idea, as a motive power, is subjugated to politics. The class conflicts have disappeared; they have been annihilated, absorbed as they are serving the interests of the whole. In place of the dangerous class struggle, fraught for the owners with unknown consequences, there appear the general actions of the nation which is united by one aim—the striving for national grandeur.

According to Hilferding, expansionist policies upset the entire world view of the bourgeoisie and replace their pacific and humanitarian views: 'The idea of peace fades, and the idea of humanity is replaced by the ideal of the grandeur and power of the state. The ideal is to insure for one's own nation the domination of the world . . . Founded in economic needs, it finds its justification in this remarkable reversal of national consciousness. Racial ideology is thus a rationalisation, disguised as science, of the ambitions of finance capital' (Hilferding, 1910, 452–4, quoted in Brewer, 1981, 98). Thus, in summary, Bukharin sees the interests of finance capital acquiring a grandiose ideological formulation, as every effort is made to inculcate it into the mass of workers (Bukharin, 1966, 109).

Karl Renner's concept of 'social imperialism' as the doctrine and practice of the whole people encapsulates this position. But as we said earlier, a significant distinction is to be made between the view of nationalism as a mere element in the development of imperialism (cf. Bukharin, Lenin) and its perception as one of the contributing factors (cf. Hilferding and especially Otto Bauer among other Austro-Marxists).

The Austro-Marxist explanation of nation

The Austro-Marxist approach to the 'National Question' is consistent with the typical 'centrist' position of the school as a whole, between the progressively more pronounced reformism of the Social Democratic parties at one extreme and the Bolsheviks at the other. In 1917 these latter were soon to take the leadership of the movement of communist parties—so renamed as to make the distinction clear and allow of no ambivalence in meaning. The sobriquet of 'Second and a half

International' (1921–3) showed something of a similar awareness of the significance of nomenclature. This 'International', inspired by the Austro-Marxist desire to re-establish an international 'centre', epitomized well the centre position occupied by the Austro-Marxists between the dismally failed Second International on the one hand and the Third International (the Comintern, 1919–43), under the leadership of the victorious Bolshevik/Communist party of the Soviet Union, on the other.

A characteristic feature of the Austro-Marxist school was the tendency to emphasize the role of a capitalist state as a preparatory agency for the future socialist society and thus to see it as not altogether an institution of negative value. The breakdown of capitalism in this reading would come as a consequence of the working of social and political forces; these forces manifested in a movement led by the working class and a political party designed to complete the process of establishing a substantively regional economic system—that 'rational interchange between man and nature' which Marx saw as a characteristic feature of socialism (Bottomore, 1978, 24). Hand in hand with the emphasis on this superstructural phenomenon went emphasis on another superstructural phenomenon: nation. Otto Bauer's *Die Nationalitätenfrage und die Sozialdemokratie* of 1907 on which Hilferding drew for his *Finanzkapital* is the largest ever single Marxist work devoted to the problem. Attacked at the time by Marxists from virtually every quarter (cf. Pannekoek, *Class Struggle and Nation*, 1912, and Strasser, *Worker and Nation*, 1912), there is a curious affinity in Bauer's approach and that of the Bolshevik 'expert' on nationalities and the national question, Josef Vissarionovich Stalin, whose definition of nation as set forth in his 'Marxism and the National Question' (1913) displays certain Bauerian features.[6] Both Bauer and Stalin seem to argue that the nation will not 'wither away' in socialism and that indeed it is only in socialism that nations may come to their full flowering. Despite Trotsky's

[6] Stalin defines nation as 'a historically constituted, stable community of people, formed on the basis of a common language, territory, economic life, and psychological make-up manifested in a common culture'. Not many existing nations would pass Stalin's test, however, for 'it is only when all these characteristics are present together that we have a nation' (J. V. Stalin, 'Marxism and the National Question', in Franklin, 1972, 61.)

attribution of the authorship of the substance of that essay to Lenin, the references to 'national character', 'common psychological make up', etc. could not possibly have Lenin as author: the thoughts articulated here are Stalin's, and, as we have observed, reveal distinct Bauerian influences.

Bauer's understanding of nation is by no means easy to follow. He does not find any contradiction between Marxist proletarian internationalism and nationalism. Nor does he feel the need, as did many other Marxists (among them Lenin and Trotsky), simply to channel and turn to account the pent-up strength of nationalist sentiment for the advancement of proletarian internationalism. Bauer has no difficulty in imagining that workers are linked at one and the same time by bonds of class and of nationalism, for to him 'cultural values' appear potentially 'neutral' and devoid of class content. Socialism will in fact purge nationalism of these national animosities which to Bauer as much as to all other Marxists were derived solely from class antagonisms. Criticized for not advocating the right of self-determination—to many Marxists a tactical device—Bauer thought cultural autonomy within the context of a multinational state would provide an adequate setting for the harmonious coexistence of nations into the future. The strong neo-Kantian overtones of his thought emerge in the form of a certain mysticism in his understanding of nation whilst at the same time he is able to fit it into historical materialism. The different (natural) conditions of life implied by the latter lead him towards Darwinism and the differentiated selection and evolution of physical types. Thus the cultural and psychological make-up of the nation derives from shared conditions of life and, consistent with historical materialism, the nation is a historical category developing over time. Rejecting any single-cause explanation of nation, and premonitory of Stalin's own later more exclusive definition, Bauer's 'comprehensive' definition sees the nation as 'the totality of men bound together through a common destiny into a community of character' (quoted in Bottomore, 1978, 107). A common history is the effective cause, whilst a shared culture and common descent are the means by which the effects are produced; a common language is the mediator of a common language (that is to say both product and producer). The common territory is a condition for the other 'elements'

· to become operative. The relationship of nation to its most
important constituent body, the state, rests on its relationship
to a territory (ibid. 103, 105). The origin both of nations and
of classes is seen to lie respectively in natural and economic
causes, and any disturbance to the existence of the nation is
attributable to the interference of classes. As Bauer puts it:

. . . our search for the essence of the nation reveals a grandiose historical
picture. At the outset, in the primitive communism . . . there is a
unitary nation as a community of descent. Then, . . . the old nation
is divided into the common culture of the ruling classes on one side,
and the peasants and small farmers on the other . . . Later, with the
development of the capitalist mode of production . . . the working and
exploited classes are still excluded, but the tendency to national unity
. . . gradually becomes stronger . . . Finally when society divests social
production of its capitalist integuments the unitary nation . . . emerges
again. The development of the nation reflects the history of the mode
of production and of property . . . (ibid. 108–9).

The fact that nations predate classes does not preclude (as it
did for Marx) Bauer's subordinating them conceptually to proper
Marxist channels:

[in the] national conception of history, which sees the driving force
of events in the struggles of nations . . . nations are regarded as elements
which cannot be reduced any further, as fixed bodies which clash in
space . . . But my conception dissolves the nation itself into a process
. . . history no longer reflects the struggles of nations; instead the nation
itself appears as the reflection of historical struggles. For the nation
is only manifested in the national character, in the nationality of the
individual; and the nationality of the individual is only one aspect of
his determination by the history of society, by the development of the
conditions and techniques of labour (ibid. 108–9).

The nature of international relations, then, if one were to
enquire of Bauer's theory, is a function of the peculiar and
enormously complex interplay of economic, social, and cultural
causes. In these states based on class division, however, one
may perceive class motive, albeit complicated by cultural
diversity, to be most significant. After the removal of class
antagonisms Bauer is not in the least troubled by the coexistence
of nations which, rather than interfering with the realization
of the Marxian ideal, make a significant contribution by bringing
the wealth of cultural diversity to the promotion of that ideal.

To complete the picture of this Marxist generation we move even further to the right to encounter the 'revisionists'. Through the work of one of the founders of revisionism, Eduard Bernstein (1850–1932), first steps were taken towards the creation of a new ideology of social democracy which was soon to become more Liberal than Marxist. Although only genetically connected to Marxism it is none the less important, for in fact it displaced Marxism in much of Europe as the principal ideology of the socialist movement, and ever since has shown a tendency to surface even from within the ranks of those other socialists who did not surrender their Marxist commitment.

Bernstein, with his open and sustained interest in international relations was indeed a rare bird in the Marxist coop, denying as he did in his explanation of the nature of international relations the characteristic Marxist economic nexus, 'the saying the worker has no fatherland, is not to be found in my political vocabulary'. He adduced a national commitment just as much as an international commitment to the working class. With such radical departures from the mainstream of Marxist (and Liberal) theories of imperialism he foreshadowed in his conclusions those of the later liberal schools of 'interdependence'. Thus, financial capital, so despised by Hilferding and others, became conducive in Bernstein's view to greater national understanding and interdependence, and he sought and found in Marx approval of colonialism.[7] In explanation of international relations, and war in particular, he concluded that it was the anachronistic fabric of the states-system itself, comprising such absurd creations as sovereignty, diplomacy, and balance of power, that was to be blamed. He had already declared the balance of power system to be outmoded as early as 1899. But to Bernstein the roots of conflict were to be found in the competition of antithetical ideologies exacerbated by a states-system that created and created anew, conflict, friction, and antagonisms. War became a necessary adjunct of the international system, the belligerency taking the form, if not of a clash of arms, then of a 'silent, or cold war'.[8] War and the 'gospel of power politics', were to be abolished, to vanish in some form of supranational

---

[7] In *Voraussetzungen*, 211, quoted in Fletcher, 1981, 328.
[8] In *RT Verhandlungen*, Vol. 295 (15 May 1914), 8888, quoted in Fletcher, 1981, 314.

political confederation with the parallel opening of a new epoch of international law. The kernel of these developments was already present in and .would flourish with the growing interdependence of all nations: they would not, in other words, be the outcome of violent revolution. When Bernstein declared before the Reichstag in May 1912 that international relations were the supreme and central issue of the age,[9] one wonders whether his arrival at such an auspicious conclusion could be reached only through the abandonment of Marxist axioms which have circumscribed the vision of so many Marxists then and since and have acted as limiting determinants on their explanation of international relations.

As for Marxists since that time, reconciliation of political and economic causes of imperialism and of international relations generally was indeed the most sensitive and divisive of the issues to be resolved. The argument revolved round such questions as whether imperialism was an optional and deliberate policy on the part of the state, in which case political conquest would be one of the attributes of a states-system (in which case also there still remained for Marxists a need to explain the states-system) and not necessarily the product of any one mode of production in particular. Alternatively, was the imperialist drive inherent in the capitalist mode of production and thus responsible for forcing certain policies on states? Or again, would the processes of imperialism have proceeded in any case (as Rosa Luxemburg had argued all along) with need neither of 'interference' nor political conquest by states?

Marxism's analytical strength is in the inseparability of economics and politics and in its rejection of the analysis of things political in isolation, or, by the same token, of the study of international politics alone. For these first Marxists international relations was a subject responsive neither to political investigation alone nor to economic investigation alone but came under the rubric of *political economy* where the study of the reciprocal and dynamic interaction of the pursuit of wealth and the pursuit of power in international relations was addressed (Gilpin, 1975, 43). To delimit the shape of the analytical

[9] In *RT Verhandlungen*, Vol. 284 (14 May 1912) 1996, quoted in Fletcher, 1981, 357–8.

framework is of course one thing, to strike the precise ratio of the relative weight to be accorded all possible explanatory factors is quite another. At a time when international relations have indeed become 'the supreme and central issue of the age' we try to trace in later chapters the outcome of the various questions and answers originating with this first generation of Marxist theories of international relations.

Part II

Marxists become also Diplomats

4 The USSR

The USSR owes its relevance to the study of Marxism and International Relations to a number of interconnected reasons. The student of International Relations does not advance far along the path before he encounters the 'Russian Question' and must decide on the nature of the Soviet superpower, and the Marxist student of international relations in particular, conversant with the notion of a state's external behaviour as a function of its domestic structure, discovers a preliminary excursion into Sovietology to be a prerequisite to his further travel. This latter must ask himself such basic questions as whether the Soviet Union is the first Marxist state (as she claims for herself); has her 'actual socialism' been since the beginning a socialism *manquée*, or has the deformation taken place at some later date? And then, in this latter event, is the 'deformed' socialism based on a brand new or on a transitional mode of production? Has its deformity led, or is it leading to, a simple mutation—of a capitalist state? If the conclusion is that the USSR is not a socialist state, is the essence of East-West relations, then, a simple mix of 'inter-imperialist rivalry', or 'ultra-imperialist co-operation'? In any other case—if, in other words (as in the Marxist perception) the Soviet Union is a 'different animal' distinguished as such by a non-capitalist nature, then it follows that her foreign policy too should be 'different' and based on radically different foundations. Exactly how radical will depend on the perception of the distance already travelled in her transit.

We have already concluded elsewhere that the Soviet Union can boast a theory of international relations. If we are to accept that she has had some success in 'transiting' away from capitalism then the delineation of a self-image and portrayal of her own location within her own cosmology becomes of crucial interest to a Marxist 'theorist' of international relations. We suggested earlier, in circumstances where there may be perceived to prevail a general dilution of Marxism and the absence of any objective criteria for the establishment of the permissible limits of such dilution, that we accept as sufficient criterion a rule-of-thumb self-designation as Marxist. The Soviet Union goes further, claiming to be not only Marxist (Marxist-Leninist) but to constitute the élite contingent of the world revolutionary forces. The official Soviet ideology and that of her ever expanding empire is Marxism – Leninism, and according to its own lights Soviet foreign policy is part of the subjective aspect of the objectively-given historical process. In Soviet theory the USSR's birth signalled the entry of the world capitalist system into its 'general crisis' the first stage of which was to last until World War II (the second stage until the onset of the decolonization process, and the third is still in progress), each stage representing an advance in Man's quest to free himself from an alienated social organization. Be that as it may, the stages have indeed been punctuated by enormous geopolitical and strategic advances on the part of the USSR. And yet, despite the seemingly irrefutable testimony of history (and of the map) a sizeable part of Western theory has taken it upon itself to deny that such advances are Marxist-inspired and/or that they are advances at all. There has been created not only a fully-fledged academic industry to investigate the non-expansion, but there has also been generated something of a vested interest and commitment to a (non-Marxist/non-expansion) argument whose ponderous weight accumulated over the years has brought its own corresponding inertia, manifest in terms of irreversibility! It is worth a thought that this industry, too, may unwittingly have become part of the 'world historical process' contriving as it has done to explain that Soviet advances are not advances and that the Soviet rule at home and in Eastern Europe is about to 'crumble' under the tremendous weight of economic and political problems caused by the usurpation and coming to power of an illegitimate government—that, in brief, we are dealing with an ordinary, albeit parvenu, superpower, fully committed to orderly behaviour within the context of the international system.

Fascinating though it might be to explore the seeming paradox of a state portrayed as 'normal' and committed to 'orderly' behaviour managing in such a short space to make the transition from humble, backward (socialism in one country) beginnings to the leadership of a global hierarchy, we must confine ourselves here to Soviet international relations theory, and will turn later (Chapter 10) to an investigation of 'Marxist sovietology' in so far as it predicates Marxist perceptions of the nature of the 'East-West' conflict. In Chapter 8 we survey Soviet and Chinese attitudes towards international law and international organization and their deployment as instruments of (Soviet and Chinese) policy, and we aim in the process to arrive at some idea of the effect the 'Marxist' powers have had on these traditional cornerstones of the states-system. In the meantime, space limits us to a brief outline in the present chapter of the main contours of the Soviet 'sociology' of international relations.

Soviet ideology and theories of international relations

Dismissed on various grounds by most critics in the Western world, Soviet theories of international relations can in that sense hardly be said to have travelled well. To many Marxists the USSR either ceased with Stalin's excesses to be Marxist or was never Marxist in the first place. And yet, when faced with the implausibility of a seemingly irreconcilable relationship between Marxism and international relations the almost impossible has been achieved. On to the received Marxist framework that committed the USSR to the class analysis the Soviet leaders/theorists managed, as the country became part of the international system, to graft a theory of international relations which thus became a theory of international order and world order at one and the same time. In other words the synchronic working of vertical axes of analyses (class and world order) brought a result that was neither one nor the other of those analytical lines in pure form, but a mix of both ('diagonalization' as we have described it elsewhere[1]). The resultant 'sociology of international relations' combines the analytical lines of states and classes and, whilst undoubtedly corruptive of both, affords a comprehensive picture of the world: a picture indeed that is more complete than many produced either by Western and Third World Marxists or by Western theorists of International Relations, inhibited as are both categories by their one-dimensional world view.

[1] Kubálková, Cruickshank, 1980, 220.

The anti-communism of Western Marxism aside, to Western theorists generally Soviet theories of international relations have proved unacceptable. The fact that the grounds for the dismissal have displayed a lack of uniformity, not to say a flexibility, might be thought to reflect upon the legitimacy of the findings, and particularly so since these (grounds) have tended to shift in sympathy with the vagaries of the relationship between the United States and the Soviet Union. Ranging the spectrum and offered as good and sufficient reasons, we are informed that Soviet theories are too Marxist(!); too ideological; or are possessed of legitimizing/mobilizing purpose but without heuristic value. Alternatively, and on the (mistaken) assumption that the 'conflation of political practice and theory' is no business of scholarship, there is the view that although Soviet 'theories' might perhaps throw some light on Soviet intentions (the self-fulfilling prophecy of the maniac) they do not contribute to our understanding of the problems of international relations with the elucidation of which Western-devised models deal more adequately. More recently it has become fashionable to suggest that with the achievement of superpower status the Soviet Union has shed ideology altogether to become integrated into the world economy. Proponents of this view see their claims borne out by a Soviet theory and practice that are allegedly increasingly Westernized, state-centrist, cleansed of the tarnish of Marxism.

The controversy centred on the relative contribution of 'ideology' to the Soviet foreign policy-making process is answered in part by an awareness of the fundamental misunderstanding about Soviet ideology. Soviet ideology is neither amorphous nor homogeneous, but consists of a highly-structured corpus of ideas whose various roles accord with their overall position within that framework. We picture a pyramidal structure to whose well-defined apex are joined equally distinct interconnected layers. The closer one approaches the base, the more important becomes a decrease in generality, to be replaced by an inversely proportionate gain in flexibility and plasticity. Whilst the apex performs a largely legitimizing role and also acts as a binding agent on the whole political system (a catalytic effect, itself having remained virtually unchanged throughout Soviet history), the heuristic role of the pyramid's lower layers, in terms of reflecting both reality and the thrust of Soviet purposes, increases as these layers (increasingly towards the base) reduce in axiomatic content and multiply the variables open to debate and research. With this said, it clearly becomes a case of misplaced rejoicing to record the seriousness of the approach and the high quality of research taking place in such areas as economics, anthropology, and theories of development in the lower layers. Such research is devised to strengthen, supplement, and provide rationalization for the higher pyramidal levels, and it is not difficult to point to instances where the research findings have 'trickled up' to set in motion precisely those processes of change to which we have referred. Thus change is confined to parts, affecting less, therefore, the integrity of the whole structure—and least of all the apex itself. With the pyramidal structure in mind it may be seen as equally erroneous to dismiss the entire Soviet ideology as 'rhetoric'; such a tendency stems from a failure to recognize the sharp decrease in 'rhetorical' content in the lower levels. Perhaps an examination of the various parts of Soviet ideology might help to clarify the situation further.

At the apex of the ideology there are a few unassailable verities. There is the moral creed and goal of communism, as well as certain elemental beliefs about the nature of society before the achievement of communism. This is the essence of the myth taught in school: essentially simple, eminently credible, widely propagated, and incidentally in these respects at sad variance with the Western Marxists who long ago abandoned the notion of simplicity and an appeal to mass comprehension (masses whose consciousness the doctrine is of course supposed to articulate), and to whom dissemination and accessibility to Marxist discourse meant too often its artificial confinement to a few of the *cognoscenti* versed in esoteric (Western) terminology. The simple story of Soviet Marxism portrays history as deriving always from the economic bases, the key to which is the class struggle. Society proceeds through stages that are dependent on the ownership of production, and which in the later stages is through the feudal order dominated by landowners and thence to capitalism dominated by the 'bourgeoisie'. When that (bourgeois) class is eventually expropriated by the workers, they (the workers) establish a new and superior form of society, socialism, which is conceived to grow into the ultimate, perfect stage of communism wherein will be realized the redemption of mankind in a society of freedom—freedom from money, work, exploitation. In a society plagued by a chronic shortage of consumer goods the promise of abundant fulfilment of the needs of all is not without an understandable appeal. Notions such as 'bourgeoisie', 'capitalist', 'feudal', 'class struggle', 'proletariat', 'communism' are themselves highly emotive and conjure up the fairy-tale creatures who people this Soviet land of Faerie. Communism as a moral and political goal takes its definition still from Lenin's formulations of 1920 and 1922 to the effect that whatever promotes revolution, and following that revolution whatever promotes the construction of communism, is seen to be good and moral. Any and all measures and instruments, including those of foreign policy, as long as they might plausibly be supposed to further the advance on these objectives, are *ipso facto* deemed legitimate and moral.

In the vagueness of the goal, and in its remoteness, there is ample opportunity to enable a relationship to be struck, or even a merger arrived at, with a notion of similarly opportune vagueness: 'national interest'. The security of the state and its defence thus becomes a prerequisite for the achievement of the goal of communism, as indeed does anything else where the meaning of 'necessary' and 'expedient' can be made to merge. That there exists a distinct possibility that the means designed to achieve the goal may in fact negate the goal is obvious. The danger becomes more acute when one considers such a definition of 'good' to represent a blank cheque which the government writes itself.

It will be remarked that no pyramidal level can be contradicted by the one immediately below. Subsequent layers in descending order add specificity in terms of concern with the actual construction of socialism/communism, on the *domestic* front and *through* international relations. As in the case of the definition of the moral and political goal the description of 'international relations' supplied in the level immediately below the apex has changed hardly at all. Consistent with the precepts of classical Marxism the world is portrayed as being in a state of unstable structural disequlibrium which is permanently inclining to change in the direction of eventual dissolution of all these structures save one—which introduces the idea of the ultimate domination of the world by a single structure with, overall, a new ideo-political consensus 'arrived at'. The disequilibrated world is no innovation but the date of final dissolution of the structures has moved progressively from 'imminent' to 'foreseeable' to 'unforeseeable' whilst at the same time the identity of the disequilibrated substructures has undergone change. What has not changed is the method of measuring the 'state of the world' or, in Soviet terms, arriving at an assessment of 'the correlation of forces'. This correlation purports to measure not only the relative strength of states and the overall condition of the states-system but goes beyond that balance of power function to apply the assessment to all other parts of the substructure and super-structure of all societies. In summary then: the belief in communism, albeit an increasingly remote prospect, coupled with the description of the world in permanently disequilibrated flux and the concept of gauging the world historical process (including the states-system), using as yardstick the 'correlation of forces', remain unchanged. The frequently recognized Soviet proclivity to accept change rather than stability as normal derives from these perceptions.

On the lower levels susceptible to change are located the long-term policies (strategies) that govern and delimit the short-term policies (tactics) at a still lower level. A tactic, say peaceful coexistence, can be promoted (as was for example peaceful coexistence in 1956) to strategy. Although such flexibility is normally confined to the upward mobility of tactics, mobility (upward or downward) in the case of strategies is not unknown. Strategy A may be replaced by strategy B if the bridge between them can be shown to be consistent with the higher ideological echelons. In that event strategy B might in fact become operational even if in total contradiction with its predecessor. A good example of the 'bridge' to which we refer is the 'law of uneven development' which once enabled Lenin's theories of imperialism to modify Marx's scheme. Again, the same 'law of uneven development' enabled the jettisoning of the 'theory of imperialism' and the application of 'socialism in one country' as strategy.

Each epoch has a number of strategies one of the main criteria of the efficacy of which is the degree of plausibility with which it invests the achievement of the goal (communism). In terms of the specifics the strategy addresses itself to the idea of a disequilibrated world and supplies important elaboration. Subject always to its retaining an acceptable consistency with the moral goal the strategy may also add significant details having a bearing on the system's transformation. Strategies share with the upper level the characteristic of refraining (as yet) from prescribing any particular course of action appropriate to any given development. This level (strategy) as a result may give to an observer the mistaken impression that its existence is owed to nothing more nor less than the serving of propaganda purposes. It is however only on the next (inferior) level that the elements (the tactical or short-term policies) seem increasingly to be bound up with thorough scientific research and the rationalization process of Soviet society—and from which some conclusion on immediate action can be derived. The upper levels of the ideology have remained surprisingly constant and have succeeded in providing a necessary continuity. Setting aside as beyond our scope such considerations as the leadership question, domestic policies, etc., we turn to the major changes in strategy and the tactical turns during the years in office of Lenin (1917–23), of Stalin (until 1953), of Khrushchev (until 1964), and of Brezhnev (until 1982).

Lenin

With the help of the theory (bridge) of the *uneven development of capitalism*, Lenin 'corrected' Marx who had located the major dysfunctional processes at work *inside* the advanced capitalist countries, and died too early to appreciate further developments in the capitalist mode of production. These comprised specifically the development of monopoly systems and, above all, the unevenness of capitalist development. To Lenin the unevenness of a fully globalized capitalism had become clear for the first time: the export of capital (necessary to offset declining rates of profit on capital) had led now to the destabilization not only of the individual countries but of the world as a whole. Increasingly there was a polarization between the developed countries and the colonies. Capitalism, it was realized, has a significant effect on the internal structures both of the 'Centre' and the 'Periphery' when it allows the deflection of the 'labour aristocracy', and with it the working class, from their revolutionary path. In real terms, the withdrawal of these crucial elements into a period of class quiescence manifested itself in the actual historical circumstances surrounding the convocation of the Second International and in the betrayal of the workers' leadership of their charges to the nationalism of their respective countries in the wake of World War I. The same circumstances tended to validate Lenin's argument that the revolutionary outbreak must now originate in the 'Periphery' (of 'oppressed countries'), and, with his theory of imperialism, could thus be seen to legitimize the October revolution in the USSR as an integral (initial) part of the Marxist world revolutionary process. In circumstances where much of this theory predated the actual outbreak of the Russian Revolution, Lenin's strategy had been one of 'world revolution'.

The inevitable need to protect the achievement of the Revolution led Lenin in the last months of his life to a reluctant recognition of the possibility of having to 'go it alone'. As far as he was concerned, however, the 'socialism in one country' thesis belonged to the same category of tactical expedients as did acceptance of the humiliating terms of the Brest Litovsk Treaty in March 1918. To this category of expedients, designed to gain time to consolidate and avoid a relapse into capitalism, belonged also the notion of peaceful coexistence which, though now ascribed by Soviet theorists to Lenin and the Decree on Peace, was subordinated to the overall strategy of world revolution of which the Soviet experience constituted only one part. The foundation of the Comintern in 1919, and the bustling early years of its existence as an operational centre for the next stages of world revolution, bore out this (tactical) interpretation of peaceful coexistence, as did Lenin's persistent reluctance to become too deeply enmeshed in an international system that was about to be overwhelmed and founder in the world revolutionary wave. Whilst acknowledging that the Soviet state was a part of the system of states Lenin saw its coexistence therein to be of very temporary duration. Soon after the October outbreak Lenin's own theory of imperialism became (even for Lenin) a mere *bridge*—to the 'survival of revolution in Russia', which is to say that 'socialism in one country' would soon be elevated to the rank of strategy, characterizing, as it turned out, the entire epoch.

The measures adopted by the Bolshevik government upon their coming to power on 7 November 1917, unusual in themselves, could be taken to suggest a genuine intention to implement Marxist precepts. George F. Kennan, for one, has noted the early Soviet moves as 'demonstrative diplomacy . . . designed not to promote freely accepted and mutually profitable agreement as between governments, but rather to embarrass other governments and stir up opposition among their own peoples' (Kennan, 1956, 75–6). The Bolsheviks, committed to the interpretation of World War I as an imperialist war and a result of rival capitalists competing in the redistribution of the world (and in confident anticipation of the world revolutionary outbreak about to explode) at first rejected traditional norms of international law and diplomacy (Chapter 8). One of the first moves of the government on November 8 was the Decree on Peace offering 'to all warring peoples and their governments to begin immediately negotiations for a just and democratic peace . . . an immediate peace without annexations and without indemnities'. Secret diplomacy was abolished and an undertaking entered into to publish in full the secret treaties of the Tsarist government and 'to carry on all negotiations absolutely openly before all the people'.

But whatever the intentions, certain imperatives in the aftermath of the revolution were not to be ignored. Both the notion of 'world revolution' and that of the 'theory of imperialism' (devised to explain that revolution's inevitability in a post-Marxian world) went by the board as far as their elevation to the status of Bolshevik strategy was concerned. It does seem clear, in the light of Roberts's explanation of Lenin's reluctance to 'be bothered' with his own theory of imperialism, that the theory from the outset had no more than a decorative or legitimizing role to play (Roberts, 1977). And it is borne out in his debates with Roy in the Comintern that Lenin had lost interest both in studying the export of capital or any of the other mechanisms by which the accuracy of the theory of imperialism could have been verified. Once come to power, and in the short time left to him, he was too preoccupied with considerations of how to keep the Bolshevik cockleshell afloat in a sea of capitalist troubles. Despite his faith in the strategy of 'Soviet revolution as the first part of world revolution', the exigencies of protecting the Bolshevik state caused him to begin the process of integrating economically, and then also politically, the Soviet state into the international system. In the process there could be no turning aside even from policies that clearly cut right across the Marxist/Bolshevik grain. The 'New Economic Policy' was adopted in 1921 to revive the ailing economy and involved a revision of the cherished idea of isolation from the international system. In the same year the Soviets signed an Anglo-Soviet trade agreement, and the violation of first principles went a step further with the acceptance by both of the European 'pariahs' (Russia and Germany) of an invitation from the British Prime Minister to attend an economic conference in Genoa where the opportunity was taken by their Foreign Ministers to conclude a treaty (Rapallo) between them (April 1922). Rapallo represented an enormous diplomatic success for the Bolsheviks since it brought *de jure* recognition from Germany (the first by a major European country). The Bolsheviks now (as Lenin put it) lived not only in a state but in a system of states.

Stalin

The succession struggle between Stalin and Trotsky after Lenin's death was fought largely on domestic issues. As far as the external affairs of the Bolshevik state were concerned the substance of the Stalin-Trotsky schism had to do specifically with the immediacy and relevance of the two contending concepts of 'world (permanent) revolution' and 'socialism in one country'. The theory of imperialism would of course have suggested the adoption of policies promoting the first of these but by now (and soon after Lenin's death) the theory of imperialism was fast becoming a mere legitimizing ornament decking the Soviet edifice. Trotsky, in his total rejection of the 'domestication' of 'socialism in one country', compared its theoretical absurdity to children's games: 'Up to the complete

world victory of the world proletariat, a number of individual
countries build socialism in their respective countries, and
subsequently out of these socialist countries there will be built
a world socialist economy, after the manner in which children
erect structures with ready-made blocks' (Trotsky, 1936, 54–5).
Trotsky's repudiation of the 'socialism in one country' doctrine
was based on traditional Marxist precepts, specifically that of
the contradiction of forces and that of the relations of
production. To Trotsky the fatal weakness in the capitalist world
system was to be found in the contradiction between its world-
wide nature on the one hand, and on the other the exclusively
nation-state-based, and thus fragmented, political structure.
Socialism applied on a world-wide scale was thus called for, and
the application of any other temporary expedient (such as a
socialism reduced to the scale of one country) made no sense;
such a reduction, far from benefiting socialism internationally,
would put it at a serious disadvantage as against its capitalist
rival.

However, the world revolution did not eventuate and in the
areas where outbreaks did occur these were complete failures.
To have taken 'permanent revolution' as the strategy would
have meant the grant of autonomy to the Comintern and Soviet
support for world revolutionary outbreaks across the globe.
Staking all, in other words, on the accuracy of Marxist-Leninist
predictions (applied to another era), they would have stood to
lose a civil war and to suffer foreign intervention. Stalin was
too much of a *state* leader and politician to gamble on such
imponderables and instead proceeded with all speed, and
ruthlessly, to subordinate other goals and ideals (including
Marxism in its entirety) to a 'socialism in one country' *strategy*;
which in the domestic context became the doctrine of
'revolution from above'. Massive industrialization, forced
collectivization (these subject to centralized planning),
concentration camps, show trials, genocide, and the elimination of any political or even intellectual opposition, were
all steps taken towards the strengthening of the Soviet state
—now presented to the world (including to the 1928 Sixth
Comintern Congress) as the bastion of world revolution. The
apprehensions, lines of potential cleavage in those areas espousing Marxism, and the siege mentality awakened, were well

summed up in the course of the Sixth (Comintern) Congress:

> She is the international driving force of proletarian revolution that
> impels the proletariat of all countries to seize power . . . she is the
> prototype of the fraternity of nationalities in all lands . . . that the world
> proletariat must establish when it has captured political power. . . .
> In the event of imperialist states declaring war upon and attacking the
> USSR, the international proletariat must retaliate by organising bold
> and determined mass action and struggle for the overthrow of the
> imperialist governments . . . all Communist parties owe exclusive
> allegiance to Moscow.[2]

The national revolution took precedence over world
revolution and the political superstructure was to determine the
march of events instead of accepting the economic substructure
as determinant of the shape and pace of the development. In its
external aspect 'socialism in one country' meant a gradual but
complete integration of the Soviet *state* into the international
system. This integration coincided in the thirties with the trials
which brought an abrupt end to the debates on international law,
now to be replaced by the Vyshinsky doctrine of international
law (Chapter 8). In the process Stalin consigned the Marxist
strictures to the apex of the ideology and, held there as part of
the revealed Word, they commanded veneration, but as far as
immediate demands and day-to-day development of foreign
policy was concerned they had been rendered ineffectual and
irrelevant. Thus the main world imperialist contradiction, that
between the oppressed and oppressor countries, was relegated
to become only one of several of the contradictions of capitalism.
The main driving force, and the 'hub' around which world
politics revolved was now conceived to be in the relation in
which the *two camps* stood to one another (on the one hand
socialism in one country and on the other those areas that went
to make up the ring of 'capitalist encirclement'). There was only
one way in which the main conflict as identified in the theory
of imperialism could be subordinated to the existence/survival
of the first socialist society. This was by arguing that within
the social formation of the world as a whole the main socio-
economic *systems* could be taken to represent an embodiment,
so to speak, of the (world) relations of production and the (world)

[2] The Comintern's 1928 Programme, quoted in *The Strategy and Tactics of
World Communism*, US Congress, 1948, pp. 121–40.

forces of production, embroiled with one another in revolutionary conflict. Apart from these formal references to Marxism-Leninism, Stalin's theory cast aside Marxist inhibitions to become a theory of international relations *par excellence*—notwithstanding the fact that the theory was confined largely to the Soviet state's relations with capitalist countries. With all of the salient lineaments of Marxism submerged, there was one unmistakable feature remaining: the predilection for subversion legitimated by the continuing commitment to proletarian internationalism. Contrary to the established practices of the ideologically homogeneous world before the inception of the USSR, there was now, as Adam Ulam observes, a state:

that would demand and enjoy all the international appurtenances of 'normal' statehood and membership in the community of nations at the same time that its professed aim and ideology was to subvert all other existing forms of government. Nothing resembling such a situation had existed since the religious wars of the sixteenth and early seventeenth centuries. Even the First French Republic did not explicitly seek the destruction of non-republican forms of government in countries with which it was not at war. Paris was not the center of an international movement with adherents in Vienna or Petersburg plotting the overthrow of their governments. 'Friends in peace, enemies in war' was the ruling maxim of international relations in the area that came to an end on 7 November 1917 (Ulam, 1980, 26).

Soviet leaders who were pleading for diplomatic recognition and trading facilities abroad were at the same time continuing to declare their hostility and interfering in the most blatant fashion in the internal affairs of those same countries. The United States and other western countries requested that such practices be abandoned but by 1933 the Soviet Union had achieved full statehood, she had been extended recognition by the major powers, and was soon (1934) to gain admission to the League of Nations. In that particular forum, as it happens, she became the strongest advocate of collective security. That such requests (and concessions) on the part of the great powers were made at all was evidence enough that the old diplomatic order had not only changed but had disintegrated. The Soviet capital, it will be recalled, was also of course the seat of an international body (the Comintern until its dissolution by Stalin in 1943) whose commitment to the dissemination of communist dogma across the face of the earth necessarily involved an infringement of the sovereignty of other states. Neither Lenin nor Stalin gave any sign of wishing to dissociate themselves from its secretariat.

A glance at Stalin's foreign policy both before and during World War II is enlightening, and his prowess as diplomat/ statesman seems incontestable with a state policy punctuated by such successes as: admission to the League of Nations, establishment of the Comintern as an instrument of Soviet foreign policy, conclusion of the Ribbentrop – Molotov non-aggression pact (and secret protocol) with Germany, and engagement in a grand alliance with the United States and United Kingdom. There is of course the essential thread of diplomatic duplicity running through the skein of foreign policy in which, though one might be tempted to acknowledge the influence of Hobbes or Machiavelli in the diplomatic designing, part at least of the attribution must go to Marx. After all, a doctrine that views all capitalist countries as tarred with the same brush, that sees them as simply hostile, with little to choose between any of them, that advocates further the maximization of inter-capitalist contradictions and their various rivalries, and recommends the exploitation of these, must surely have provided some of the inspiration for Stalinist diplomacy. In the process Stalin, against all the odds, had contrived to put the USSR on the map and involve that state in the states-system. A Trotskyist—or a present-day world-system theorist (Chapters 6 and 10)—would deny the possibility of a piecemeal transition from the capitalist world economy in favour of an *en-bloc* shift, and to such theorists the participation of the Soviet state in the states-system could in itself be taken as proof of that country's renunciation of real Marxist ambitions. It cannot be denied that many important Marxist precepts went by the board, or were substantially modified; nevertheless the leadership, by their own lights, never swerved from the reiterated commitment to Marxism, and who, in the presence of such ambivalence, amidst a plethora of interpretation, and faced by a bewildering choice of direction, could say what destination lay at the end of any particular path? It is significant, after all, that, with the possible exception of the Soviet-German non-aggression pact, it was in contemplation not of foreign but rather of domestic policies that

Western Marxists were led to conclude that Soviet Marxism was defunct. Those among them who had not already reached the conclusion in the 1920s were brought to that position at different points in the thirties. There were notable exceptions, as for example Sweezy, who as late as 1942, in his classic work, *The Theory of Capitalist Development* (1968, first published in 1942), still envisages revolutionary transitions along the lines of the Soviet experience to take place. The break with the Soviet Union has of course done serious damage to Western Marxism for undeniably the Soviet record of participation in the states-system, was, and continues to be, punctuated by remarkable successes. Many early Marxists, in circumstances of failed world-wide revolution, would have settled for the idea of a Marxist superpower. Soviet participation in far-reaching decisions in partnership with her wartime allies over the parameters of the new post-war international order, would already have been a hard act in any other scenario (short of world-wide revolution) and, one suspects, a difficult one to stage-manage by any other impresario.

There is no doubt that Stalin's theory of international relations is a conglomeration of *ex post facto* justifications for courses of action already taken. In the accomplishment of giant feats of social engineering a parallel for which might be found in the Pharaoh's labour methods in the construction of the Pyramids—Stalin took serious liberties with the 'rules' of world history as identified by historical materialism. All superstructural phenomena, and particularly the state, had now become tools for building what by (historical materialist) rights they should have been 'reflecting', namely the socialist economic substructure. The Hegelianization of Marxism begun by Lenin in his voluntaristic reading of Marxism is thus complete: the process is to be seen in the state/party surrogate of class, in the re-writing of the dynamics of class struggle, and in the notion of 'revolution from above'. All of these together with Stalin's authoritarian rule, making a mockery of major Marxist precepts. It is at this point, and aware of that indictment, that Marxists outside the USSR rally *in defence of Marxism*, insisting in the main that the USSR in its ascent to power has ceased to have the right to continue its ride on the coat-tails of Marxism. Since we return to their argument in a later chapter let us here note only the major innovations (Marxist or otherwise) in Stalin's approach to international politics.

In addition to the overall doctrinaire (and practical) stress placed on superstructural phenomena, and particularly in regard to the theoretical elaboration of the internal and external roles of states (Kubálková and Cruickshank, 1980, 135), there were other changes no less important made in Stalin's world view, and in its Marxist justifications. In theoretical terms, the essence of the doctrine of 'socialism in one country' as a Marxist theory of international relations was the retrospective redefinition of class conflict on a world scale so as to shift its main (oppressed versus oppressor) axis (as defined in the theory of imperialism) to become the relation of the USSR versus 'capitalist encirclement' by the rest. Whereas in the theory of imperialism class conflict was seen always to emanate from within *one* social formation, its obverse side (with the proviso that the struggle of superior and inferior modes of production might constitute a source) could always be seen to be exploitation—at the level of individuals or nations. The class struggle in all Soviet theories since, is to be located not between modes of production within one social formation but between social formations based on different modes of production. These coexisting (capitalist and socialist) social formations have been designated socio-economic systems and the coexistence of states of which such systems are made up is seen as a major form of class struggle. The political conflict within the interstate system is thus elevated so as to represent class struggle. In such a portrayal imperialist relations are de-emphasized and forever subordinated to the major line of ('two camps') confrontation which as early as 1920 Stalin had referred to as 'the hub of present day affairs, determining the whole substance of the present home and foreign policies of the leaders of the old and the new world' (Stalin, in Franklin, 1972, 85). Stalin in his theorizing tended to underestimate or even to overlook both the proletariat in the capitalist countries and the national liberation movement in the colonies, and the two-camp doctrine presaged a line fully utilized by his successors. He anticipated these later developments in another respect: he corrected Lenin on the connection between capitalism and war. In this version, although wars amongst capitalist countries would continue to be a concomitant of capitalism, between capitalist and socialist countries they were no longer inevitable. Unfavourably disposed commentators saw in this a Stalin concerned that the increasingly powerful USSR, in trying to bring about internationally that which the historical process was so dilatory in providing, namely a socialist economic basis in the USSR and the world-wide revolution, might find herself in (military) confrontation with the rest of the world.

The theoretical model after Stalin

The 'socialism in one country' strategy worked. To its headlong industrialization process the authoritarian state was able to divert one-third of the GNP and maintain a growth rate of eight per cent. In addition to what is seen in Marxism-Leninism as the 'internal' function, the state in its 'external' role was called upon to withstand a number of external threats. Emerging victoriously from World War II (named the 'Great Patriotic War' to emphasize the heroism of the nation) 'socialism in one country' was in the ideological van of a country on its way to becoming one of the world's great powers.

Socialism in one country was by definition self-centered, introverted, defensive and, as a theory of world politics, necessarily truncated: the xenophobic fear of 'capitalist encirclement' cast a long shadow. But the new post-war correlation of forces obviously demanded a new strategy, and the forms that the strategy might take were limited to two. World revolution would involve the launching of a frontal attack from the fortress. Fully aware of the hazard inherent in that option, Stalin chose the alternative, which, as it happens, has become the main strategy of his successors ever since: the strategy of 'coexistence'. He had signalled the adoption of the strategy as early as the twenties (a rare prescience considering the hindsight quality that characterized much of his 'theorizing'):

It is more likely that, in the course of development of the world revolution, there will come into existence—side by side with the foci of imperialism in the various capitalist lands and with the system of the lands throughout the world—foci of socialism in various socialist countries, and a system of these foci throughout the world. As the outcome of this development there will ensue a struggle between the rival systems, and its history will be the history of the world revolution (Quoted in Sweezy, 1968, 356).

Less prescient however was Stalin's grasp of the implications of the quantum jump in destructive capacity that flowed from the development and proliferation of nuclear weapons, and in fact he discussed quite cheerfully with Molotov a third world (atomic) war which would result in the global victory of socialism and the final demise of capitalism (it was left to Khrushchev to realize that since the 'atomic bomb does not observe the class principle' such a war would not discriminate between capitalism and socialism and that both would perish). Thus was born a strategy for world revolution that had its origin in the arsenal of tactics where, as Marcuse pointed out, it functioned as a soporific to lull capitalists into a sense of false security and keep them from any purposeful attempt to resolve their contradictions (Marcuse, 1971, 67). An assessment of change in the correlation of forces, and consequently in the description of the world, was made by Khrushchev at the Twentieth Party Congress in 1956. The revised strategy involved no change in the 'topmost' level of Marxist-Leninist ideology— and indeed the 1980s were expected to see the construction of communism in the Soviet Union. The analysis continued to see the world in a state of disequilibrium, with capitalism now in a new (third) stage of 'general crisis', and with the correlation of forces coming into propitious imbalance so as to favour a socialist victory. On the ideology's lower levels, however, there occurred a rare flurry of upward and downward interchange, a period of unprecedented movement in the levels—unprece- dented, that is, if one excepts the frantic (continuous) activity in social science research (bottom level) which, with a virtually unlimited franchise, worked (and works) ceaselessly at the rationalization of society in the post-Stalinist years. Khrushchev's reassessment went further. The 'zone of peace' was introduced to suggest that the newly independent countries, rather than forming part of the capitalist system (as one of that system's contradictions), be joined with the socialist countries. Where previously (in the Stalinist period) only a token support had been afforded to indigenous communist parties as members of the Comintern, now the inclusion of these countries in the zone of peace meant that bolder *diplomatic* intercourse on the inter-state level could prevail. The zone of peace concept allowed the USSR to enter into diplomatic relations with countries (often still capitalist in nature) even where their regimes carried out programmes of persecution of indigenous communists. Thus construed, the notion incorporated ex-colonies, the people's democracies, and the Soviet Union—in other words half of mankind. Although officially the analysis was alleged to be based on a reassessment of the correlation of forces, consideration of the inevitability of the broaching of a nuclear dimension in the next war provided the setting for what appeared to be (after Lenin) the first comprehensive global model of world politics. To an extent the main outline of the model has remained unchanged to the present and so we may relate its statements to developments across the entire post-Stalinist period.

The new model of international relations loses the introverted and capitalist states-oriented focus of its predecessors. It is both a theory of the states-system and at the same time a theory of world class conflict, with appropriate modification. The result is that both of these in many respects mutually contradictory components are compromised by the synchronic influence of a 'contradictory' pull by, on the one hand, the dictates of historical materialism and, on the other, that of the states-system. Our examination of the states-system must therefore be prefaced by, and constant reference be made to, historical materialism—as the other (opposed) influence. Marxist historical materialism postulated the clear division of the world according to the predominant mode of production and class struggle. On the one hand there is 'capitalism', which, far from displaying any 'encircling' capability, is in an advanced stage of crisis; particularly has this become evident as, in the process of decolonization, each successive part of its once substantial domain (territory and treasure) has been removed. It is riddled with problems and internal contradictions made more acute by the workings of the scientific and technological revolution[3] and which capitalism has shown itself historically to be

---

[3] The scientific and technological revolution is a concept much relied upon in Soviet theory. As important as was the Industrial Revolution to capitalism, the processes of that revolution lays the 'material-technological foundations' of communism. The concept is inconsistently applied in so far as it reintroduces a considerable degree of determinism into international relations whilst retaining domestic voluntarism. The demise of capitalism is largely a result of this objectively given process, 'assisted' by the world revolutionary forces, as the subjective factor. Domestically,

incapable of resolving. The final confrontation between the forces and the relations of production is inescapable. On the other hand, and standing in dialectical contradiction to capitalism, are the 'world revolutionary forces'.

However, these findings of historical materialism (evocative of Biblical sheep-and-goats imagery) are modified by recognition of the fact that the world is politically divided into states. Equal under (international) law though these may be, with equal access to diplomatic intercourse, to international organizations, and to the legitimate use of force in a peculiarly anarchical international environment, the 'sovereignty' of some, according to the strictures of historical materialism, is by no means sacrosanct. So it comes about that when the two levels are superimposed on each other there emerges a substantially modified notion of international system: states are not of a uniform nature but differ one from the other according to a 'content' determined by the prescriptions of historical materialism. Thus we have capitalist states, socialist states, and the states of the Third World. The sovereignty of the two latter *vis-à-vis* capitalist states is inviolable and indeed is vigorously argued as a useful bulwark against inroads into their progressive nature. In contrast, the sovereignty of capitalist countries is relative in so far as it is subordinated to the pursuits of the 'revolutionary forces' in their midst. The sovereignty of the socialist states with regard to each other (and to the USSR in particular) is eroded by the countervailing objectives and considerations of the world class struggle. It is a formulation with which Brezhnev was quite unjustifiably credited. Thus historical materialism rationalizes what to the non-Marxist is unacceptable or indeed duplicitous, namely that the internal structure of a country may not only determine its foreign policy but also its degree of imperviousness to encroachment by different parts of the international system. Furthermore, historical materialism points to a range of actors in international politics other than states. These include groups of states and various bodies located within a state's frontiers and which by virtue of their belonging to the 'world revolutionary process' are transnational in character.

To elaborate this last point: we have first of all two 'socio-

however, 'socialism has to be built'. Without conscious effort the advances of that same scientific and technological revolution do not appear to be as assured as they are assumed to be within the domains of capitalism (see Kubálková and Cruickshank, 1980, 217).

economic systems' made up of states. A socio-economic system, whether referred to as commonwealth (as is the socialist), bloc, or world, is not a political alliance but rather 'a socio-economic class political community which determines the unity of the objective interests of its states in the struggle between the two systems' (cf. Gantman, 1969, 56; Granov, 1975, 73). The two systems are therefore 'offsprings' of the two antagonistic classes, poured so to speak into state containers. The socio-economic structure of the Third World is not as yet finalized but is to be found in a grey area over which the tug of war between the two systems ranges. This triangular configuration will be replaced in due course by bipolarity as the Third World countries 'choose either the capitalist or socialist path'. The final step is of course the emergence of a monolithic socialist world from that penultimate bipolar collision. In this historical, materialist portrayal, too, the behavioural patterns of states are determined by their being either capitalist or socialist. The socialist states are well-disposed, the capitalist countries ill-disposed, the type of behaviour expected of each deriving from their respectively superior/inferior internal structures. An additional consideration beyond the overall correlation of forces might operate in the case of the Third World countries, whereby a country still capitalist in nature or pro-capitalist in orientation might still merit the accolade of Soviet friendship. And so against world capitalism stand the revolutionary forces, consisting not only of those countries which have already experienced their revolution and are embarked on the construction of socialism/ communism, but also all of the anti-capitalist, anti-imperialist countries, classes, parties, and other organizations located in the Third World—not to speak of the anti-capitalist Trojan horse already installed in the capitalist countries themselves. The 'world revolutionary forces' is by no means an empty concept and in its ranks can be numbered, first, the sixteen or so countries with communist parties in power, and, second, a 'revolutionary movement of the working class in the capitalist countries' amounting to some eighty Soviet-accredited communist parties in non-communist countries with a following of approximately 46 m. members (the estimated world communist party membership in 1981 was 76.6 m. (Staar, 1982) and had risen by 1982 to an estimated 80.6 m. (Wesson, 1983); and third, the national revolutionary movements of 'revolutionary democratic parties' and 'countries of socialist orientation'. The latter are considered to be the vanguard of the national liberation movement and differ from the Soviet bloc countries in that even though the national economy in the majority is dominated by the state sector the final break away from the world capitalist system has yet to be made.

The Soviet model consists of two partially overlapping triangles corresponding to the three groupings of *states* (the capitalist and socialist socio-economic systems and the Third World). The three main groupings of revolutionary forces and the socialist system of states form part of both triangles, otherwise the location of other revolutionary forces is within the capitalist system and in the Third World. As to *relations* amongst the actors so identified, there is here an absence of perceived uniformity, for although the content of the relation might appear substantially the same, the quality of the relation depends entirely on the nature of the countries involved. It is a situation that we have elsewhere described as a participant-determined typology of international relations. To complicate the matter further, we have to recognize different types of policies directed by states towards other states which, joined and merged with the reciprocal policy response, constitutes a *relation*: as for example (in theoretical terms) does the origin of the relation of Cold War, or of *détente*. Thus, using the Soviet Union's own expository and terms we identify the following policies:

Socialist states towards capitalist states:	peaceful coexistence	Stage 1: Cold War (capitalism prevails)
Socialist states towards socialist states:	socialist internationalism	
Socialist states towards progressive forces in the capitalist states and in the Third World	proletarian internationalism	Stage 2: *détente* (socialism prevails)
Capitalist states towards socialist states:	anti-communism	
Capitalist states towards capitalist states:	contradictions	
Capitalist states towards Third World states:	Neo-colonialism	Stage 3: new Cold War
Third World (progressive) states towards socialist states:	proletarian internationalism	
Third World (progressive) states towards capitalist states:	national liberation movements and anti-colonialism	
Third World (progressive) states towards Third World states:	proletarian internationalism or capitalist contradiction	

Clearly the most important of these relations is *proletarian internationalism* from which the others, including socialist internationalism and national liberation movement, flow. From across the entire spectrum it is the main *class* principle. Other relations—and peaceful coexistence most particularly—can be discussed only in full awareness of the synchronic workings of proletarian internationalism which at all times underpins and acts as modifier on peaceful coexistence. Proletarian internationalism since the time of Marx and Engels has been seen as a quintessential part of the doctrine, rejecting as it does the nation-state partition of the world and substituting for it division by class: 'proletarian internationalism expresses the community of interests and the solidarity of the working class and the working people of all lands, their concerted action in the struggle for the revolutionary transformation of society' (Zagladin, 1973, 441–2). The principle has been substantially diluted in meaning, however, as the compass of the world progressive forces has also come to include a good deal more than the 'proletariat'. It is now rather a 'progressive forces internationalism', and legitimizes the 'all-round support' and 'aid' for these groups in the similarly stepped-up continuing struggle between capitalism and socialism. In reality it means that such 'all-round support' or 'aid' is forthcoming *irrespective* of the relations at *governmental* level between the socialist countries and those (capitalist or Third World) countries in which the particular 'detachment' of the revolutionary forces is located.

In contrast to proletarian internationalism, *peaceful coexistence* is *not* a class principle but an exclusively inter-state *strategy* of the states of the socialist socio-economic system towards the countries of the capitalist socio-economic system. Correctly put, the somewhat loosely termed 'peaceful coexistence' should properly read 'the peaceful coexistence of states of different socio-economic system'. Inseparable from the principle of proletarian internationalism to which it is subordinate, peaceful coexistence supplements proletarian internationalism and will vanish with the capitalist system. It means that 'all controversial problems that arise between countries with different social systems must be solved by peaceful means', and in its working acts as a shield for proletarian internationalism by preventing world-wide class contradictions from leading to nuclear war. The principle serves also as a curb on the assumed aggressive nature of capitalism whilst simultaneously creating favourable conditions in which can take place the people's struggle for national and social liberation. Peaceful coexistence is a specific *form of class struggle* which leads to the victory of socialism. It neither conjures up the idyll of reconciliation nor does it modify the nature of capitalism or of socialism; both systems remain antagonistic.[4]

In justification of the concept of peaceful coexistence the Soviet theories manage to relate the concept to that of class struggle. Peaceful coexistence, we are told, is an expression of two out of three forms of class struggle, namely the economic and the political. In the third, the ideological form, it simply never can apply. There can be no ideological compromise and Soviet writers state and restate this to the axiomatic conclusion, for they have the impression that it is to the area of ideology that the West would most prefer to believe that peaceful coexistence applies. In economic terms, peaceful coexistence means a competition to 'demonstrate the advantages of the socialist system' and to derive at the same time as much advantage as possible from the (still) economically and technologically superior West. In the political and military field, where peaceful coexistence also applies, it does not entail any absolute commitment or guarantee that war will be avoided, and particularly would such a commitment be out of place for wars of national liberation movements. Peaceful coexistence aims neither at a 'balance of power' (balance of terror) nor at the maintenance of the status quo. The parallel commitment

---

[4] Only a handful of Western authors, and that only in the 'New Cold War' atmosphere of the 1980s appreciate this important aspect of the Soviet concept of peaceful coexistence, and on it based Soviet strategic doctrine, which is therefore dissimilar from the US version. As Kolkowicz pointed out, Western theorists have ethnocentrically and arrogantly defined and prescribed the theories, such as massive retaliation, flexible response, deterrence, assured destruction, escalation dominance, limited war etc. on the assumption of their absolute correspondence with Soviet strategic thought: '. . . our knowledge and understanding of the vital political, social, and pre-policy values and processes in the Soviet Union remains marginal . . . And so we tend to focus our attention and responses on Soviet military capabilities, on the threat-potential, and on other stereotypes . . . [a] "strato-babble" ' (in Mickiewicz and Kolkowicz, 1983, 154–5).

to the principle of proletarian internationalism makes this, the Soviets' own interpretation, uncomfortably plausible. *Détente*, in this reading, replaced *Cold War* as a *stage* of the relationship between capitalism and socialism, when, as a result of an unfavourable 'correlation of forces', capitalism became obliged to yield to the pressures of the peaceful coexistence drive and, however reluctantly, to acknowledge all of the principles on which the concept rests.

Thus the international system in the Soviet portrayal is a transitional community in which 'Kantian' universalism practised by the USSR is gradually replacing the Hobbesian conflict-based nature of capitalist international relations. In fact, subjected to the pressures of peaceful coexistence the co-operation of these latter is demanded. Peaceful coexistence introduces a peculiarly Grotian factor into the international system, whereby capitalist states are made to co-operate as part of the effort to transform the world. In this Soviet portrayal there is indeed a prototype of the new 'international society' which shares values, institutions, and the goal of transforming itself into a world (communist) society.

This is of course the weakest and least credible part of the Soviet cosmology. For, if anything, the 'socialist system' or commonwealth is in reality more reminiscent of a suzerain-type system depriving lesser states of any meaningful modicum of autonomous statehood. The apparent inconsistency of a socialist world system still organized into states is an acknowledgement of the fact that the states-system is a fact of life and as such the barriers of statehood of the socialist states are accepted as a useful bulwark against capitalist encroachment. Internally, within the socialist community, the meaning of state sovereignty we are informed, has radically changed: a question we shall return to in Chapters 6 and 8. The easiest way of explaining the meaning of the term 'socialist internationalism' as a basis of the relations amongst the socialist countries is by reference to peaceful coexistence. Whilst peaceful coexistence (directed towards and applicable to the capitalist countries) includes '[c]omplete equality, respect for territorial integrity, state independence and sovereignty and non-interference in domestic affairs' (cf. Miroshchenko, 1966, 67), socialist internationalism since the 1957 Communist Summit formulation includes all of these plus the additional 'fraternal mutual assistance and mutual support' (quoted in McNeal, 1967, 99–100). The addition of this 'qualitatively new factor' not only changes the meaning of these other principles that socialist internationalism shares with peaceful coexistence, but adds a moral (and also legal!) right and duty for these states to 'protect their unity and mutually assist one another in the struggle against capitalism', as well as to 'co-operate and mutually assist one another in building socialism and communism in a comradely manner' (Mrázek, 1976, 79). Thus socialist internationalism places a moral (and legal) duty upon all socialist states to assist in the joint protection of socialist achievement— and, in practical terms, legitimizes intrusion and interference in their affairs. But so far as it can be argued that proletarian internationalism is at the root of socialist internationalism (which is no more than the application of the former to the relations of states) the 'Brezhnev doctrine' or 'doctrine of limited sovereignty' as it has become known in the West, is deeply embedded in Marxist – Leninist thought, Brezhnev in effect simply having restated an already well-established principle.

In the Soviet portrayal of the fragmented states-system it is then logical that all concepts associated with the states-system such as state, sovereignty, war, intervention, international law, and diplomacy are filled with different class content, and are never seen essentially as general concepts, and thus Soviet theory, by definition, always stops one step short of its Western counterpart because its class approach precludes it from reaching the same level of abstraction. The Western construct of 'national interest' is regarded by Soviet theorists as a deliberate emasculation of the class content of international relations.

The Western Marxists would not be particularly flattered by the suggestion that there is a peculiar convergence between their attitudes to state and those of the USSR. A 'regional' concept (as for Poulantzas), state is in Soviet theory also a positive, worthy institution, an important 'committee' in the organization of society on behalf of the leading classes. A Khruschchevian concept, now enshrined in the new Soviet Constitution, introduced the idea of the state as no longer a dictatorship (of the proletariat) but, with the removal of class differences in Soviet society (and whilst socialism is still building), a 'state of all the people' (Brinkley, 1972, 387 ff.). It is a concept, as

Brezhnev pointed out, as part of his conceptual contribution to Soviet Marxism-Leninism, that is consistent with a 'developed socialism'.

The Soviet model of international politics is neither neat nor elegant, as once was Lenin's theory of imperialism. It contains a good deal of description of the world and also a good deal of normative (wishful) thinking—this particularly in regard to the socialist countries. Even with so many actors, groups, and subtypes, 'ifs and buts', the Soviet model recognizes the 'world historical process', and thus probably shows a more realistic awareness of the essential complexity of international politics than is provided by some others in the West. And yet this Soviet attempt to reconcile the concepts of international and world order has been dismissed with the simple diagnosis of 'schizophrenia' by some commentators (cf. Zimmerman, 1969).

5 The PRC

Like the USSR, the PRC is another giant *state* which legitimizes its domestic and foreign policies by reference to Marxism – Leninism; and again it is a Marxism explicitly modified to suit *national* circumstances. The PRC came into existence only in 1949, and took up her United Nations membership as late as 1971. With a similarly belated diplomatic recognition (by the United States only in 1979) Chinese sorties in the field of international diplomacy are understandably also of relatively recent origin. In the first ten years, as an 'orderly' member of the Soviet socialist commonwealth, the PRC was in no position to arrive at an autonomous conceptualization of the world that would differ substantially from that of the Soviet, nor could she venture into foreign policies independently of her powerful ideological partner. Thus when the Sino-Soviet split (whose origins harked back to Comintern days) opened in the early sixties into a wider breach, there was little of recent relevance to hand that might act as a theoretical basis for an independent understanding of the world. As it turned out, Mao's political resourcefulness was equal to the task of breaking the tyranny of the Soviet model (Sweezy, in Burke *et al.*, 1981, 215) and it was his theory of contradiction of the revolutionary transition, as applied to his country, that gave both a promise to the Third World at large, and to Marxism, a universal applicability (cf. Amin, 1980, 208). But Mao's major contribution to Marxism definitely does not lie in the devising of theories of international relations. Whereas it is usually agreed that although he attempted frequent analyses of the international situation (as did the various party conventions), and issued foreign policy directives from time to time, nevertheless he contrived no personal theory of international relations to approach that, for example, of Lenin (Jashek, 1978, 366).

The 'three worlds' theory attributed to Mao received official endorsement again in 1981. The theory's implementation in PRC foreign policy initiatives postdates Mao and in its Marxist content has in any case been the subject of critical comment— as indeed has its usefulness other than as a basis for ordinary Realpolitik—in the decade since its official promulgation in 1974. This is largely because in the important years (since 1978) the PRC embarked on a programme ('four modernizations') in which many commentators quite correctly draw a close comparison with the early years of the Soviet 'socialism in one country'. It is in such periods that many of the ideological articles of faith become removed to the apex of the ideological pyramid (Chapter 4) where they remain until the achievement of prescribed diplomatic goals, in this case the attainment of great-power status for China by the turn of the century, predicated on massive advances in the industrialization field. The dictates of 'socialism in one country' in the USSR also implied, first, the task of establishing the country in that 'system of states' before making a way up through its hierarchy. Clearly such a course is a *prior* concern for any Marxist state. Or, as the Chinese themselves put it: 'The establishment of diplomatic ties is nothing but a form of relations between two countries. It cannot alter the (political) system of either side'.[1] The goals of Marxism were not allowed to entrammel the approach, although a skilfully deployed Marxism could sometimes smooth the path.

The study of Chinese foreign policy has in its subject-matter a much shorter history than has the study of sovietology, although they have in common many of the arguments and the divisions that traditionally divide students of Soviet society. As to China's Marxist credentials, such as may be established from the direction of her foreign policy, those who see the PRC as pursuing an outright power-politics line seem to have been vindicated by the onset in recent years of a number of Chinese foreign policy initiatives that have run counter to any, let alone Marxist, theoretical guidelines.

The shape of her Marxism when the PRC reaches her 'Soviet 1956' remains at the moment a matter of conjecture. We proceed

---

[1] Ch'iao Kuan-hua's address on the 'Current Situation of the World and Peiping's Foreign Policy', *Classified Chinese Communist Documents*, A Selection, p. 546 quoted in Yin, 1983, p. 50.

in the present chapter to survey the Marxist roots of the 'three worlds' theory to show that these are firmly established in a Chinese Marxism whose flexibility should serve as a deterrent to those who would prematurely rejoice at the theory's having been superseded by the dictates of the Chinese 'four modernizations' campaign, or by de-Maoization.

The 'three worlds' theory

In terms of its inspiration the three worlds theory develops some of the earlier of Mao's concepts such as an 'intermediate zone between the Soviet Union and the United States' (1946), 'two contradictions and three forces at work' (1957), and a 'second intermediate zone' (1964). Along the way the theory touches also on Mao's ideas of 'one world', 'two families', and the train of thought of which the 'division of the world into three' appears to be the end product. The theory can also be seen to embrace his theories of contradictions and of the United Front which have generally been taken to form the foundation of Chinese (Marxist) foreign policy. Already on 22 February 1974, in an interview with Kaunda of Zambia, Mao actually used the words in an observation that the world was split into three worlds. Soon afterwards (12 April 1974) the first fully elaborated statement of this theory was contained in an address by the then Vice-Premier Deng to the Special Session (Sixth) of the General Assembly of the United Nations (the same session incidentally which was called to discuss the New International Economic Order). All pro-Soviet Marxists dutifully attacked the theory, including Albania, China's only loyal ally in the aftermath of the (Sino-Soviet) split. The attack was joined by neo-Marxists in the Third World: Samir Amin who for long had taken a pro-Chinese position in his writing declared that the Chinese had 'bent the stick too far' by which was meant a too great leaning back from the foundations of Soviet theory. In a repetition of the Soviet action in cutting off China in 1960, China now within a year of the publication (1977) of the Albanian critique stopped all aid projects to that country. After Mao's death in 1976, in an unusually lengthy 35,000 word rebuttal, Renmin Rebao defended the 'three worlds' theory as a Marxist and Maoist theory ('Chairman Mao's Theory'), making for a Chinese—or for that matter for a Marxist—a rare excursion into the theory of international relations. A year later however, in February 1978 the 'four modernizations' campaign was officially proclaimed that accelerated the country's passage along the path of industrialization. As far as foreign policy was concerned, there followed what was for a Marxist state a strange sequence of diplomatic initiatives: the proliferation of economic, political, and strategic ties with Japan was followed by similar arrangements with western Europe and the United States that made China into something of a *de facto* partner of that coalition (Trilateral Commission) of conservative capitalist global actors (Kim, S. S., 1981, 437). These manoeuvres coincided at home with sharp criticism of the late Chairman and his mistakes. China's activities in the Third World and her attitude for example towards Angola, Pakistan, Sri Lanka, Sudan, and Chile came in for heavy criticism from Marxists who saw it as 'reactionary'. To many Marxists across the world the USSR by comparison constituted a positive force for progress and for the advancement of the national liberation movement in the Third World. To add to the widespread confusion into which the commentators (as much as the PRC herself) have been thrown in recent years further evidence of the depths of duplicity plumbed by her leaders was provided by their obvious prepared-ness to negotiate an improvement of state-to-state relations with the Soviet Union. Only the manoeuvring of the latter country in the wake of World War II could have presented the commen-tators with so tangled a diplomatic knot to unravel.

The 'three worlds' theory from the Marxist point of view is certainly innovative for in important respects it presages the world-system theory dear to the hearts of the more radical circles in Western and Third World academia. The theory's claims to originality are quite soundly based however since it is in harmony not only with the thoughts on world politics of Mao but also with those of one of the first Chinese Marxists, Li Ta-chao. In presaging the world-system theory an important departure from Soviet, and even from Western thinking on the subject is made when Li Ta-chao setting aside a Marxist axiom disconnects foreign policy from the state's domestic structures. He sees the foreign policy of a state as determined by that state's overall position in the system with regard to the system's main

contradictions. The fact that identification of these contradictions is assumed in this case makes China once again into the
'Middle Kingdom' and the 'three worlds' theory into a grand
theory of Chinese nationalism. The theory offers an unusual
conceptualization of world politics and certainly distinguishes
it from a Soviet cosmology which despite its idiosyncrasies bears
a close (if superficial) resemblance to, and coincides to a large
extent with, the Western symbols of 'East', 'West', and 'Third
World'. It is only the Third World that the 'three worlds' theory
shares with these others. In the Chinese version, the First World
is comprised of the United States and the Soviet Union, the
Second World includes all that is left after the Third World has
accounted for the developing countries of Asia, Africa and Latin
America. Thus:

1. *The First World* consists of only two countries, but they are
those at the pinnacle of the international hierarchy: they are the
two imperialist superpowers which deal in wholesale exploitation and oppression. Between them, through subversion, interference, aggression, and economic exploitation, all other
countries are brought under their thrall. Owing largely to the
fact that they possess nuclear weapons and participate in an arms
race, their dealings are a threat to world peace—the potential
causes of a war which the Chinese (with a degree of uncertainty
only as to when and where) regard as *inevitable*. Whilst each
of the superpowers seeks nothing less than world hegemony,
the 'contradiction' between them is 'irreconcilable' (*détente*
therefore in that reading being no more than a dangerous
illusion, a fraud amounting at most to the appeasement of the
USSR by the USA). In reply to the serious criticism that putting
a socialist and capitalist country into the same category is
unMarxian, the Chinese supplied a detailed analysis of the
transformation which the once socialist USSR had undergone
on the way to becoming a true imperialist superpower on the
offensive, whilst the United States, the older (and indeed the
less culpable of the two) is in a stage of relative decline. The
socio-economic foundation of the USSR is seen as a special
variety of monopoly capitalism, and, it is claimed, the entire
six characteristics of imperialism as identified by Lenin are
readily apparent in the case of the Soviet Union. The social

imperialism of the USSR is the more invidious since she flaunts the label of 'socialism'—whilst abusing the moral heritage of Lenin and Marxism – Leninism. As a monopoly capitalist country the Soviet Union is considered to be far more centralized than the United States ever has been, and has a much more advanced capability for mobilizing and militarizing her people and economy. Because she is economically still the weaker of the two superpowers, the Soviet Union has a higher expenditure on weaponry and the military, and is necessarily reliant on military power to achieve her world hegemonistic aims. Thus, although strictly speaking both of the countries of the First World are imperialist superpowers, the Chinese perceive essential differences and feel the need to distinguish between the two. In so doing, and having in view a counterbalance to the Soviets' mounting advantage in the context of the 'main' USSR – USA 'contradiction', their preference was, at least in the first years, for an accommodation with the United States.

2. The features that characterize a *Second World* country are more difficult to discern. So ill-defined are they that one is obliged to arrive at the definition by elimination: in other words, the country concerned is so designated by virtue of its possessing none of these criteria that properly belong to the First and Third Worlds. If there is any particular feature characteristic of the Second World country it is a dualism in its nature. Thus, whilst some still retain neo-colonialist relations of one form or another with Third World countries, they themselves are in varying degrees controlled, threatened (or bludgeoned) by one of the superpowers in its hegemonistic aspirations. In the process, it might be noted, those which once belonged to the socialist bloc (in the Chinese view now defunct) are made into overt *dependencies*. Together with the countries of the Third World, those of the Second share the desire to rid themselves of the superpower yoke and to assert their national independence and sovereignty.

3. *The Third World* embraces the developing countries located in Africa, Asia, Latin America, and the Balkans (Albania, Romania, Yugoslavia) which suffered long from colonization, from imperialist oppression and exploitation. Despite their political independence, for them the task remains one of

removing colonial influence, developing their national economy, consolidation, and generally investing with meaning their national independence and status. The conglomerate of Third World countries is extremely powerful in terms of the size of their territories, populations, and wealth of natural resources; 'they constitute a revolutionary force propelling the wheel of history and are main forces combating colonialism, imperialism, and particularly the superpowers'; and, nurturing a powerful desire for liberation and independence, they have already scored 'splendid victories'. Of these countries, China, in her own perception, sees herself for various reasons as their natural leader.

The Chinese concept of 'world' obviously differs fundamentally from the Soviet concept of 'socio-economic system'. In both cases we have an attempt at reconstituting a kind of 'global class' along the same Marxist lines, and yet the end product differs dramatically in the two readings. Whilst in both cases the 'global classes' are clearly broken up into states, in the case of the Soviet socio-economic systems the states of each 'system' are homogeneous. It is a consideration that does not appear to preoccupy the Chinese who find it possible to place side by side in one 'world' countries possessed of very different socio-economic structures. The two superpowers (the USA and USSR) of the First World, despite an initial Chinese designation of the nature of the Soviet system as 'social-imperialist' (but tending more recently to accept her openly as a socialist country!) are quite obviously different in their socio-economic foundations. The difference is even more pronounced in the case of the Second World, where such 'ex-socialist' countries as Czechoslovakia and the United Kingdom find themselves placed side by side in the one category. The puzzling question is how can such a serious conceptual divergence as exists between the Chinese and Soviet approaches be possible when the two derive from the same ideological root. Which, in other words is the 'more Marxist'?

We have argued elsewhere that neither of these two variants is either implied in classical Marxism or is completely inconsistent with it (Kubálková and Cruickshank, 1981, 179). The difference seems to derive from the selection of a focal plane onto which the Marxian relation of substructure and superstructure is projected. For the Soviets the focus chosen is quite clearly that of separate *states*, thus enabling the retention of Lenin's dictum of the dependence of foreign policy of a country on its domestic structure, from which point they are led to the conclusion that countries of the same socio-economic substructure share certain predispositions in regard to their foreign policies which unifies these countries in a socio-economic system. It is of course a highly state-centristic and USSR-centristic point of view that distributes countries into 'socio-economic systems' according to their foreign policy relations with the USSR. The PRC's view is no less state-centred and self-centred although the state-centrism enters, as it were, through the back door. In the three worlds analysis the *world* superstructure and substructure are seen as fragmented into those of states arranged into 'worlds' according to their relation to the 'world class struggle'—defined needless to say by China. The placement of a country is thus determined by the country's level of performance in the external balance of world forces relevant to the principal contradiction of a given stage of world (as opposed to interstate) politics. As the Chinese put it, what appear to be 'relations between countries and between nations in the present-day world . . . [are seen] . . . in essence . . . to bear directly on the vital question of the present-day class struggle on the world scale'. Relations between states are based on relations between classes ('Chairman Mao's Theory', 11). In fact the Chinese argue that all the Marxist classics used the same approach: they employed the analysis of the international class struggle as a starting-point and saw the major configurations in the world as by no means stable but highly changeable (ibid. 16). In this reading the three worlds are three world classes, with world imperialism (the two superpowers) on the one hand and the international proletariat (of which in the Lenin – Stalin – Mao tradition 'every national liberation movement forms a part') on the other, locked in a contradiction. Between these two there is the 'dual-natured second world', comparable to 'national bourgeoisie', which can be won over by the Third World and may be 'united with' in the struggle against the hegemonism of the two imperialist superpowers (ibid. 17).

The state centrism of the Chinese theory of global class

relations is apparent in a close coincidence of the designation of superpowers, 'second and third rate powers', and 'middle and small powers', to correspond respectively with the three worlds distinction. The category of 'superpower' is in fact by definition connected with 'First World' and 'imperialism'. Consequent upon the functioning of the uneven law of the development of capitalism, what was once a handful of imperialist powers is reduced now to only two. Beyond those two, and set apart by the absence of capability to contend for world hegemony, the remaining imperialist powers are relegated to a secondary place. The features conceived to distinguish the superpower in the Chinese reading include, first of all, the existence of a state apparatus controlled by monopoly capital in its most intense form—and therefore greater in degree than that obtaining in any other country. Second, they 'carry on economic exploitation and political oppression' and 'strive for military control on a global scale'; and, last but not least, each superpower sets exclusive world hegemony as its goal and to this end makes 'frantic preparation for the world war' (ibid. 19). Thus imperialist superpowers are defined both in class and behavioural terms, and it is against such a definitional background that repeated Chinese denials that she herself could ever become a superpower should be seen—and which in that light alone makes sense. The Western notion of 'superpower', either as a power unrestricted in its reach in terms of global geography, or (in nuclear terms) a country possessed of a second-strike nuclear capacity, is clearly one of her aspirations. China styles herself a 'great power', or one of the smaller medium powers: the Third World, which consists of 'oppressed nations, oppressed countries, and socialist countries' (in other words, of people) is her natural constituency.

The critique by Stalinist Albania, which now regards itself as the world's sole Marxist – Leninist state, is interesting. There, objection is taken by Albanian Marxists to the Chinese eradication of the concept of socialism, and hence of the contradiction between socialism and capitalism perceived as the main contradiction of the epoch. It is also wrong, it is claimed, that imperialism should be reduced to the two superpowers and that an attempt is made to differentiate between the two imperialisms, elevating one above the other. Similarly mistaken is the call for a United Front (of all) to confront the two superpowers, since it implies the PRC entering into dealings with reactionary Third World regimes: 'According to this logic, the oil sheiks, who deposit their oil money with the banks of Wall Street and the City are allegedly fighters against imperialism' (quoted in Satyamurthy, 1978, 1950–1).

None of this is to suggest that a case could not be made out for the Marxist credentials of the 'three worlds' theory as a theory of three world classes. Indeed, we have argued to the contrary. However, most critics of that theory stress in their writing the second of the two sides that characterize the Marxist theory of international relations, namely that it regards states and nations as constituent amalgams of the global classes. Samir Amin, for example, pointed out that the 'three worlds' theory appears to be 'based exclusively on the national factor, reduced in this case to the shape and place of nations in the system . . .' and that it 'does not explain reality if it is taken literally and if one reduces all reality to the national factor . . . substituting nations for classes . . . states and nations are realities not of course independent of class but not reducible to class' (Amin, 1980, 221). In fact the 'three worlds' theory enables a full integration of China into the international system, allows her a place in the system of states, and further legitimizes intimate relations with both (or either one) of the two superpowers.[2] It is at one and the same time a theory of global class and a theory of inter-state relations which identifies only two enemies—even then contriving to co-operate with one of them against the other. In some respects it would seem to resemble more closely the rules of balance of power (the enemy of our enemy is our friend) with, as Kim has observed, Chinese strategic thinking closely paralleling that of the United States (Kim, S. S., 1981, 438).

As a matter of fact the 'three worlds' theory has been seen as a reversal of Lenin's theory of imperialism from which it claims to derive, and replaces his theory with a 'theory of superpowers' (Jashek, 1978, 381). According to the 'law of uneven development of capitalism' it is possible to argue with the Chinese that the number of imperialist powers becomes eventually reduced to two, who, far from co-operating in a

---

[2] To add to the terminological confusion the Chinese use the principle of peaceful co-existence as defined in this model with regard to *all* states, not only with regard to capitalist states (as in the case of the Soviet model).

collusive relationship (as Kautsky predicted), vie with each other for world hegemony, and along the way oppress in varying degrees other countries. Their warmongering is regarded as virtual catastrophe (to use Luxemburg's terms) in the face of which the 'United Front' of all (second and third worlds joined with, if need be, one superpower against the other) is the recommended solution.

Is the 'three worlds' theory an exercise in cynicism on the part of an aspiring great power/superpower trying to dissimulate her nationalist aspirations by veiling them in Marxist global imagery? The theory is certainly not lacking in flexibility. It has been pointed out that in the earlier years it supplied the rationale for China's isolation from, and hostility towards, both superpowers. The seventies were characterized by hostility towards the USSR and co-operation with the United States, and there are recent indications that the wheel may have come full circle, that the PRC might return to its earlier relationship with the USSR either to join with her against the United States or to play the two superpowers off against one another. All or any one of these attitudes would be perfectly compatible with her 'three worlds' theory.

Li Ta-chao and the three worlds theory

To impute such motivations might be to do the PRC a serious injustice, for although any one of the interpretations as to motivation might be correct, a too ready acceptance would be to run the risk of overlooking the tradition of Marxism as it has developed since its first grafting on to the Chinese environment. Marxism in China has taken on features that are uniquely Chinese and that correspond to the unique circumstances of Chinese culture.

The appurtenances of Western civilization have always remained alien to China since she first entered the modern world. The accommodation of China—or for that matter of any Marxist state—into such a product of Western civilization as the states-system has proved difficult; in the case of China the complications are multiplied. Apropos the USSR we said that it was a question (in practice and in theory) of a mix of horizontal (state) and vertical (class) axes: in the case of China we have to take into account a third (Chinese) dimension. China never saw herself either as a nation-state or as a political or 'sovereign' subdivision of a larger order or system. The ancient Chinese civilization in fact points in the opposite direction: corroborated over a period of centuries by Confucian philosophy the image was retained, until the nineteenth century, of China as the 'Middle Kingdom'—a notion perpetuated to this day in the Chinese characters for China ('Chung-Kuo'). In this portrayal China was in herself a world order, with the 'outside' constituting a 'barbarian' periphery. There is nothing in Chinese tradition remotely resembling the principle of sovereignty or the idea of *ius gentium*; these and other notions having to be 'imported' from their 'outside' place of origin—to assume in a Chinese context a slightly different meaning.

Marxism was of course one such alien doctrine, with the Chinese host body (unlike nineteenth-century Russia) totally unprepared for the foreign implantation. Likewise, the nature of the Chinese revolution when it arrived, as compared to the Russian revolution, was also to show fundamental differences. The task of the Chinese revolution was to salvage an entire civilization in danger of extinction from external (European) encroachment by powerful nation-states. It had, moreover, to set in reverse the processes of internal political and social decay already set in motion by the working of capitalist forces. In these circumstances, Marxism appeared (paradoxically enough) to offer the world view most appropriate for the accommodation of China in the international system, in which direction the country was already being steered. Chinese thinkers had already in the nineteenth century come to grips with the idea of 'imperialism' and Liang Ch'i-ch'ao, in 1902 well in advance of any Marxist, defined it as 'the industrial power of the citizens of a nation [which] has been fully developed domestically and must flow to the outside' (Hoffheimer, 1979, 255–6). Underlying Liang's conception of imperialism there was always the suggestion of international *racial* conflict and imperialist exploitation of the Oriental peoples as a form of class struggle on the international level. It was an undertone that was also to run through the thoughts on imperialism of Li Ta-chao (one of the founders of Chinese Marxism) and, later, of Mao.

In fact it was only through development of the theme of

national imperialist exploitation that could have paved the way of Marxism into China. The country lacked a developed urban proletariat, the supposed vanguard element elsewhere of the class struggle. Quite clearly, also, pre-Leninist Marxism, with its assumption of the existence of capitalist economic relations had little to offer China in the second half of the nineteenth century. There remained only one possibility of inferring Marxism's relevance for China and of channelling the enormous potential of the doctrine to the future of that country. It is for us of particular interest that Li Ta-chao grasped that international aspect of Marxism that resulted in the doctrine's introduction in China as first and foremost a theory of international relations. As Meisner has pointed out in his important study, if China lacked a developed urban proletariat to carry on the class struggle *internally*, then the whole nation had to be looked upon as part of the world-wide forces of proletarian revolution (Meisner, 1973, 154). At an early date, therefore, Li Ta-chao had recognized the way by which China could make her entrance upon the stage of world history and become part of the swelling tide of universal progress. Thus Marxism became from the very beginning an instrument of Chinese nationalism. The term 'nationalism', being also of course an alien term, had best be replaced: instead of saying that Marxism was to serve nationalism, the restoration of the great Chinese civilization, the Middle Kingdom, made a much more acceptable proposition.

In this way the idea of a 'proletarian nation' was born, a distant echo and an inversion of Marx's notion of 'national class', revised to fit a very different context, to conform to European circumstances, and to serve radically different ends. From his first encounter with Marxism Li Ta-chao saw the class struggle not as a process taking place within individual countries but as a single world struggle. The conflict was not between different positions in the process of production, but between the forces of darkness represented by international capitalism and the powers of regeneration represented by the flood-tide of Bolshevism.

The notion of the 'proletarian nation' was first put forward in an essay that appeared in January 1920 entitled 'An Economic Explanation of the Causes of the Changes in Modern Chinese

Thought'. The crucial factor in modern Chinese history, he contended, was that economic changes in China resulted from the intrusion of outside forces, this in contrast to Western countries where economic changes derived from internal developments. Thus the suffering of the Chinese people under the pressures of world capitalism was much more severe than that of the proletarian classes in the various Western countries who were oppressed only by their own national capitalist classes. So great in fact was the impact of imperialism upon the Chinese economy, and so severe the oppression of the Chinese people, that 'the whole country was gradually transformed into part of the world proletariat' (Li quoted in ibid. 144). The implications of this argument were clear, essentially that if China was a proletarian nation, China was entitled to a proletarian world view: 'in the world economy of today China really stands in the position of the world proletariat'. This does of course present a most interesting interpretation of a nation's consciousness (*mutatis mutandis* its superstructure) as a reflection not of its own economic substructure (which in that event would have China not as a proletarian but as a pre-capitalist feudal state) but of the whole world in which, through the medium of the states-system, a nation's nature is conferred by the system as a whole. Thus China was both economically and ideologically qualified to participate in the world proletarian revolution. Li Ta-chao wasted no time in substituting the identification of the source of China's misfortune from his pre-Marxist formulation of the 'guns of the Europeans' to become 'international capitalism', and for China's 'rebirth' he substituted the 'great mission of mankind' and proletarian internationalism.

The nationalism inherent in the theory of the 'proletarian nation' is obvious. There was the implicit assumption that class differences within China have dissolved in the face of China's external enemies. If, then, the entire Chinese nation was 'proletarian', the national struggle and the class struggle were one, and nationalistic interest and motivations were sanctioned as legitimate forms of China's contribution to the world revolution. The theory in fact implied that China had a special role to play in the international proletarian struggle, for if indeed the whole Chinese nation was proletarianized, then China was presumably more revolutionary than the capitalist nations of the West. These nations might have large proletarian sections, but they still appear on a world scale amalgamated as imperialist aggressor states. The 'proletarian nation' theory raised China to a position of superiority, for the revolutionary struggle thus redefined had no longer anything to do with oppressor and oppressed classes but instead with oppressor and oppressed nations; and from among the latter 'proletarian' China was in the van.

From this reasoning there emerges by implication a theory of nation that contrasts sharply with Marx's theory of proletarian internationalism and of nation. Li ta Chao argues along similar lines to those of Otto Bauer to the effect that characteristics peculiar to a nation can determine the particular history of that nation. National characteristics constitute a most powerful motivating force in the special experience of each nation—not by any means a unique train of thought, for other Asian and African Marxists arrived at the same conclusion, but Li Ta-chao proceeded further to argue that behind national antagonisms there lurked racial differences and prejudices. The blame rested with the Europeans for whom there was 'nothing else to speak of except Christianity, and as far as their world view is concerned, they think that there is only the white man's world' (ibid. 188–90). According to the European world view 'all nonwhite peoples were destined to occupy a position of permanent inferiority':

The white peoples [see themselves] as the pioneers of culture in the world; they place themselves in a superior position and look down on other races as inferior. Because of this the race question has become a class question and the races, on a world scale, have come to confront each other as classes . . . the struggle between the white and colored races will occur simultaneously with the class struggle. The Russian Revolution is evidence of this. Although [members of] the white race participated in the Russian Revolution, the oppressed-class colored races also took part, and the object [of the revolution] was to resist the oppressor-class white race. Thus it can be seen that the 'class struggle' between the lower-class colored races and the upper-class white race is already in embryonic form, and its forward movement has not yet stopped (ibid. 191).

It is a view expressed not infrequently by Marxists of non-European origin at that time. For example Sultan-Galiev, a Tatar communist, and an Assistant Commissar for Nationalities under Stalin (purged with many others from the communist movement) also made the distinction between the Western proletariat, which was a social *class* and Eastern *nations* which were entirely proletarian because of the economic conditions imposed upon them. Pushing this opinion even further, he argued that once the victorious Western proletariat replaces the Western bourgeoisie as the dominant class it will automatically inherit its attitude to the national question. Sultan-Galiev envisaged a colonial communist International which would have defended the interests of the proletarian nations against the advanced countries (d'Encausse and Schram, 1969, 36).

Mao and tactics

We return to Mao, and employing once again the imagery of the pyramidal figure (Chapter 4), and in the hands of a Marxist state the locating of ideology at certain of its levels, we argue that Mao's major contribution to the Chinese approach to international relations is to be found in enhanced theoretical sophistication and in the grounding of that theory on an enormous *tactical* flexibility. Thus, whilst the upper ideological levels (and particularly those at the apex) have remained Marxist – Leninist in essence and add little to the message (the world is in the process of traversing a lengthy, arduous route towards communism in accordance with the findings of historical materialism), Mao proceeded to reinforce and legitimize the twin bulwarks of his theoretical position: the theory of *contradictions* and the theory of the *United Front*. The theoretical underpinnings are not original, deriving in the case of the United Front from an old Bolshevik doctrine of the twenties, and in the case of his contradictions from the classical Chinese philosophical principle of Yin Yang (the endless reciprocal interaction of direct opposites). However, in this latter regard, by substituting the Marxist value of conflict for the Confucian value of harmony, Mao was to make a fundamental break from the traditional Chinese image of world order. As with Marx, and for that matter Soviet Marxism – Leninism, the principle of the contradictory had a profound influence on Maoist thought and Mao believed in the interaction of contradictions as a moving force present in all things. 'Everywhere in the world there are contradictions. If there were no contradictions there would be no world' (quoted in Schram, 1969, 92). 'Society develops "at all times" through continual contradictions.' And in fact, the 'law of contradiction in things, that is the law of the unity of opposites, is the most basic law of materialist dialectics' (ibid. 194–5). It is an awareness (as Kim points out) that leads Mao to the perception of a conflict-based human nature as forming yet another category. But to Mao (unlike Hobbes) conflict/contradictions are inherent in the social process itself rather than in the biological or psychic make-up of man. Human nature after all is like clay in the potter's hand—endlessly malleable; and the remoulding of the world is therefore predicated on the prior shaping of man's world outlook (Kim, 1979, 59).

Because the presence of contradictions is universal, and since all relations are inherently contradictory in nature, it becomes obvious that it is the distinction between types of contradictions that matters, equally important is the identification of principal and secondary contradictions and, last but not least, the degree of 'handling' to which the contradictions lend themselves—and the degree of dexterity of that manipulation. Contradictions are (as they were for Lenin) either antagonistic or non-antagonistic, the distinction revolving round their derivation from the class struggle. The antagonistic are resolvable only in revolution. Contradictions will exist even in communism, and beyond 'handling' them there is no way of eradicating them completely.

To Mao the contradictions are, Manichean-wise, all related to the concept of people—as the embodiment of 'good'. Mao, like Li Ta-chao before him believed that backwardness represents a great advantage secreting as it does a seed—of youth and progress. The notion, whilst consistent with the military application of the theory to produce a novel perception/assessment of strength ratios (weakness in strength: strength in weakness), represents also a departure from Lenin and Trotsky who so often deplore the backwardness of Russia and see in it nothing but a hindrance. Unlike the Chinese Marxists, their Russian counterparts were preoccupied with the idea of the proletariat and its central role in the historical process—deriving not from backwardness but from that special relationship to the means of production. To Mao, by way of contrast, poverty *per se* and not occupying any special position *vis-à-vis* the relations of production, qualifies for a place in the revolutionary mission, and inequality becomes a virtue. Hence Mao always argued against the cities ('dens of iniquity') and for the more virtuous countryside—a distinction that led not only to the concept of the countryside encircling the cities, but also the *world* countryside (the Third World) encircling the world cities (the industrialized zones) ('Chairman Mao's Contribution', 26). It is in this light that one should read Mao's references to the small and the weak as opposed to the big and strong—a moral juxtaposition derived as much from precepts of Mao's (fifth-century) strategic inspiration Sun Tzu' as is the Maoist revolutionary tactics and strategy itself. In this way a small country can defeat a large one and a weak can defeat a stronger, not only because of superior strategy but because from the 'people' (equated with the 'good' pole of every antagonist contradiction) there emanates an aura of real power. Therefore, as soon as the people embark upon their own liberation struggle they become invincible, and the outcome is inevitable. The road to victory might well be tortuous and daunting but the victory itself is historically preordained:

Innumerable facts prove that a just cause enjoys abundant support while an unjust finds little support [as in Soviet ethics, clearly just and good are seen here to merge]. A weak nation can defeat a strong, a small nation can defeat a great. The people of a small country can certainly defeat aggression by a big country if only they dare rise in struggle, dare to take up arms and grasp in their own hands the destiny of their country. This is a law of history (ibid.).

Within this broad context and by reference to the ubiquitous web of contradictions the decision-maker is given *carte blanche* in regard to the actual formulation of foreign policy. In all of this there is, however, only one contradiction designated at any given time as the principal contradiction and that necessarily determines the development of the others. The task of leadership is to identify that one contradiction and then to concentrate on its resolution. The resolution of the secondary contradictions is subordinated to the correct resolution of that one. The actual method of 'handling' the contradictions depends on their nature: the antagonistic responding only to armed struggle. Mao's idea of guerrilla warfare and the protracted war—his major contributions to Marxist revolution—are in fact refinements of methods for the resolution of important (domestic) contradictions.

As in Marxism, Mao accepts the idea that war is the continuation of politics and is a means of resolving contradictions: whether between classes, or nations, or states. In terms also of crucial distinctions Mao, in company with his fellow Marxists, distinguishes between two kinds of war: the just and the unjust; and two kinds of violence, revolutionary and counter-revolutionary (with denunciation or approbation to correspond). Another important Maoist distinction is made between revolutionary and global war. The former is essentially a domestic affair for every oppressed nation, and despite the advent of the nuclear age is still to be encouraged since such violence can be kept under control and held apart from the second (global nuclear) variety. This latter type of war necessarily takes the form of inter-state conflict and is therefore to be avoided.

The reach of Mao's concern always stops short of the whole world order, viewing the world in the manner of other Marxist statesmen, through the prism of 'one country'—whose place within the world order is of cardinal importance. The conclusion reached by a number of students of Chinese foreign policy is that the whole history of the foreign policy of the PRC confirms the fact that her formulation in the last analysis involves the identification of that perpetually changing hierarchy of contradictions, the further identification of the principal contradiction, and the joining in a 'United Front' with all the other 'floating' elements and factors not directly connected to the main contradiction. In this context, the history of the Sino-Soviet split is in Chinese eyes a history of the USSR coming ever closer to, and finally being part of, the principal contradiction. Underpinning the 'three worlds' theory therefore are a number of contradictions the most important of which are readily identifiable: first, there is the contradiction between the oppressed nations on the one hand and imperialism and social imperialism on the other; second, that between the proletariat and the bourgeoisie in the capitalist and revisionist countries; third, the contradiction within the imperialist ambit and between imperialist countries; and fourth, the contradiction between the socialist countries on the one hand and imperialism and social imperialism on the other.[3]

There is a surety in the concept of the United Front and the theory of contradictions, a confirmation of the fact that even should the Sino-Soviet gap again close, or at least a working relationship be established, such a circumstance will not necessarily invalidate the 'three worlds' theory. Chinese confidence in her own superiority, well grounded experience in self-reliance, and foreknowledge of an auspicious future, these together with endorsement of all of them in the Maoist version of Marxism hold a promise that in the end they will prevail. In the slow but sure ascent of China through the hierarchy of the international system there is no reason to suspect that the path she has so far followed and the signposts along the way, are mistaken.

[3] *Peking Review*, 29 April 1969.

6 Resisting 'Proletarian Internationalism'

Instead of the expected fulfilment of the century-old promise of world-wide Marxist revolution, there is now, some seventy years after that solitary Soviet ('socialism in one country') experience, a sizeable part of the states-system made up of states going by the name of Marxist,[1] and in virtually every other state there exists at least one and often several Marxist parties/Marxist inspired movements. In this and in the following chapter we extend our enquiry beyond the theories of international relations and the Marxist international politics of the USSR and the PRC to examine those of these others. In the process we look at relations among the various Marxist contingents, and the reciprocating effect of their relations with the states-system.

Marxist international politics

The exact figures are difficult to establish but according to some accounts between 1918 and 1980 alone armed force was used

[1] We adopt the classification of these countries suggested by Wiles:

Group One consists of those countries that are first of all full members of the Council for Mutual Economic Assistance (CMEA) subdivided into the 'core' (Bulgaria, Hungary, Romania, East Germany, Poland and Czechoslovakia with Romania maintaining a degree of independence in foreign policy). Second, the non-European members: Mongolia, Cuba and Vietnam.

Group Two are countries designated as socialist who are not members of the CMEA and are at present outside the Soviet influence: Albania, China, North Korea, and Yugoslavia with their relationship to the USSR permanently subject to change.

Group Three are what has been designated as the New Communist Third World: the countries that have proclaimed themselves *voluntarily* Marxist-Leninist, are not members (as yet) of the CMEA but receive substantial aid from the USSR: Angola, Mozambique, the PDR of Yemen, Ethiopia, Afghanistan (now under Soviet occupation), Laos, Cambodia, Grenada (till 1983), and Nicaragua (since 1984).

Group Four consists of 'doubtful' cases such as Madagascar, Benin, Congo-Brazzaville, Guyana, and Somalia whose development might take them into Group Two or Three (Wiles, 1982, 13 ff.).

offensively by self-proclaimed Marxist countries between 35 and 40 times. In more than half of these instances the USSR was involved, in four or five it was China and Vietnam, and in one or two, eight other socialist countries were embroiled. Of the total of 16 socialist countries, 11 resorted to armed force for other than defensive purposes (Stojanovic, 1983, 8). Even a less startling count would seem to constitute an indictment of the validity of the Marxist thesis that conflict in international relations is coterminous with capitalism and co-operation is with socialism. But of course the point to be made once again is that the Marxist classics did not consider the possibility of a coexistence of capitalism and socialism, let alone that such an (albeit transitory) coexistence would take the form of *states* coexisting in a *states-system*. When Marx and Engels refer to socialism and communism as devoid of conflict it is in the context of a socialist or communist *world society*, a society devoid also of states.

Marx and Engels expressed concern for (indeed condemned) the possibility of that piecemeal transition to socialism in 'one' or 'several' countries which has in fact taken place. 'Proletarian internationalism', such as the USSR claims to practise, was to Marx and Engels an alternative principle for the organization of mankind, superior to that on which the states-system is based. Indeed, all indications from that group of states which have been the subject of Soviet experimentation with 'real' (or 'actual') 'socialism', as it came to be called, point to their preference for the operation of an ordinary variety of international relations within the 'ordinary' states-system. Their preference it might be thought, could derive from dissatisfaction with their massively powerful suzerain's interpretation of 'proletarian internationalism' and her maladroit conduct of their relations. But whether for that reason, or because *any* definition of the concept that transgresses 'orderly' participation in the international system would prove similarly unacceptable, it is to be observed that resistance to Soviet domination is not framed in Marxist terms but in those of the states-system.

The fact that these Marxist contingents show a tendency to adjust faithfully to its anarchical, oligarchical structure, and to assimilate its instruments instead of unshackling themselves from that system, adds further strength to the seeming paradox.

It is in any case undeniable that participation in international politics and a facility in the deployment of its traditional instruments has served admirably such aspirations as the geopolitical aggrandizement of the larger among them and has helped preserve the autonomy of some (not all) of the smaller. At the very least the process of their integration into a Marxist empire has been slowed.

In other words their theories of international relations, rather than being economically determined and a function of their domestic structure, become a function of their overall position within the states-system in general and of their relationship with the suzerain (USSR) in particular. Thus the distinction usually made between three categories of 'powers' ('small, regional, great') in the study of International Relations, when applied to the respective approaches to international relations of these Marxist contingents, sheds a curiously informative light on their nature. Traditionally the concern of a minor power has always been restricted to the preservation of territorial integrity and political independence whilst that of a great power has been the fashioning of a new international environment (in its own image) in close accord with its own interests. The regional power's aspiration has been to create a favourable regional environment in the process of attaining global political status (cf. Aron, 1962, *passim*).

In the case of the Marxist contingents the spectrum is somewhat wider as we have to add categories that are 'outside' the states-system on either side of the 'small-regional-great' power range. At one end are the Trotskyists who in their lack of a formal attachment to a permanent home in any particular state (Shipley, 1977, 1) are the only 'contingent' untouched by the stigma of nationalism and states-system and can thus boast a true internationalism. Rejecting the Bolshevik fragmentation of world revolution, their abiding animus is a hatred of *state*, both capitalist *and* socialist, proclaiming a theory of international relations to correspond. At the other end of the range are those Marxist states in Eastern Europe whose sovereignty and autonomy are already a mere formality, and who have no right whatsoever either to formulate their foreign policies or to articulate the attitudes towards international relations on which such policies would otherwise be based.

Except in special circumstances and in the writings of dissidents (an area to which, along with the Trotskyist theories, we shall return) there are in these parts of the world no alternative Marxist theories of international relations. More often than not the dissidents or aspiring Marxist group are preoccupied with the preservation or the achievement/recovery of national independence and sovereignty: a somewhat un-Marxist concern in the circumstances. The Soviet definition and implementation of proletarian – socialist internationalism has produced fiercely defensive nationalisms and anti-Soviet sentiments rather than seeking and finding their reward in overtaking and superseding the states-system—as prescribed in classical Marxist texts.

The Soviet innovations

Marx and Engels neither spelled out in any detail the future of inter-communal relations nor stated what was meant by 'proletarian internationalism' in a post-revolutionary period. The First and Second Internationals were equally reticent on the subject and in fact more than anything else the organizational structures of these bodies bore a resemblance to those of the League of Nations! The Soviet definition of 'proletarian internationalism' became based quite logically on the main Leninist innovation, the concept of a highly centralized Communist Party. Hence it comes as no surprise that the main features of the Soviet notion of a superior brand of international relations are based, first, on the principle that such relations are based on the deployment of Communist parties, and, second, on the conduct of inter-state relations following similar lines to those operative in inter-party relations. Thus *Communist parties* in the Soviet model function as a kind of super-government, operative at levels both alongside and above the state itself. Even in countries where the communist party is not in power such parties still differ substantially in role and purpose from their Western parliamentary counterparts. Their role goes well beyond victory in elections and participation in parliamentary affairs, and their purpose is the replacement of the existing order with a party regime designed to transform man and society (McNeal, 1967, 3).

In negotiations between a communist country and a non-

communist country it is of course in the former the communist
party which, holding a monopoly of power, formulates the broad
lines of domestic and foreign policy. Since the conventional
government would hardly contemplate entering into transactions on a government-to-party (instead of government-to-
government) basis the relation has all the appearance of a
perfectly ordinary diplomatic exchange. In the case of relations
between two communist states there will be maintained
additionally a system of diplomatic relations running in parallel
with the inter-party network. This means that inter-party
ideological differences can be, and have been, 'resolved' by the
more drastic, more coercive instruments of the states-system,
including war, threat of violence, the breaking off of diplomatic
relations, abrogation of international treaties, and the like. The
powerful communist parties in France and Italy which came
together in the seventies in a movement loosely referred to as
Eurocommunism[2] had promised, even before they first came
close to victory at the polls, to return to a more conventional
Western parliamentary style party and in their inter-party
relations introduced features characteristic of inter-state
relations! This plank in the Eurocommunist election platform
was reinforced in a 1977 meeting when the CPI and CPF agreed
to treat their relationship on a state-to-state basis, institutional-
izing 'fraternal diplomacy' and respect for the 'sovereignty' of
the parties concerned and 'non-interference in one another's
affairs' (MacLeod, 1980, 193).

The Soviet definition of 'proletarian internationalism' as a
basis for her relations with other Marxist contingents is similarly
based on the extension of the Leninist notion of a highly
centralized Soviet Communist Party. The principle was first
applied with the formation of the Comintern, an organization
designed to act as a sort of International Communist Party,
sharing such features with the Soviet Party as a similar structure
and procedures, and a unified set of rules as set forth in Lenin's
Twenty-One Conditions (1920) for admission into the Comintern. Significantly, also, the Soviet-led body designated each of
the national 'sections' that went to make up the one giant
international Party as 'Communist'. There took place in the
Comintern forum, particularly in the early years, serious

2 But also in Spain, Greece, Japan, Great Britain, Belgium, Mexico, Australia.

debate between Marxist participants from all over the world, and it was only when some of the 'sections' came to power in their own states that arguments developed on that international platform assumed the status of inter-state conflicts and became unmanageable. Mao, Kun, Ho (then known as Quoc), Tito (then Broz), Dimitrov, Togliatti, and Ulbricht all took their place in this Soviet foreign legion and submitted to the leadership and dictates of the CPSU. Returned to power in their own countries however they then established their own version of that Party with, as we have observed, the escalation of interparty into interstate conflicts as a consequence.

The Comintern over a period did indeed wield an absolute dominion over her 'sections' which unfortunately was not commensurate with the quality of its counsels. Among the mistakes was the 'advice' to the young Chinese Communist Party to support the Kuomintang, the results of which are still with us today. The advice to the German Communist Party was to oppose the social democrats rather than unite with them against Hitler; again with tragic repercussions. The list goes on, to become a catalogue of failure. The intellectual damage done by the Comintern to Marxism was similarly world-wide in its effect and, as it turns out, has proved irreparable; it was largely the fact that the 'sections' of the Comintern were subject to similar constraints to those placed on Soviet society that proved unacceptable to many Marxists based in the non-Communist world. And yet, although the Comintern (and its two International predecessors in their eighty years of existence) failed to stage (or even to assist) any successful revolution, there grew from that main (Comintern) stem all the main 'deviations' of the right and of the left. The Trotskyists, who formed their own (Fourth) International, the Chinese, the Yugoslav, the Vietnamese—all the major Marxist variations grew from CPSU/Comintern roots that, in the last analysis, could trace their germination to the October Revolution.

The Comintern was only one of many international organizations devised to serve the purposes of the Soviet empire of that time or since, such organizations having for members either communist parties, communist states, or in some cases less formal gatherings with a membership open to both the particular state or states concerned and to communist parties.

After World War II, and continuing the tradition of the Comintern, the Cominform (Communist Information Bureau) was the provision of a common platform to integrate the people's democracies, and the communist parties of Italy and France, into the Soviet orbit. These East European countries have since, under Soviet leadership, become organized into the Warsaw Pact and the CMEA (Comecon) and into some thirty other regional technical organizations with countries from other groups invited to participate informally or as observers (cf. Szawlowski, 1976).[3] Beyond this somewhat scaled-down area of Soviet implementation of the Marxist universalist vision there exists no other permanent pan-communist organization on the lines of the three Internationals that would be open even in principle to communist states or parties. Instead there are various irregular gatherings of parties in and out of power in various denominations and mixes. The Congresses of communist parties in power are used as opportunities for multilateral communist meetings, but even there, and ever since the serious divisions among the communist communities surfaced in the late forties, there has been a marked preference on the Soviet part for bilateral contacts and for the conclusion of bilateral, rather than multilateral, treaties. In the event of something 'going wrong' with the multilateral arrangements on which the entire system of international (communist) organizations would rest, there is still the parallel web of bilateral treaties 'of friendship and co-operation' to ensure that the political, and particularly the military, structures remain unimpaired.

Proposed alternatives to 'proletarian internationalism'

Following closely on the heels of the establishment of a plurality

[3] The whole gigantic economic and military complex of the international organizations of the communist countries is completely dominated by the USSR and is conditioned by the overwhelming disproportion of forces between the 'senior' partner and all the remaining forces combined: over 3:1 in the military field (plus the Soviet monopoly of nuclear weapons) and over 2:1 in the economic field. This is also reflected in the absolute dominance of the Russians in the top positions in the WTO and Comecon, and in the fact that Russian is, in almost all the organizations, the only working language. This power imbalance renders quite clearly such special ('socialist internationalist') features of these organizations as unanimity in voting meaningless (cf. Szawlowski, 1976, xvi–xvii).

of socialist states (people's democracies) in Eastern Europe, pressures against the Soviet-inspired and Soviet-enforced interpretation of 'proletarian internationalism' began to mount. It turned out that only an East European core was 'caught' with seeming permanence in the net—and the situation of that core was rendered irretrievable by the refashioning of proletarian internationalism, to become socialist internationalism. Arguments amongst those Soviet-led socialist movements (that were capable of argument) have focused mainly ever since on this theme. As far as resistance in Eastern Europe was concerned, the East-West geopolitical/strategic considerations that had worked from the beginning to frustrate such resistance in these countries continued in ever-intensifying operation.

As we have remarked, however, not all of the parties involved could be denied a voice, and in an interview with *Nuovi Argomenti* in 1956 Palmiro Togliatti spoke of 'polycentrism'. It was the year of 'destalinization' in the socialist countries, and for the first time the fallibility of the leadership and of its 'socialism in one country' thesis was admitted. It was also in 1956 that the 20th Congress of the CPSU crowned its revised ideological directions with the institutionalization of the possibility of 'separate roads' to the socialist/communist goal, to correspond to the individual national circumstances of the particular country. The process of fragmentation was further developed with a Chinese (and Albanian) challenge aimed directly at the Soviet leadership: specifically at the wisdom of its foreign policy attitudes and at its alleged departure from ideological purity and/or from Marxism, or from socialism. The Eurocommunist Italians took the opportunity to speak of a 'new internationalism' and the French of 'international solidarity' as their own alternative to the Soviet version of 'proletarian internationalism'. These alternatives in their Italian version (1979) envisaged the acknowledgement of, and complete respect for, national sovereignty, advocated a process of disarmament and the eradication of military and political blocs. The French communists, too, called for 'wider, more just and egalitarian international relations', and respect for the sovereignty of nations. In fact, these alternative approaches, including that of the Chinese, seem in large measure to be a neatly contrived antithesis to the Soviet thesis—and to the statement of Soviet foreign policy. The Eurocommunist case in particular hinged largely on the perceived contradiction between the Soviet foreign policy of *détente* of the seventies with the West, and their own revolutionary ambitions. Criticizing the Soviet policy of peaceful coexistence on the grounds of its perpetuating the status quo in Western Europe, the assault on proletarian internationalism was frontal. By far the most dangerous of the proposals for the USSR was that which envisaged a socialist Europe (including also the East European countries) in opposition both to the United States and to the Soviet Union.

The extent of the Eurocommunist parties' dissatisfaction could be gauged from the direction and substance of their attack. Among these, before the election defeat that shelved Eurocommunism as a meaningful practical force, was: the rejection of 'proletarian internationalism', assertion of their right to an independent policy even if it were to conflict with the state interests of the USSR, insistence also on their right to criticize the Soviet Union and to reject the Soviet model as a basis for their own transformation. Other hardly less significant 'anti-Soviet' measures were adopted: the name Leninist was dropped from the Spanish Party's name and the French went so far as to give up the idea of the dictatorship of the proletariat. Calls for non-alignment resounded throughout the movement and the French referred ominously to an omnidirectional nuclear strategy (*tous azimuts*). The Spanish communists devised a relatively autonomous conceptual framework of international relations, the main theme of which was the establishment of a distinction between nuclear parity between the United States and USSR on the one hand and the multilateral military alliance system on the other. The former was endorsed as positive whilst the latter was rejected in favour of non-alignment and a call for the disbandment of all military blocs. The Eurocommunists' foreign policies otherwise were rather sketchily drafted and with many inconsistencies. Theirs was a liberal variant of communism with the emphasis on democracy and adjustment (although by no means complete adjustment) to the West European democratic traditions, whilst along the way a rapport was established with the Romanians and Yugoslavs. The worldwide interest in the phenomenon that had been aroused abruptly ceased when in 1978 the Eurocommunist chance was lost in the elections, in the course of which it was pointed out that there was no such thing as 'Eurocommunist behaviour', for the parties differed too greatly from one another and their 'Eurocommunist' proposals were by no means novel—boasting as they might a lengthy pedigree reaching back in various ways not only to Bukharin, Trotsky, and Luxemburg, but also to Kautsky and Bernstein. Their greatest disappointment was the failure to extricate themselves from the Soviet connection. With the exception of Santiago Carillo's defiant posture the Soviet Union had never been openly challenged as non-socialist, nor had her foreign policy anywhere in the world been criticized as non-revolutionary. In fact the whole episode had shown that the West would be unlikely to act as 'the cradle of the communist renaissance', or that such a renaissance 'would emanate from the Eurocommunists' (Steinkühler, 1982, 323).

Theories of international relations of aspiring or oppressed Marxist regimes

In countries on the verge, but not yet Marxist, theories of international relations are to be found in the context of revolutionary tactics and military writing, and of manuals on strategies devised for the purpose of the coming-to-power of Marxist political leaders. Preoccupied as these works inevitably are with 'national strategy' the internationalist dimension tends to become obscured, vague, overlaid, or lost sight of, unless the particular national revolution happens to coincide with the struggle against a foreign intruder (such as imperialism of external origin, colonialism, national oppression, etc.). The sole, or chief, purpose of theories of international relations is often an attempted justification of the introduction of Marxism into a new milieu in which Marxism has not previously been 'applied'. Lenin's theory of imperialism or Li Ta-chao's concept of 'proletarian nation' are examples. A later example is Amilcar Cabral's new theory of imperialism in which he has as surrogate for the class struggle (absent in Africa) the mode of production as motive force. Again, Cabral, like Lenin and Li Ta-chao before him, has no purpose beyond the incorporation of his 'national' circumstances into the Marxist ambit. His purpose (akin to that of Gramsci's 'theory of international relations'), far from the exposition of international relations, is an explanation of the revolutionary failure in the West and the contriving of a new, improved strategy to deal with capitalism in the metropolises or ex-colonies. Unless such politicians become the 'diplomats' their theories of international relations, having performed their 'bridgehead' role, fade as a rule into the background, to be replaced by considerations of other more immediate domestic concerns.

In East Europe the concern for international relations is similarly obscured. These countries retain only a nominal sovereignty as separate states, a formality that permits merely their (separate) echoing of Soviet voting on the platforms of international organizations. None is allowed a 'separate' interpretation of world affairs however, nor, therefore, any independent promotion of foreign policy. *Romania* in this context constitutes an exception, although often one that is over-emphasized. Romania is in fact another instance of the denial of the interconnectedness of the notion of dependence of foreign policy on the domestic structure of a country, for *domestically* she is one of the most oppressive of the Soviet-style regimes, and yet of all the socialist countries has the most 'liberal' of foreign policies. She managed not only to stay outside the Warsaw Pact but was able to strike an independent (of the USSR) foreign policy in relation for example to Israel and to West Germany. Romania protested also against the Warsaw Pact invasion of Czechoslovakia in 1968 and sided with maverick Eurocommunist parties against the Soviet Union—most notably at the 1976 East Berlin Conference. Lately, however, she has again moved closer to the CMEA and to the Warsaw Pact, despite her failure to comply with the Soviet boycott of the 1984 Olympics. We may in fact regard Romania's relative independence as no more than the case of a successful 'socialism in one country' application made possible by a unique concurrence of factors. Unlike the other socialist countries Romania did not destalinize in the fifties and her then leader, Georgiu Dej, an imitation Stalin, in order to stay in power, contrived to establish a special relation with the Soviet Union. The less exposed Romanian geographical position (than the others of East Europe) together with her considerable mineral resources was to a large extent responsible for the privileged status.

It is remarkable that in the vociferousness of the dissidents in the socialist states, or in the wealth of their thinking on a wide range of topics, little is heard from them of international relevance. Of course the dissident movement has not yet constituted itself internationally and so it is perhaps small wonder that whilst proposals for 'internationalism' are forthcoming from East Europeans none is explicit about the organizational make-up nor of the tactics to be employed by this international alliance (cf. Oleszuk, 1983, 535). With such rare exceptions as the East German Marxist Rudolf Bahro's *The Alternative in Eastern Europe* (1978) which possesses a distinct internationalist dimension and awareness, the dissidents' calls seldom go beyond a critique of the Soviet model imposed on their countries or beyond demands for modifications of the relationship with the Soviet Union. Logically, their brand of Marxism (socialism with the 'human face', etc.) is predicated on national autonomy and sovereignty, but to the ways and means for the achievement of these conditions they spare hardly a line. Their immediate goal usually takes the form of a demand for 'equality' in the relations of states (as expressed in the Czechoslovak Action Programme of 1968) or calls for 'peaceful coexistence' in preference to the 'socialist internationalism' of which these countries are recipients, or, more rarely (less subtly), the call for outright neutrality.

Bahro's work manages to overcome this introversion but he too fails to handle the vexed 'national question'. Where precisely is the nerve centre, he asks: 'Does it not lie in the national confinement of opposition ideas? The national phenomenon is a very important fact.' Its roots lie in the 'historical and present uneven development of peoples, giving rise to the opposition between national interests' (Bahro, 1978, 333). Reminiscent of a Trotskyist argument he explains the great-power politics component in Soviet foreign policy as derivative of the encirclement of the USSR and her competition in the arms race. Bahro's dream is once again of a socialist world society, an 'association of communes into a national society and association of nations in a contentedly co-operating world' (ibid. 453). Until that happy eventuality, however, Bahro, unlike most of his East European dissident colleagues, is capable of a wider, more refreshing international perspective through which to view his country's misfortune. That perspective is along East – West and North – South lines of conflict carrying with it also the implications of nationalism which, he asserts, the Soviet leadership is provoking beyond endurance both inside and beyond its (Soviet) borders (ibid. 333).

In fact Marxism (after all the doctrine of the oppressor) appears in the East European countries to be under serious threat. In the circumstances it is hardly surprising that the ideologies that seem to supply a need appear to be a mix of nationalism, religion, and populism. It would not be going too far to say that the renaissance of Marxism that we have seen in the Western world, and the undoubted success it has enjoyed in the Third World, are paralleled in the countries to which it was brought by the Red Army, by the doctrine's gradual decline. However, it is most unlikely that the crumbling of East European 'faith' is to be followed by a loosening of the bonds of the Soviet 'socialist commonwealth'. As a matter of fact students of Soviet international organizations (Szawlowski, 1976), of Soviet international law (Hazard, 1971), and of the Soviet economy (Lavigne, 1983) are united in their opinion that more integration, rather than less, is indicated despite, or because of, the problems arising within the East European commonwealth.

Non-alignment

In the hands of communist states the institution of non-alignment has served a multitude of purposes and has proved a highly effective way by which small powers who entertain at least regional power aspirations may advance upon their goals. The doctrine has assisted others to maintain their socialist characteristics and at the same time preserve a certain independence; in this category a Yugoslavia independent of the Soviet Union and a Cuba independent of the United States. Undeniably, of course, geopolitical distance has been a main factor in both cases. Yugoslavia discovered the usefulness of the device in contriving to prevent her incorporation with the rest of East Europe in Group One. Cuba, located in the other hemisphere, and thus soon to become invaluable to the USSR as the sole available (and it seems reliable) agency in that hemisphere, managed to strike a relationship with the USSR that confers upon her the distinction of being the only known critic of the Soviet Union for that country's too liberal application of 'proletarian internationalism'. Unlike the first subgroup of Group One, and along similar lines to Vietnam, Cuba quite obviously benefits from her membership in the CMEA—to the estimated tune of between $8,000,000 and $10,000,000 subsidy daily. Whilst the Marxist credentials of the concept of non-alignment might be somewhat dubious, a side effect has been its enormous attractiveness to Third World countries whose membership since the sixties has climbed to upwards of eighty. In the circumstances of the Cold War's East-West division it has supplied a platform from which may be launched such radical demands as those embodied in the programme of the New International Economic Order, and with a Marxist (Tito) among the concept's three founding fathers non-alignment certainly warrants a mention in our present context.

Tito's idea of non-alignment has been seen as proof of Yugoslavia's aspirations to global political status through its venturing into self-management as an alternative (domestic) ideology and model and in the maintenance of a high-profile foreign assistance programme quite out of keeping with her minor-power status. The idea of non-alignment, since it was aimed specifically at the refashioning of the international environment as a whole, must be expected to confer a special status on any state which could legitimately claim leadership of the movement (Ramet, 1982, 66). It is a cynical (though not necessarily incorrect) interpretation of Yugoslav intentions, which, needless to say, they themselves vehemently deny, arguing that over and above her occupying a place as a truly non-aligned country, Yugoslavia has also a unique commitment to world peace and human progress. No apology is made either, for the frequently remarked nationalist implications of non-alignment for, as is pointed out by a foremost Yugoslav theoretician (himself credited by Tito with the main theoretical guidelines), 'the so called "nationalism" of which the non-aligned countries are frequently accused does not hamper the process of mankind's integration, or detente, co-operation, rapprochement and unification of peoples; rather, by their policies and struggle, they actually pave the way for such a development' (Kardelj, 1976, 106). The concept's rationale according to Kardelj was the protection of small states against the division of the world into blocs by which non-alignment helps 'maintain the system of international relations that took shape in the imperialist epoch' (ibid.). What, then, exactly is the meaning of the term?

According to conclusions reached at the Cairo Preparatory Meeting held in June 1961, the major features of the movement comprise its support for national independence and abstention from all conflicts connected to the Cold War Great Power conflict. Thus non-aligned countries pledge themselves not to enter any multilateral military alliance that is concluded in the context of Great Power conflict—with, exceptionally, membership in regional defence organizations. Neither in the case of a lease of military bases to a foreign power should such concessions be made in that context. The movement was specifically designed to be based on the coexistence of states with different political and social systems, with its foreign programme emphasizing peaceful coexistence, equality in interstate relations, and the end of colonialism (quoted in Willetts, 1979, 3).

The origins of the movement are usually traced to the Afro-Asian Conference held in Bandung in 1955. The twenty-nine participating countries ranged from the communists (China and North Vietnam) to the Western Allies (Turkey, the Philippines, and South Vietnam) although the conference brought together all of the independent countries of Africa and Asia at the time with the exception of Korea and Israel. Willetts claims 1956 as the date of origin when Tito, Nehru, and Nasser began a period of close co-operation that was to culminate in the non-aligned Conference at Belgrade in 1961. As one might expect, the motives of three such different leaders were correspondingly varied, and only those influences on the Marxist (Tito) are relevant to our present concern. Tito's main motive was a continuing concern for his country's independence *vis-à-vis* its former Soviet ally, and in fact the Yugoslav had been historically the first Marxist leader (preceding even Mao by some years) to challenge the Soviet Union's domination, and to survive. The special circumstances of Yugoslavia's situation at the time (lacking in other East European countries when their 'moment' arrived) included in the early years the absence of Red Army support for the installation of the communists in power. Therefore, although preparations were set afoot for the incorporation of the country into the USSR (and subscribed to by many prominent Yugoslavs including Kardelj) the Yugoslav communists owed little of their success to the Red Army.

The escalation of mutual hostility and withdrawal of all Soviet aid from the country followed Tito's request for time to set a timetable for the transition (seen by the Soviets as dragging his feet), and as feelings ran high the Yugoslavs embarked on changes to their socio-political structures and the promotion of an economic model of self-management and market socialism that differed widely from the Soviet situation. Floundering in the unfamiliar climate of Cold War and seeking to recoup the losses of the wartime conferences, the West welcomed Tito's advances and the opportunity of acquiring a well-located ally, and so in 1953 Tito, for his part in constant fear of Soviet invasion, signed a treaty with Greece and Turkey, becoming thereby a *de facto* ancillary member of NATO. Following his assurance to Churchill ('we are your allies'), the Balkan Treaty in 1954 (with Greece and Turkey) became a formal military alliance.

Stalin's death made possible a *rapprochement* between his successor, Khrushchev, and Tito to such effect that by 1955 Tito had abandoned his Balkan alliance, dropped his Western commitments, and instead of the concept of 'peaceful and active co-existence' now favoured the Khrushchevian notion of 'peaceful co-existence' with all of the implications of that concept. It was a pattern—the Yugoslav alternation in East – West alignment— whose swings followed closely the vicissitudes of the Cold War and the flow of events, whereby, for example, the strains exerted on the Yugoslav-Soviet relationship by the Hungarian crisis in 1956 swung Tito once again towards the West: and the counter-swing duly followed. However, his inclination in the direction of a new concept, non-alignment, became in the meantime more pronounced, and in the end turned out to be the one relatively stable factor in Tito's strategy. In 1961 'peaceful co-existence' gave way in Yugoslav foreign policy to the notion of a simple 'coexistence', a modification that brought with it a closer kinship to the semantic preferences of his non-aligned (non-Marxist) friends, Nehru and Nasser.

Notwithstanding the vagaries of Tito's foreign policy and the cynical interpretation that it often attracts, there is no doubt (as distinct from the cases of the PRC or of the USSR) that the Marxist-Leninist theory is for Yugoslavia more than a mere embellishment or an *ex post facto* justification for *ad hoc* opportunistic policies. Yugoslavia is a Marxist – Leninist state, a fact attested to by the lines of development of her society as by the directions pursued by her foreign policy. The country shares a number of common features with the Soviet model such as the single-party system, the suppression of dissent, and the commitment to Marxism – Leninism as the only acceptable framework of political ideas. Her leadership professes furthermore a determination to implement the guidelines of that framework. An alternative reading of the balancing act between West and East would see the lean to the West made necessary in order to avoid incorporation into the Soviet Group (One) alongside other East European countries—a development that would bring with it an inevitable *de facto* loss of sovereignty. On the other hand the inclination towards the East precluded the loss of Yugoslavia's Marxist – Leninist system that could result from a too close dependence on and exposure to the West. In other words, Yugoslavia is an example of a small Marxist state, with aspirations that can only be guessed at, balancing between East and West and yet managing to retain unmistakable Marxist features. In her achievement of that status, in addition to the advent of a Tito, the presence of propitious international circumstances was a main consideration in her 'socialism in one country'. The two main such influences were the onset of the Cold War and availability of a plausible ideological line of 'retreat', an alternative to both East and West: that of the doctrine of non-alignment—already subscribed to by the leaders of two important countries.

Trotskyism

The Trotskyist movement is world-wide and has a relatively small but enthusiastic following whose sense of direction is more often than not impaired by unfortunate division both inside and outside its official international representative body, the Fourth International. Trotskyism may in many ways be seen to constitute a bridge between our present chapter and that dealing with Western Marxism. Trotskyists are not diplomats (indeed, in so becoming they would by definition cease to be Trotskyist), but rather political activists following the Marxist dictum that there is no Marxism without a political movement (the political involvement therefore becomes mandatory for a Marxist). Yet as activists Trotskyist successes have been limited in the extreme, hampered often by the fact that there was no place for them within the states-system—and so no vested interest in its retention. In that part of the history of the group since Trotsky's laying of the organizational foundations following his expulsion from the CPSU in 1927 and exile from the country (1929), the Trotskyists failed to stage any successful revolution. Their lack of success was due in the main to their keeping (or being kept at) a distance from any state power centre including the Soviet, with the essay in partnership in Mrs Bandaranaike's Sri Lankan government constituting a rare exception. Participation in a number of guerrilla campaigns in Latin America and in student demonstrations in Western Europe were similarly inconclusive.

Whilst such non-participation may be seen as one of the chief obstacles in the path of Trotskyist development, it is nevertheless in keeping with their credo, and specifically with the rejection (as theoretically and practically nonsensical) of 'socialism in one country' experimentation. Instead they can boast of having followed the true path of Marxist universalism. Further, owing to their failure to participate in international power politics their doctrine lacks that fragmentation of principles that has followed participation in the states-system by fellow Marxists whose roots, like their own, go back to Comintern days. And yet, paradoxically enough, their own fissiparous tendencies are even more pronounced than are those of their fellows, taking the form of doctrinaire argument and the division into splinter groups and factions. Thus hobbled by their own internecine feuding, their political sights are set no higher than the targeting of established parties for infiltration; aiming usually at the various labour parties across the globe.

With Western Marxism the Trotskyists share (as well as a home ground) the commitment of many to the belief that it is not the national liberation movement in the Third World but rather the urban proletariat in developed Western capitalist countries that is the main agency of revolution. So Trotskyists oppose the 'Thirdworldism' of many neo-Marxists, which, in the tradition of Franz Fanon, Lin Piao ('countryside encircled cities'), Baran and Sweezy's *Monopoly Capital*, and Herbert Marcuse's *One Dimensional Man*, writes the urban proletariat off as the vanguard element. With the Western Marxists they share, too, the displeasure with the Soviet Union on grounds, however, that they adduce differently. For the Trotskyists the USSR is too conservative and does not lend enough support to world-wide (permanent) revolution. In other words their distaste derives from the international dimension rather than (as for the Western Marxists) from the oppressive (domestic) features of the Soviet regime. If anything, for the Trotskyists the Soviet practice of proletarian internationalism would be—as it is for the Cubans—too liberal, too loosely applied, and so they (like the 'Marxist Diplomats') see the Soviet economic structure as essentially *socialist*, with the 'deformations' of that system mainly of a superstructural nature and derivative from an *international factor* (the absence of world-wide revolution). Like the Western Marxists (and unlike the 'Marxist Diplomats'), the Trotskyists produce the most important modern theoretical work in the best tradition of classical Marxist – Leninist writing. Livio Maitan's analysis of China is one of the first attempts at a Marxist sinology (Maitan, 1976) and Ernest Mandel's writings on economics, on the Soviet Union, and on world affairs in general, ranks him as one of the most important of modern Marxist scholars. Most notably in his *chef d'œuvre*, *Late Capitalism* (1975), Mandel attempted a full analysis of the capitalist mode of production in its declining (or 'late') stage within the context of an increasingly complex capitalist development taking place since the thirties. In that work he explains the post-war boom and recent economic crises in the economies by reference to his major theoretical innovation, the 'long waves' of alternating expansion and relative stagnation— an exposition that leads him to a prediction of intensified inner capitalist contradiction and thence to armed violence to protect 'surplus value' and a dramatic reduction in the rate of profit. The economic analysis as set forth does not appear to invalidate the major Trotskyist 'theory of international relations' whose outlines seem to have remained intact since its promulgation as the Fourth International Transitional Programme of 1938. The 'three sector' theory of revolution contained therein is repeated again in another major Trotskyist document, the 'Dynamics of the Revolution Today' (1963).

The belief that there are three fronts to the world revolution reveals an underlying Trotskyist division of the world into three parts, characterized by different socio-economic structures: these are, first, the 'developed' capitalist countries; second, the 'underdeveloped' capitalist countries: and third, the 'deformed workers' states' of East Europe, the USSR, the PRC, etc. The world revolution constitutes a whole whose various parts as they are fought on those three fronts have reciprocal effects (Frank, 1979, 109). The Trotskyists identify, in other words, three parts of a one-world revolutionary process: the classical or proletarian revolution in the developed capitalist countries, the colonial revolution in the underdeveloped capitalist countries, (where it tends to become a permanent revolution), and, third, the political anti-bureaucratic revolution in the 'deformed workers' states'.

Such a reading of the world situation is based on a logical extension of a Leninist analysis contained in his theory of imperialism—and without the 'socialism in one country' staging post. The Trotskyist reading adjusts to the course of world events after Lenin's death, and the whole analysis is derivative of the belief held in common with Marx and Engels (and arguably also with Lenin) that the worldwide 'permanent revolution' was the only form of revolution possible. That the permanent revolution (presumably still in progress) was halted in mid-flight as a consequence of the betrayal perpetrated by the working-class leadership, a leadership comprised both of the social-democratic (of which Lenin was of course aware in his theory of imperialism) and of (subject of a recent revision) the Stalinist. Therefore, the Trotskyist argument runs, the process by which the revolution was carried first to the periphery before reaching the heart of the capitalist system was in no way part of an inevitably sequential development but resulted essentially from a combination of leadership betrayal and of a function of what might be termed the unstable equilibrium that exists between the fundamental antagonistic social forces on a world scale. It is also believed, however, to be a reflection of the long-term structural weaknesses of world capitalism as indicated for example by the Soviet leadership, who, despite repeated economic and military attempts, have been unable to restore the capitalist mode of production in the USSR.

To all intents and purposes the Trotskyist analysis addresses itself to the unmodified Marxist goal, and their 'working model' of international politics is one which, of all the other Marxists surveyed in this chapter, bears least the impress or taint of the states-system. The Trotskyists are certainly no 'Diplomats' in the sense that one might perceive to be the Soviet, Chinese, Vietnamese, and Cuban. Neither, in their commitment to the world-wide revolution, are they nationalists. The Trotskyists are not 'Professors' since for them the hallmark of their connection with a political movement and commitment to political action moves them well away from that category. In their romantic, Utopian (and unrealistic) designs, the Trotskyists are 'revolutionaries' and one is prompted to wonder whether it is at this juncture that they are most out of joint with the times and structures in which we live, and whether their 'maladjustment' lies in their having become victims of the world's political structure—a structure that militates against Marxist universalism and which scatters the revolutionary ferment (working ceaselessly, the Trotskyists would assert, not through but against the institutions of world politics) into fragmented impotence.

For us to choose to focus on international relations gives rise to a serious injustice: or so would claim the Trotskyists and the early Marxists (except the 'Diplomats') and some Western Marxists. Their horizons are elsewhere. For us to search for a theory of international relations in their writings would in their eyes appear as little relevant as would the judging of a marathon runner by the way he walks. It is a feeling that would be shared by the category to which we turn in Chapter 10.

7 The Third World and the 'Brocade Bag'

Writing on the Third World has an unfortunate tendency to become dated before it even goes to print. The unsecured political structures of Asia, Africa, and Latin America, the shifting intra-regional relations, the degree of immiseration of a geometrically increasing population, all show a proclivity to change from month to month—invariably for the worse. At the same time such influences upon these areas as flow from the cross-currents of the Cold War and superpower involvement, together with assessments of the 'correlation of forces', are all similarly subject to constant fluctuation, and make the situation difficult to 'freeze' long enough to make useful long-term evaluation. And yet, platitudinous though the observation may be, it is in these areas that the future of the whole of mankind will be determined.

These are the 'new states' that gained independence *en masse* only in the fifties and sixties and whose collective presence inside the states-system constitutes one of the most visible strains on a system that is endemically subject to such strains. Areas that once were debarred from membership of the exclusive European club for lack of standards of civilization are now reformed into upwards of 120 independent states occupying much of the world's territory, and already hold within their borders by far the largest proportion of mankind. Moreover the ratio is widening: to the extent that very soon only a relatively small fraction of the world's population will inhabit the cradle of 'international politics'—and will still be in possession of, and consuming, an infinitely larger proportion of the planetary cake than (on a head-count basis) would be their entitlement. Small wonder that the political leaders of the 'new states' and jurists refer to the 'common heritage of mankind' on which to base their claims for a restructuring, redistribution, reorganization of the political and economic rules of the game that so far would be more applicable to the era of European 'classical international politics' than to the modern globe-encompassing system.

Although Marxism was designed by its founders for other times and circumstances, with an intended application to the anticipated majority of the populations of the twenty or so European states, the doctrine, with characteristic flexibility, has proved itself adaptable enough to become a powerful intellectual and ideological foundation for Third World claims. As far as Marxism is concerned the transference from a revolutionary agency (the proletariat) that is rapidly running out (according to the redefinition of class structure in Western societies by such modern Marxists as Poulantzas and Olin Wright) is none too soon, and the shift from the de-proletarianized Western centres to areas and populations once described by Marx and Engels as 'barbarian' or 'nations of peasants' may turn out to have been just in time. Marxism, ahead of the rest of the 'common heritage of mankind' has been 'redistributed' and taken over in these substantial parts of the earth's surface by new owners.

The contemporary relevance of Marxism in the Third World derives from a number of sources. There is a clear temptation to apply to Marxism's new home the old Marxian categories intended for the internal relations within states between a growing proletariat and the bourgeoisies. The portrayal is, in the new circumstances and to all intents and purposes, hopelessly wrong or irrelevant, and yet perhaps it may prove to have been only 'prematurely wrong'. We are reminded of Gramsci's reference to the wisdom of Luxemburg's comment that we often discard thoughts as outdated, when there is nothing wrong with them—either the mistake is in our faulty appreciation *or* developments have still to catch up. There is, for example, no doubt that the world is *polarized* into rich and poor countries and that the widening gap recalls forcibly to mind the Marxist thesis of the absolute immiseration of the proletariat. The revolution (and in that reading the world has not as yet experienced one) will occur when the disparities are stretched beyond all endurance.

But there are a few snags in such an application of the doctrine. There is in the first place the difference between dreams of wish-fulfilment and a social theory, and Marx, after all, was engaged in the construction of a social theory in which each step in the reasoning was carefully referenced, based on economic analysis and empirical findings. Furthermore, his analysis referred without question to the relations of classes and in no way to the relations of states. In that (class) context he believed it possible actually to point to the article which to him represented the surplus value misappropriated by the (capitalist) system—a misappropriation he referred to as exploitation. Exploitation of increasingly larger sections of the proletariat led him to the realization that there existed serious injustice in the system and of the need for its replacement, the conclusion being that capitalism was not only an unjust but also essentially a defective mode of production.

There is therefore the fact that the Marxist categories in order to fit the needs of new owners require serious adjustment, which does not of course mean that such an obstacle should prove insurmountable or beyond the resources of those sufficiently hard-pressed. Guidelines for such adjustment have in fact already been set, and particularly in a seminal work by Lenin presented at the Second Congress of Comintern in 1922. In his *Theses on the National and Colonial Question* it was explained to Li Ta-chao, Mao, Ho Chi Minh, and the other future Asian, Latin American, and African Marxists (for many of whom this was their first introduction to Marxism) the lines along which adjustment to the doctrine would have to be made to have it relate to those revolutionary transformations so needed in the Third World.

Marxism gave the widest currency to the term 'imperialism' in the simple message that there is a causal connection between the deplorable state of affairs that characterizes virtually all of the Third World and the (in many cases) centuries-old colonial arrangements only recently terminated. In coining the term 'Third World' Alfred Sauvy intended to parallel the French Third Estate whose demands had led to the outbreak of the French Revolution and the coming of a new 'dawn' for liberty and equality. Although a prescient enough selection of a name in many ways, in yet others there are dissimilarities in the two situations. So unlikely a venue is the states-system for a sympathetic hearing of the real issues that lacerate the Third World communities, and (even less likely) for the adoption of other than perfunctory measures for their correction, that the implications of the adoption of such measures can only be a matter for academic speculation. The states-system would as a first consideration have to be restructured as an *international society* possessed of powerful, commonly held values and concerns. The transformation would have to go one step further with the implementation of the provisions of such documents as the New International Economic Order as well as the United Nations Conference on the law of the Sea (UNCLOS) Draft Convention, and the general economic principles on which international society should be based. This would be an embryonic world society still consisting of states but based on the all-pervasive principle of distributive justice with economic and political structures designed to correspond. There could emerge, on the other hand, a new states-system from what would have turned out to be no more than a rearrangement with some (still sovereign) states guaranteed economic and political privileges: an interchange, in other words, of the have and have-not positions. In this connection most authors refer to Adelman's study which showed convincingly that such transfers of privilege and the reduction of inter-state inequality does not necessarily lead to the reduction of inequality within these states, often the very reverse (Adelman and Morris, 1973). That particular imbalance might lead to the formation of a new political structure altogether, with a return (after the three-century states-system interlude) to some variant of a world-state.

There are two serious contenders only too ready, one assumes, to undertake the task of leading such a restructured community—with lesser aspirants standing by. Since there is no way in sight in which the serious ideological differences that separate the two leaders can be overcome, the idea of a 'coalition government' of the world-state is out of the question. But in any case there is little likelihood of the contingency arising since rocking the political and economic (states-system) boat could be a hazardous exercise for either of the two superpowers, who stand to lose so much in the event of an upset—and might also be for anyone else with a stake in the system.

In this regard the term 'Third World' is grossly misleading in so far as it implies the notion of distance from *both* the First and the Second World, that is from the West and East respectively. In the fifties (before Sauvy coined his phrase) and in the sixties it could apply to a situation in which there existed only the People's Republic of China, Vietnam, and Cuba (and of course Mongolia), with a demonstrable orientation towards the East when these areas were not always thought of as a 'Communist Third World'. In this connection the situation was more realistically interpreted by the USSR (see map, p. viii), which anticipated that as the number of Third World countries increased (portrayed in Soviet theory as the grey area to be won over by the 'East'), so a number of other Third World countries would choose the Soviet model. Thus, by virtue of the changes they were obliged to make to their own socio-economic structures, they became in Soviet theory part of the socialist socio-economic system—without even membership of any of the Soviet sponsored 'regional' organizations. It goes without saying that regardless of what may or may not be the theory, Soviet practice in the Third World has had its fair share of mishaps and failures, and unfortunately it is with such failures that Western commentators in large part have developed the (misleading) tendency to become preoccupied. In Western convergence theories that became popular in the years of *détente* in the seventies, some writers developed the argument that the Soviet Union, seeing her own increasing involvement in an interdependent (one) global economy, gives up the struggle (the struggle being the inevitable conflict situation implied by the existence of two separate socio-economic systems locked in a zero-sum relationship), from which point it was but a short flight of author's licence to have her surrender her revolutionary aspirations in these (Third World) areas.

Another, more alarming, reading of the same facts might see in retrospect Soviet behaviour in the Third World to have been an attempt simply to exploit to maximum advantage her foot in the door of the capitalist world comprising *both* the capitalist metropolises *and* the ex-colonies. Mistakes were outnumbered by successes. Some Soviet protégés fell from power in such countries as Iraq (Qasi), Ghana (Nkrumah), Indonesia (Sukarno), Algeria (Ben Bella), Mali (Keita), and there was a hurried Soviet departure from Egypt, and more recently from Somalia. On the other hand there were successes (in mentioning some of those we refer to Wiles's Groups of states (above, p. 117)). Whilst some of the 'Old Communist Third World' are by now independent of the USSR (China, North Korea) others

(Mongolia, Cuba, and Vietnam) have been 'promoted' to Group One with the 'irreversibility of their position' (cf. Wiles, 1982, 20) marked by full membership in the CMEA. Another bloc of states fall into Group Three, comprising the 'New Communist Third World' (Angola, Mozambique, the PDR of Yemen, Ethiopia, and Soviet-occupied Afghanistan). In that category also belong Laos and Cambodia as satellites of Vietnam and the PRC respectively, and till 1983 Grenada ('Cuba's Laos'). Wiles lists in Group Four Madagascar, Benin, Congo-Brazzaville, Guyana, and Somalia as 'doubtful' cases whose final allegiance to the USSR, to Marxism – Leninism (or to both) is still to be determined. Other instances of success in the formation of Marxist regimes include that of Bengal which plays a key role in the Indian Congress government coalition. There are also a number of insurgent groups throughout the Third World supported either by Cuba, the Soviet Union, the PRC, or Vietnam, and making a steady contribution to the continuing 'export of revolution' elsewhere.

In addition to Marxist advances in individual countries there are not to be overlooked the demands made by the volatile collective of the Third World acting in concert. The non-aligned movement, of which one of the founding fathers was a Yugoslav Marxist, has exercised an enormous popular appeal on the newly-liberated countries and soon revised the tenor of its agenda from questions of decolonization to focus on the economic concerns of the Third World as a whole. Essentially, from the platform of the non-aligned movement through the medium of the Third World's core *Group of 77*, collective demands have been made for the implementation of such programmes as that of NIEO and UNCLOS. Third World 'advances' are thus made on the basis of individual states whose regimes claim to be able to secure a more equitable domestic order (including those regimes declaring themselves to be Marxist – Leninist) as well as the collective calls using the forum of the United Nations and the easy majority in the General Assembly for formulating and giving vent to their various grievances.

Underestimation (or overestimation) of the affinity between the Third World and the USSR can be a temptation for commentators. There are certain easily discernible limits beyond which the USSR will not support the Third World's claims, and Soviet sources make the limits clear. First of all the USSR totally rejects the all-embracing conceptualization of North-South (acceptance of the idea would clearly have her fall into the [culpable] North). Any such admission of the accuracy of the concept would also negate the Soviet's own portrayal of the main world contradiction, seen as a conflict between capitalist and socialist socio-economic systems. Essentially, the USSR claims that neither the Soviets nor their Tsarist predecessors ever ruled colonial empires in the Third World and therefore need take no responsibility for their plight—a line of reasoning developed by Lenin in his theory of imperialism. As it turns out, this denial of any responsibility is also from a purely practical point of view particularly auspicious. For the USSR, as Western observers are at pains to point out, does not in any case have enough to offer of economic aid to the Third World, let alone participate in an automatic transfer of wealth from the countries of the North to those of the impoverished South. It is quite obviously true that many of the Soviet economic problems do in fact coincide with those of the Third World countries. Both are in urgent need of technology (of whatever degree of sophistication), and both have what seems to be an insatiable hunger for Western credits. On the other hand, neither requires markets or materials—this last characteristic being the weakness of the West! There are of course good reasons for such shortcomings on the Soviet side. Her superpower status has clearly been achieved at the immense cost of diverting into military spending between 15 per cent and 20 per cent of her GNP, a massive sum when set against the relatively small 5 per cent deployed to the same end by the United States. The USSR simply cannot compete with the West in meeting the demands of the Third World: the economic co-operation (on the basis of the 'division of labour') by which she seeks to tempt into her orbit the Third World countries is not by any means her strongest suit, and in fact the strength of her appeal lies in other directions. She is, after all, committed (since the Khrushchev era) to the global rather than to a mere continental strategy and is therefore badly in need of (global) bases. In the circumstances it seems understandable that the methods to be used in order to acquire such bases are not economic but mainly political, military, and ideological—aiding where possible sympathetic Marxist – Leninist regimes to come to power. The fact that these regimes thenceforth have Soviet encouragement for the maintenance of close economic co-operation with the West (sometimes seen in the West as having something to do with a Soviet readiness to surrender the ideological commitment) is designed for the purpose that it actually achieves, namely the incorporation of some Third World states into her orbit with Western support, at Western expense. In the course of debates such as those following NIEO it comes, therefore, as no surprise that the USSR on many occasions, having set the debate going, has preferred thereafter to act with restraint on substantive issues.

Such debates offer the opportunity also of driving a wedge between the ex-colonies and the ex-metropolises, and of politically (not, as we have remarked, economically) separating them. Therefore as much as the USSR rejects the idea of her own inclusion in 'the North', with similar vehemence she challenges the Western notion that there is an interdependence between the (undivided) North and South. The suggestion of the possibility of a friendly resolution of North – South problems meets with a similarly resolute denial, in accordance with which the interpretation of NIEO as a set of cosmetic adjustments (implied by the Western interdependence thesis), or the argument that perceives an inherent relationship between the North and South, she refers to as blatant neo-colonialism, drawing attention to the fact that she alone is the Third World countries' 'sole (natural and most reliable) ally'.[1] Soviet writers link that new version of interdependence to the old version of 'building bridges', not this time between East and West but between North and South. This she regards as counter-revolutionary—it also relegates the USSR and her entourage into the unimportant, shabby backyard of the North, and places her as a bystander in any real resolution of the North – South problem.

The Soviet attitude to the Third World is of course complicated by China which, particularly at the height of the Sino-Soviet hostility, busied itself (tirelessly) with 'unmasking'

---

[1] G. Bondarevsky, V. Sofinsky, 'The Non-Aligned Movements and International Relations', *International Affairs*, Aug. 1976, p. 50.

Soviet advances towards the Third World as 'social-imperialist', exposing in the process such euphemisms as 'international division of labour' as thin disguises for Soviet social-imperialist ambitions in the direction of world hegemony. The Soviets in turn wasted no time in reciprocating by deriding each and every move the PRC ever made. As Kapchenko, for example, pointed out, 'since China's admission to the United Nations the Chinese representatives have not come up with a single sensible or constructive proposal'.[2]

The assessments vary but in the circumstances the USSR has not done badly from the furore caused by the North – South debate so far. After all, NIEO's origins are with radical liberal or Marxist interpretations and are not owing to any Soviet inspiration or initiative. It will be recalled that the idea sprang from the non-aligned movement and only more recently became a subject of direct Soviet attention. In any case it is only recently that a North – South division, which until a few decades ago was a relatively minor contradiction in one of Stalin's two 'camps', grew to its present magnitude. Anti-imperialist, radical liberal, and Marxist feelings all converge on the issue of North – South despite the differences that will in the long run separate them. In other words to resort to the highly emotive terms of historical materialism in order to establish the causal connection between the world's poverty and the colonial masters might be seen as a form of conceptual overkill. The radical liberal argument alone can lead to the call for distributive justice—as also it may well make reference, and an appeal to justice in international society. But the sweep of Marxist notions and parlance carries its own excitement and appeal by way of which there emerges the 'plan' or grand design for development in sequence—in this case from complaints of 'exploitation' to revolution, to restructuring of the whole global economic system, to 'adjustments' also to the political superstructure of the world. But perhaps the point to be emphasized is that the radical liberals and Marxists are fellow travellers for a considerable distance, of which only a short way has so far been travelled. There is thus an easy ideological understanding between most of the Third World countries who only need to feel deprived and anti-imperialist—or simply anti-

<hr/>

[2] N. Kapchenko, 'The Thirty-second Session of the United Nations General Assembly', *International Affairs*, Dec. 1977, p. 94.

Western—to find themselves casting their vote along with the world's Marxist states.

There is another side to the underestimation of Soviet and Chinese participation in the Third World's plight: that is the *over*estimation of one aspect of (particularly) the Soviet involvement there. There is in this regard the assumption that countries such as Vietnam and Cuba are directly comparable to the Soviet East European satellites in their foreign policy subordination and obedience to Soviet policy directives. The term 'war by proxy' has been used to describe the deployment of their Third World satrapies to wage wars on behalf of their respective Soviet and Chinese masters. The use of the East German troops and East European weaponry has seemed to confirm the connection. However, unlike the situation in East Europe, the characteristic feature of those countries of the New Communist Third World, Cuba and Vietnam in particular, is that their proclamation of Marxism – Leninism (albeit subscribed by small incumbent élites) has been both voluntary and genuine. As Wiles points out, these countries may or may not be satellites, but (except in the case of Afghanistan) the élites do not feel that way (Wiles, 1982, 14–15). Their appearance as mere satellites confuses the fact that they decided of their own volition to become such. In the case of Cuba and Vietnam it required no great insight to perceive that their 'national interests' would be furthered by orbiting around a great body; or, as in the case of Yugoslavia, around another 'body' (non-alignment) to protect her independence. The *voluntary* conversion of Cuba to Marxism – Leninism may with good reason be attributed to her proximity to the United States and an unwillingness to submit to that country's Gleichschaltung policies in her Latin American sphere of influence. The selection of a 'protector' at the safe distance of half a world away is equally understandable and the enthusiastic adoption of Marxism – Leninism *after* Castro's coming to power did no damage to (indeed served to preserve) the Cuban revolutionary identity as well as her autonomy. The Marxist – Leninist success story of Vietnam's admission to the CMEA in 1978 (regarded in Marxist state circles as the 'final vows') is that of the Comintern-inspired adoption of Marxism in Indochina seen right from the beginning as the most suitable method for attaining independence and the realization of

Vietnamese nationalist aspirations. On this ground alone the argument therefore can be sustained that the seed of Marxism does not have to be imported into the Third World by the Red Army, as it was into the countries of Eastern Europe, but may be sown directly by indigenous nationalist forces. Whether the USSR or China assists in the germination process the resulting growth is self-sustaining and is capable of developing its own indigenous mutation. The question then arises of the position of the other states in the 'Communist Third World'. Specifically, have they developed their own 'three worlds theories' or do they consider themselves inhabitants of a world adequately described in the Soviet theory?

The two countries which so far have never destalinized still follow Stalin's precepts in their development processes. Beyond the guidelines of development Albania found in Marxism also a refuge from possible incorporation into the Yugoslav federation. Describing herself as the only Marxist – Leninist state in the world today, Albania, like North Korea, practises diplomatic isolationalism and economic autarchy as far as possible in an attempt to preserve doctrinal purity. The North Koreans, similarly concerned, coined a phrase that gained popularity in Third World circles: *Chu ch'e* ('national identity') that describes in economic terms near-autarchy, and is combined simultaneously with 'psychological decolonisation' (Lee in Wiles, 1982, 308) with overtones of a philosophical nature. 'The *Chu ch'e* idea is based on the philosophical theory that man is the master of everything . . . [it provides] a powerful weapon to grasp the world intellectually and transform it.'[3]

Cuba

From the point of view of creating new variants of Marxist theories and practice of international relations, the two oldest (apart from the PRC and Mongolia) in the group referred to as Marxist (or Communist) Third World have been Vietnam and Cuba. Cuba and Vietnam in their domestic and international experiences have in fact been not infrequently compared (cf.

[3] Kim, Yoon-Soo, 'North Korea's Relationship to the USSR: A Political and Economic Problem', in *Bulletin of the Institute of the Study of the USSR*, Munich, June 1971, quoted in Wiles, op. cit. 308.

Schnytzer in Wiles, 1982, 351). Both are separated by 'safe' geographical distance from the USSR, both are poor. Both fought their own revolutions and only after these were won chose a friendly tie with the USSR. Both countries are threatened by hostile great-power neighbours and because in both cases these powers happen to be arch-enemies of the USSR the strategic value of Vietnam and Cuba to the USSR is as a consequence greatly enhanced. Both have made similar foreign policy decisions within the context of demonstrably independent foreign policies and—what is also strongly forbidden to orbiting East European communist countries—have allowed large numbers of their populations to emigrate. Both countries have sent their troops abroad in efforts to advance other countries' 'revolution'—and although Soviet interest in such activities has lent these excursions an air of 'wars by proxy'—have done so on their own initiative rather than as Soviet puppets. Indeed Cuba engaged in the export of revolution even before entering into her friendship with the USSR. Vietnam, no doubt following the Cuban example (of 1972) and thus not as apprehensive as she might otherwise have been of the irreversibility of such a move, joined in 1978 the CMEA. Thus with her membership also of the IMF and the World Bank Vietnam became the only country to be fully signed up in both economic systems.

Both countries have also been compared in different ways to Yugoslavia. Ho has been described as the Vietnamese or Asian Tito who kept up an acrobatic balancing act between an even larger number of powers than Tito's act handled. Cuba and Vietnam are active also in the non-alignment movement, and Cuba (since the seventies) has gone as far as vying with Yugoslavia for leadership of the movement. Their very different reasons for joining non-alignment reflect the wide-ranging interpretation of which the philosophy of the movement is capable. Yugoslavia sought refuge in non-alignment against possible Soviet retaliation, and therefore maintains that the characteristic of the non-aligned movement is not necessarily keeping equidistant from all of the great powers but seeing rather the Third World to be 'under threat' from all of them. Just as the Yugoslavs sought in non-alignment protection from Soviet retribution for Tito's deviation from Marxist – Leninist orthodoxy, so Cuba sought refuge in non-alignment from the

USA—and to guard against the possibility of her abandonment by the USSR. A position (or positions) that meant that whilst Cuba's Third World activism could never be 'bloc neutral', by creating a constituency in the Third World she could raise the diplomatic cost to both superpowers for policies unfavourable to Cuba (Leogrande, 1982, 169). Yugoslavia then has proved herself capable of the conceptualization of Soviet interference as a threat. Not so Cuba, who in fact since her *rapprochement* with the USSR and full entry into the Soviet bloc echoes the Soviet saying that socialist countries are the sole 'natural ally' of the movement. That position, argues Cuba, will not change so long as the Third World countries need foreign aid and until their South – South co-operation develops to the point of freeing them from any foreign aid ties. Thus political differences, always present in the non-aligned movement, came into the open as Cubans along with other radical new states tried to drag the whole non-aligned movement closer to the USSR. An operation that met with enthusiastic Soviet support and whose achievement would have fulfilled an undisguised Soviet ambition. So far at least, however, these moves have run into opposition which has been fuelled by the Cuban involvement in 1978 in Ethiopia and by the Soviet invasion of a non-aligned country (Afghanistan) in 1979. Cuba will certainly persist in her radicalization attempts. Her criticism of the USSR in the sixties centred on the idea of peaceful coexistence. And again, Cuban criticism of the Soviet interpretation of proletarian internationalism has been that the interpretation is far too liberal and non-militant.

The Vietnamese and Cuban roads to Marxism – Leninism are of course strikingly different. Vietnamese Marxism derives from the early years of the Comintern and the writings of Ho (then Quoc) on Marxism date from the twenties. In the case of Cuba (as in the case of countries across the whole Latin American continent) the road to Marxism was a good deal more complicated. The early Latin American (Peruvian) Marxists Jose Carlos Mariategui and Victor Raul Haya de la Torre came to the conclusion in that era (as did Ho Chi Minh and Li ta Chao at roughly the same time) that Marxism does not apply to Latin America. Haya de la Torre argued that whilst imperialism could be considered the last stage of capitalism in Europe, it was in fact only the first stage of capitalism in Latin America, and only later, with the development of capitalism, would the proletariat have developed sufficiently to enable it to carry out its revolutionary task (Sigmund, 1980, 21 ff.). Much later, in the works of Che Guevara and Regis Debray on guerrilla warfare and on theories more appropriate to Latin American conditions, the conclusion was reached that in the absence of the historical revolutionary vanguard, rather than await the formation of a Party to lead them (formed in Cuba only in 1965 with a first congress in 1975), the guerilla army, conceived of as constituting the revolutionary agency, should take the initiative into its own hands. The most significant Latin American theoretical contribution to Marxist thinking on international relations however was not Cuban: the *dependencia* theories (Chapter 10) developed in the sixties by the (not necessarily Marxist, despite similarities in the terminology) Latin American Left. Notwithstanding protestations of non-Marxist roots (cf. Osvaldo Sunkel), a whole tradition of Marxist theories right across the globe owes its *modern* beginnings and subsequent rediscovery of Marxism to this Latin American (*dependencia*) school.

The main Cuban innovation is not to be found in the area of Marxist theory but in the conduct of her foreign policy. With little or no thought to the theoretical foundations of her policies, the most significant of these continues to be in her practice of exporting revolution, in defiance and in breach of the principles on which the states-system is based. But at least in the early sixties such exports could claim to be made with some justification—as a demonstrably defensive measure on Cuba's part. Isolated economically and diplomatically by the United States and with the continuation of her revolution in danger of being interrupted from that quarter at any moment, Cuba encouraged wide-ranging terrorist and guerilla activities right across Latin America. These first stages were dismal failures and the practice was discontinued to allow a revaluation of her policies to take place, to afford also a breathing space in which to develop her economy and soon also, to enter into a new and closer relation with the USSR in the seventies. The export of revolution then resumed and, combined with Cuba's increasing prestige in the non-aligned movement, led to the relationship with the USSR becoming increasingly intimate. On her own initiative Cuba dispatched 36,000 troops to Angola in 1975/6 and, having assisted the revolutionaries to victory, found herself eligible, with her newly-won prestige, for the non-alignment leadership. Her involvement alongside the USSR in Ethiopia in 1978 however brought a reversal and at least temporarily weakened Cuba's chances of bringing the non-aligned (movement) closer to the socialist bloc. Cuba, because of her position, and in the circumstances, has little choice but to preserve her revolutionary identity by continuing the practice of her 'war by proxy' and by 'exporting' revolution to various parts of the Third World. Methods already tested in these areas were used with considerable success when in the eighties the Cuban leadership again turned its attention to Latin America as the prime target area. There in the Caribbean and in Central America, thanks to the Cuban involvement, a substantial American (US) commitment has been made, tying down significant quantities of men and *matériel*. A Latin American potential has been tapped, and already (no small part of the Cuban success) is the triggering of a psychological fear in her giant neighbour of 'another Vietnam'.

Vietnam

When in 1975 South and North Vietnam unified and in 1978 consummated the union with membership in the CMEA, it was indisputably a coup for the Soviet socialist bloc. Vietnam, with a population of over 60,000,000, is the third largest country in the world to call herself Marxist. Moreover, despite her poverty the country maintains the third largest standing army in Asia and harbours an old desire to unify the whole of Indochina. Also, despite her poverty, she is already a new power centre. Another state prepared to wage proxy wars, she simultaneously advances her own as well as what are obviously Soviet ambitions in her region. The incredible success of the Vietnamese revolution, fought largely by her own methods against all odds (close ties with the USSR being only recent), has given rise to exhaustive enquiry as to the methods used to achieve such success. Less work has gone into discovering the role of 'Vietnamese Marxism' in that success and the relevance of 'Vietnamese Marxism' to other Third World countries. For the unification of Vietnam in 1975 represented another major coup for Marxism on the long road that started with the Indochinese Communist Party formed in 1930 in the era of French colonialism, that survived the years (1940–5) of anti-Japanese resistance, and that played a part in the 'heroic war of independence' (1946–54) before its consolidation period (1954–9). There followed the years of struggle against the United States in the war in South Vietnam, Laos, and Cambodia, culminating in the Paris Agreements of 1973, and the unification.

Three elements are to be recognized as the ingredients of Vietnamese Marxism: the Leninist, the Maoist, and an indigenous Vietnamese component. The idea of a revolutionary party based on the leading role of the proletariat, the class alliances, and the central importance of violent struggle is obviously Leninist. From Maoism there comes the concept of the protracted war, a rural strategy, a permanent people's army, and the idea of the united front. The Vietnamese contribution (as the Vietnamese themselves admit) is the unique capacity for flexibility and adaptability to mould these features to the different setting of their own national circumstances. Duiker sees the uniqueness of the Vietnamese component as lying in the co-ordination of political, military, and diplomatic initiatives so as to seek out and magnify the opponents' weaknesses; there was a quality of uniqueness also in their use of diplomacy to 'orchestrate the international situation'. The unmistakable message for the Third World was to the effect that a victory for a small country, even when opposed by the concentrated power of an advanced Western nation, is possible (Duiker, in Turley, 1980, 68); or as Ho Chi Minh himself put it, 'For the first time in history, an oppressed nation defeated the aggression of a mighty imperialist power, won back national independence . . . ' (Ho Chi Minh, 1973, 213).

These features without doubt derived to a large extent from the personality of the founding father of Vietnamese Marxism. Ho Chi Minh's training included his early encounters with Leninism on the platform of the Comintern in the twenties, and the years of experience, theoretical and practical, both in the USSR and in China. Until his death in 1969 he led his country's anti-colonial struggle for national liberation. Ho Chi Minh himself describes best his first contact with Marxism – Leninism

when during his years in France he read (reprinted in
L'Humanité) Lenin's *Theses on the National and Colonial
Question*:

In those theses, there were political terms that were difficult to
understand. But by reading them again and again finally I was able to
grasp the essential part. What emotion, enthusiasm, enlightenment and
confidence they communicated to me! I wept for joy. Sitting by myself
in my room, I would shout as if I were addressing large crowds: 'Dear
martyr compatriots! This is what we need, this is our path to liberation.'
Since then, I had entire confidence in Lenin, in the Third International
('The Path which led me to Leninism', in Ho Chi Minh, 1973, 251).

The unique figure of 'Uncle Ho' as one of the greatest
revolutionary leaders invited comparison with Tito, with the
Indians Roy and Ghandi, with Mao. Such comparisons only
underscored the uniqueness, Ho having had an unusually broad
cosmopolitan and polyglot background and possessed of a keen
awareness of Western, Marxist, and Confucian values. In the
Confucian tradition (unlike Mao) he cherished peaceful means
and adopted a moralistic approach. He despised individualism.
He was an unwavering nationalist who (again unlike Mao) never
hesitated in his priorities. His nation came before classes. Where
Mao was a philosopher, the pragmatic Ho was too busy to look
beyond the immediate tasks of the national-liberation struggle
and was not concerned with Marxism as a philosophical system.
The operational milieu for Ho was very different from that of
Mao: where in the Chinese conceptualization the 'other part'
of the contradiction consisted of all Western powers, for Ho
Vietnam provided a colonial situation with only one master and,
with the metropolis's (France) strong proletariat a possible
revolutionary ally. As early as 1924 this combination was
emphasized by Ho: 'Capitalism is a leech with two suckers, one
which sucks the metropolitan proletariat and the other that of
the colonies. If we want to kill this monster, we must cut off
both suckers at the same time. If only one is cut off, the other
will continue to suck the blood of the proletariat, the animal
will continue to live, and the cut sucker will grow again' (quoted
in Willmott, 1971, 71–2).

Little of Ho's writing was taken up with attempts to arrive
at a particular world view either at that time or after the
revolution and here he took his rough outline from Lenin's

model. Ho's first essay in serious Marxism was the writing of the first Vietnamese Marxist textbook. As the first of its kind in Indochina it offered a simplified version of Lenin's two-stage concept of revolution: first of all the revolution leading to national independence for all colonies, to be followed, second, by the final destruction of world capitalism. Characteristic of all early Third World Marxism was its omission of any mention of a proletariat, but it contained (with obvious intention) reference to the peasantry (the bulk of the population), who were seen as similarly exploited. The nationalist features of Vietnamese Marxism are too pronounced to be overlooked even in Ho's earlier writings. As he said in this connection in 1951, 'Disregard for the peculiarities of one nation while learning from the experiences of the brother countries is a serious mistake, is dogmatism . . . undue emphasis on the role of national peculiarities [on the other hand] and negation of the universal value of the great basic experiences of the brother countries will lead to grave revisionist mistakes' (quoted in Duiker, 1981, 77).

Gareth Porter has pointed out that 'poverty of insights into Vietnamese policy-making in past literature . . . [resulted] from the failure to see Vietnam's response to changes in world politics' (in Turley, 1980, 227) and in fact the theory that comes closest to a Vietnamese theory of international relations is that of the 'focal point' in the global political struggle. Within the identical image of the world shared with the Comintern and the USSR the nationalism of Vietnam introduced a discordant element: the location of the 'focal point', that is to say the question of revolutionary priority. Whilst in the Comintern years the 'focal point' had been the USSR's socialism in one country and the Vietnamese commitment to the 'duty of revolution' (which consisted essentially of defending Soviet actions), the change took place at the earliest possible moment at which Vietnam was in a position to assert her independent nationalist statehood and acquire for the first time a 'national interest'. In the first years of independence after 1945, at a time when the USSR had reached a stage of global power, the Vietnamese were in fact anticipating the objections of the Chinese by arguing that the revolution would not await Soviet readiness—i.e. not as the Soviets would have wished, to await the achievement of parity with the United States. As Porter shows, as soon as the Sino-Soviet split occurred, the Vietnamese drew closer to the USSR and offered stern opposition to the Chinese proposal either to fragment the existing socialist bloc or set up an alternative. When an independent Vietnam was eventually established, and desperately seeking recognition by as many of the great powers as possible, the USSR was preoccupied with global considerations and her belated recognition came only after that had been extended by the PRC (1950). Although it had been under consideration for some time, serious discussion about the identification of the 'focal point' followed Vietnam's momentous victory, with the Vietnamese arguing that the point at which the struggle between the two camps had been joined was not the USSR but Vietnam—the implication being that the socialist bloc should have been focusing on Indochina and not on Europe. The ensuing years constituted the peak of Ho Chi Minh's diplomatic manoeuvres when he contrived to synchronize the clearly conflicting 'national interests' of the USSR and Vietnam. His pragmatic approach allowed him to shift from one socialist side to the other in accordance with what he perceived to be the Vietnamese interest. That interest for long put the country on the side of the Soviet Union, and even in 1956, when the Soviets announced the idea of peaceful coexistence, the Vietnamese were prepared to adjust to the principle—although (as for Cuba) the notion was essentially hostile to their interests. In the sixties a more independent Vietnamese line was again adopted with a tendency for the country to move closer to the Chinese. However, the American onslaught on Vietnam in 1965 again brought the theory of the 'focal point' to the forefront and the 'world revolution' became again redefined as the 'Vietnamese revolution'.

As a result of the notion of a 'focal point' there was always a second meaning to Vietnamese statements about world revolution made in the forum of the UN to which she was admitted in 1977. Although Schnytzer argues that the likely direction of Vietnamese allegiance in the continuing Sino-Soviet split is not easily deduced from the history of Ho's struggle for power in Vietnam (Schnytzer, in Wiles, 1982). Soviet support, forthcoming for Vietnam's crash industrialization programme, caused Vietnam to relocate the focal point simultaneously in both the USSR and Vietnam. Hence she has agreed to support until further notice Soviet proletarian internationalism and also to play the part of proxy in the wars with neighbouring Laos where her drive towards union corresponds fully once again with Soviet interests in the region.

In his Last Testament Ho Chi Minh urged a Vietnamese contribution towards unity among the fraternal parties on the basis of Marxism – Leninism and proletarian internationalism in a way that 'conforms both to reason and sentiment'. A few months before his death in 1969 he expressed confidence that the 'fraternal parties and countries will have to unite again' and also predicted the defeat of US aggression ('Testament' in Ho Chi Minh, 1973, 361). He was right on the second count but not on the first. Nevertheless he appeared to have captured the purpose to which Marxism, as redefined by Lenin, was put in Vietnam and elsewhere in the Third World, by oppressed and underprivileged *nations*:

There is a legend in our country as well as in China, about the magic 'Brocade Bag'. When facing great difficulties, one opens it and finds a way out. For us Vietnamese revolutionaries and people, Leninism is not only a miraculous 'Brocade Bag', a compass, but also a radiant sun illuminating our path to final victory, to socialism and communism ('The Path which led me to Leninism', April 1960, in Ho, 1973, 252).

8 Marxism, International Law, and International Organizations

Marxists add their own quota of problems to the many theoretical problems attached to an enquiry into international law. Encountered by all students of the subject are such questions as whether it is to be regarded as 'law' at all—and if so in what relationship does international law stand to municipal law? What is the nature of international law in a deeply fissured, widely fragmented world lacking in shared values? Because special Marxist problems (created for Marxists by Marxism) are from the same roots as those of the Marxist doctrine of international relations generally, international law is of particular interest in our present context.

In the traditional Marxist view, law, including international law, together with state(s), is part of the social superstructure which is determined by the economic substructure—a determinant that resolves itself essentially into one of class relations. This has two very important consequences. First, theories of international law and of international relations are always, in Marxism, closely connected. This is in contrast to their non-Marxist counterparts which may remain theoretically disconnected, or indeed stand in contradiction (cf. Hoffman, 1963). In fact, within the Marxist approaches the doctrine of international law can be seen as the quintessence of the rather more general doctrine of international relations and as such tends to magnify problems which theories of international relations might otherwise manage to ignore or set aside. The second consequence is that non-communist Marxists in the West and in the Third World, whilst ready to express (however peripheral) an interest in international relations (Chapter 10), are less than willing to give consideration to international law as one of their Marxist 'problematiques'. The problem of the nature of international law would not after all respond to a simple 'repudiation' as in the denial of the orthodox superstructure – substructure relationship that features largely in Western Marxist and neo-Marxist writing. As the pressures brought to bear by the Third World in the United Nations for the creation of a 'new' international law increase, we can expect the focusing of more explicit Marxist attention on that subject. The Soviet, East European, and Chinese writing on the 'new' international law might help to anticipate the thrust of arguments still to come.

It is significant that whilst theories of international *relations* formulated in the USSR, in the PRC, and in East Europe were not the subject of much serious enquiry on the part of their Western counterparts, the Western community of international jurists, numbering in their ranks such distinguished names as Hans Kelsen, R. Stoessinger, John Hazard, K. Grzybowski, Ivo Lapenna, to name a few, not only followed attentively the convolutions of the (Soviet) Marxist doctrines of international law, but also have given them very close consideration. A relatively minor interest to date in the case of the Chinese legal doctrine is understandable, having for long had its derivation in the Soviet, to which it bears a close resemblance. The 1950s and 1960s alone saw a Chinese output on the subject of more than 500 publications, but the effect of the ravages of the Cultural Revolution on the Chinese doctrine, and on international law as an autonomous subject, have yet to be fully overcome. Moreover, whilst the (enormous) official Soviet output on international law leaves little doubt as to official Soviet views on the subject, the Chinese position still awaits its final elaboration. The Chinese, apparently aware of their doctrinal weakness and the ambivalence, have tended to avoid taking positions in international forums on purely legal questions, in itself a factor contributing to the confusion regarding their position.

Unlike Western studies of International Relations whose many approaches simply seek to diminish or to exclude the official statement of Soviet and Chinese positions, Western legal philosophers could not by definition indulge such cavalier attitudes and were obliged to question the relevance to the international community of communist statements. Specifically, this was done with a view to finding answers to the question of the extent to which the peculiarities of the

Marxist doctrines, and particularly the practice of international law in its Soviet, Chinese, and Third World (advocate of the 'new' international law) domains is to be regarded as one of the factors (or pressures) of change on international law. Most Western international jurists seem agreed on the existence of serious pressures for change, not to be confused with their disagreements in regard to their several formulations of methods and contingency plans. The question as Professor Hazard puts it is 'should Americans work for a breaking off of relations with jurists engaged in restructuring international law, or should they remain in the conference rooms to attempt to preserve what they can of the law they revere?' (Hazard, 1979, 13).

In the present chapter we turn first of all to an outline of the various Marxist doctrines of international law, not so much for their historical interest in the context of Soviet and Chinese thinking on international relations and foreign policy but rather as a reservoir of interpretation on which the future of international law and international system must draw. For Western international legal writers agree that Marxists have *not* explained international law in a manner that is even by their own Marxist lights theoretically watertight, and so it is difficult to accept any of the positions as unquestionably Marxist. Second, we attempt to distinguish the main pressures on international law acknowledged by Western international lawyers and will try to establish which of these can be seen to be (Soviet) Marxist inspired. We then try to discover which changes (if any) in international law and international organizations effected in this century can be attributed to the Soviet Union.

The Soviet and Chinese doctrines of international law

For a Marxist legal philosopher who believes that the states-system is based on fragmented socio-economic foundations to attempt to explain the 'class' nature of *one* universally valid system of international law the task is difficult. For whilst the nature of municipal law as a class instrument can in theory be dealt with, the difficulty of resolving the problem of whose base *international law reflects* in the socio-economically fragmented world is infinitely greater. Unless one argues, with the Soviets (after much ideological soul searching), that behind the appearances there is a plurality of systems, or at least of principles of international law also, the difficulty of explaining one system of international law in class terms is virtually insurmountable. This is not to say of course that answers may not be attempted. If the proponents of the world-system approach were to tackle the problem, their likely conclusion would involve the simple eclipsing of the problem. In the holistically-conceived (*one*) world-economy, the *one* international legal system would of necessity be of a capitalist nature, and despite the 'anarchic' political fragmentation of the states-system, the legal system in world-system thinking would resemble, rather, municipal law. In the world-system approach the question of several systems of international law would not of course arise, nor would the possibility of socialist international law. Either notion would represent a conceptual absurdity. In approaches based on the view of the world as socio-economically fragmented the answer would approximate the position of such approaches to the question of state. If international law were to be construed analogously with the concept of the 'relative autonomy of state', with its 'autonomy' and its co-operative and organizing role stressed, then still the question of its nature in a world of heterogeneous social formations would remain unanswered. Then there are those theorists who see the world as comprised of heterogeneous social formations but who view the state *and* international law as class *instruments*. For these the range of possible answers is exhausted by the logical combinations of one, two, or three systems of international law (despite single-system appearances) to correspond to two or more types of socio-economic social formations.

In the Soviet Union in particular the enquiry was by no means of a scholastic nature; for a 'wrong' answer might well conjure up a heretical non-socialist nature for the Soviet state, for its foreign policy, and for the aspirations of the leadership. And so, predictably, Soviet legal philosophers were soon dissuaded from attempts to find answers, and, instead, justification was sought for the Soviet Union's uninhibited use of international legal instruments in pursuance of her foreign policy. Small wonder then that the debate was punctuated by 'samokritiky', dismissals, demotions—and executions, of the more forthright authors. It is a sad irony that (just as Soviet family law once recognized a collective paternity) the formula eventually worked out and that remains current doctrine has a 'collective father'. In the officially-adopted legal doctrine now finally compiled, and brought together largely in the work of G. I. Tunkin, it turns out to be a highly eclectic composite of the work of many of Tunkin's less fortunate predecessors—some of them still unrehabilitated, though highly-esteemed.

The Soviet doctrine of international law in our present context is of interest because for the last time in the Soviet Union of the twenties and up to the Stalinist purges of the mid-thirties Soviet legal philosophers made a contribution to Marxism as a heuristic tool. Then, since the purges and for the whole of the Stalinist era and the interlude of 'destalinization', the Soviet international legal doctrine was an instrument fully in the service of Soviet foreign policy. The statement of the Soviet doctrine of international law tends to corroborate our reading of the Soviet theory of international relations (Chapter 4), and is corroborative also of the correlation of strength of the Marxist doctrine of international relations in Marxist regimes which depends on the overall position (perceived, real, or in aspiration) of that country in the states-system. The corollary is that the degree of concern evinced by a regime in regard to the subversive uses to which international law might be put by hostile states may be correlated with the degree of consolidation or instability of the state in question. The stronger the Marxist state the readier it will be to participate in the system of international law: the weaker the state (whether through its early stage of consolidation, etc.) the less willing will be its participation. In these latter circumstances, in the case of the strong state the higher will be its regard for the instruments that contributed to its ascendancy. In the weak state, hand in hand with the reluctance remarked goes an exaggerated respect for the concept of sovereignty (in the Chinese case to the absurd point of making any intercourse with other states impossible (cf. Scott, 1975, 250)), and certainly the stronger the Soviet Union has become, its earlier inhibitions and distrust have given way to a more felicitous regard for both international law and international organizations—to a point where the dictates of the states-system prevail over Marxist doctrine. Significantly also, the USSR in the early stages showed a marked lack of enthusiasm for functional co-operation (opposition to the inclusion of the Economic and Social Council into the organizational structure of the United Nations is a case in point) and was prevailed upon to reverse her position only in return for a guarantee of her sovereignty through the medium of a (duly granted) Security Council veto. The principle (correlation of strength with attitude to international law) seems to hold good also for the countries of the Third World. As Boutros-Ghali points out with surprising candour, theirs is a situation of a collective of radical states amongst which none has as yet the strength to predominate; or, preoccupied with internal development, has not yet had the will to make the attempt. The tenor of United Nations debate (as for example in the Conferences on the Law of the Sea) frequently attests to the fact that until further notice the Third World is defending its 'collective sovereignty'—something which the Soviet Union in her 'socialism in one country' isolation could not have achieved.

In asserting the general validity of the correlation of the strength of the state and the nature of its international legal doctrine we hasten to emphasize that nihilism in relation to international law clearly implied in orthodox Marxism is a position seldom contemplated either by the Soviet, by the Chinese, or by the radical Third World states. There was never much doubt as to the Soviet acceptance of international law and, when the invitation was forthcoming there was little hesitation on the part of these states to participate also in international organizations. Such nihilism as did make its appearance in Soviet attitudes of the early post-revolutionary years was short-lived in theory and in practice. V. L. Verger's *Pravo i gosudarstvo perekhodnogo vremeni* [Law and State of the transitional period], published in 1924, pronounced the teaching and practice of international law superfluous and suggested that it be removed from the curriculum in expectation of the impending world revolution. In the area of municipal law, also, there were moves to abolish the hierarchy of tsarist courts and generally carry out a simplification of the judicial system. In the foreign policy field (Commissar of Foreign Affairs) Trotsky, for example, gave notice of the impending 'closing of the shop', and as a matter of fact, the Bolshevik government did embark initially on a policy of disengagement from the states-system and from international law and international organizations. It gave notice that it had no intention of fulfilling Tsarist Russia's commitment to the Alliance, inveighed against the Treaty of Versailles and, specifically, against the Covenant of the League of Nations. The protocol of diplomatic ranks and usages established at the Congress of Vienna was not adopted by the Soviet diplomatic service until much later, when it became obvious that the setting aside of diplomatic protocol disadvantaged Soviet emissaries, and indeed practical needs soon asserted themselves. In all areas compromise prevailed: whilst awaiting the coming revolution Lenin accepted the fact that 'we live in the system of states'. In March 1918 the devastating terms of the Treaty of Brest-Litovsk gave the Bolsheviks their first introduction to international diplomacy—and imparted another taste to the revolutionary brew. It was indeed a humiliation for a signatory government, committed to the destruction of the states-system, to have to sit down with the emissaries of his Majesty the German Emperor, His Apostolic Majesty the Emperor of Austria, and the King of Hungary. But, as Professor Ulam has argued, it remains an open question whose humiliation in the long run was the greater and which was the more long-suffering, the Soviet Union or the states-system. Whatever the effects on the states-system of the Soviet 'intrusion', on the Soviet side the adaptation and corruption of Marxist principles was manifested in such developments as the Bolsheviks' first involvement with peace-oriented organizations when in 1928 they signed the Kellogg-Briand pact (general treaty for the renunciation of war as an instrument of national policy). Her entry into the despised League of Nations in 1934 and accession to a large number of international organizations (such as the International Metric and Telegraph Union) confirmed the fall from Marxist grace. On the eve of the establishment of diplomatic relations with the United States in 1934 there came the actual honouring of some of the Tsarist debts (the Litvinov Assignment).

Whilst the nihilism of the early stages soon disappeared there still persisted the expectation of the *withering away of law*. 'Fairly soon' were the operative words distinguishing these early stages from the later years. Later, whilst both the Soviets and the Chinese were still committed to the 'withering away' notion it came to be regarded as so remote an outcome as to have no need of reflection in the doctrine of international law. It makes sense, therefore, that two of the most important authors of the early years, Korovin and Pashukanis, could speak of 'international law of the transitional period', a time when to Pashukanis the commitment to the withering away process was so clearly in prospect that the 'socialist international law' which the USSR now propounds would have seemed completely nonsensical. The watershed between the early and late periods is to be observed with the onset of the intensive industrialization and collectivization programmes carried out by Stalin since the 1930s under the rubric of 'socialism in one country' and 'revolution from above'. The prescriptions of these meant that no longer could such distractions as the 'withering away' of state and law be indulged, and instead that both state and law be portrayed as strong and positive—instruments of socialism. The meaning of this shift in the sphere of international law was the rejection of the use of 'bourgeois' or 'neutral' international law and the gradual building of a case for an international law which if not yet 'socialist' would at least already have undergone qualitative change: a dramatic boost in authority commensurate with the Soviets' increasingly muscular international presence and influence. E. A. Korovin, author of the first Soviet book on international law (Korovin, *Mezhdunarodnoe pravo pere-khodnogo vremeni* [International law in the transitional period], 1924) argued that the mere existence of the USSR brought a change to international law. He attempted to show that the superstructural reflection of the meeting of the bases on which the two systems rest is new because although it is no longer capitalist, neither is it yet socialist. In referring to Soviet innovative practices, in addition to those mentioned above, Korovin cites the refusal to recognize capitalist capitulations and extraterritoriality, the Soviet reclassification of ambassadors, and the advocacy of total and general disarmament to prove that the 'transitional' law is in fact of a hybrid nature. The position he takes quite clearly allowed for the probability of a protracted period of coexistence and the gradual evolution into a 'socialist international law' that would prevail world-wide. The explanation of international law was to be made mainly in terms of the class struggle although a marginal possibility of co-operation was allowable in, for example, the field of trade. However, 'communication on the basis of intellectual unity (solidarity of ideas) between countries with bourgeois and socialist cultures is excluded in principle, and the corresponding body of legal norms becomes without object . . .' (ibid., 2nd edn., 1925, 13, 16). Some years later, Korovin qualified this opinion with a 'pluralistic' theory of international law based on the idea of almost completely separated juridical 'spheres' or 'circles' characterized by just such a 'solidarity of ideas'. There was first of all 'the circle of the mutual relationships of a group of European states' and especially of the Great Powers. There were, second, a number of other 'circles' comprising the body of rules governing the relationships of the European second-rank states. This category embraces also the capitalist states together with their colonies. Then, third, Korovin has as his third circle the limited juridical circle of the international law of the transitional period 'regulating the modalities of the relationships between the socialist state and its bourgeois counterparts' (Korovin, *Mezhdunarodnoe Pravo*, 1928, 52). This last circle was the most important in Korovin's legal imagery. However, his prescriptions were found wanting in terms of a clear class definition and had to be withdrawn. He persevered with his notion of a plurality of systems—refined eventually after his death into two systems of international law (general and socialist) that gained acceptance by the regime.

E. B. Pashukanis's (1891–1937) ideas on the subject gained for a time prominence over the theories of Korovin. Pashukanis's main concern was that in the event of the emphasis placed on international law (as socialist or neutral) proving too strong, or indeed if the case for the establishment of a separate system altogether were to be pressed too convincingly, that the USSR might not be accepted into the international legal community; towards the achievement of that most desirable goal a callow Soviet regime was prepared to overlook the bourgeois nature of that community. In the event, Pashukanis's chief error, however, lay in the admission of the bourgeois nature of international law and the implication that the USSR as participant might also be so designated. Whilst Korovin's relatively minor theoretical misdemeanours were to recede, to allow his being given another chance to redeem himself at the end of twenty years in retreat, the errors of Pashukanis (who disappeared in 1937) were too serious and all that could be done for him was a partial rehabilitation in the sixties.

Pashukanis, using precisely the same arguments as Korovin, had reached diametrically opposite conclusions. Despite the 'transitional period', he argued, international law remained essentially unchanged. He wrote two works on international law, the first of which was one chapter in the *Entsiklopedia gosudarstva i Prava* [Encyclopaedia of State and Law] (1926). The second was published as *Ocherki po mezhdunarodnomu pravu* [Essays on International Law] in 1935. Particularly in that first work can be seen the direct influence of his general doctrine of municipal law on his ideas of international law. In a most original Marxist argument, only recently fully appreciated by Western philosophers and sociologists of law (and rejected by them) Pashukanis applies Marx's writing on political economy and its major categories by analogy to the sphere of law, inferring that Marx actually had a coherent theory of state and law. Thus, in what has ever since been known as the *commodity exchange theory of law* Pashukanis drew a parallel between the logic of the commodity form and the logic of legal form in so far as both are universal equivalents; both (in appearances) equalize the manifestly different (unequal) commodities (the object of the labour that produced them) paralleled in the legal form by the varied citizens of the polity, the subjects of rights and obligations. The implications for the Marxist theory of the transition are obvious. Specifically, instead of an envisaged transition to new legal forms there takes place the *dying out* of legal form altogether. And so the conclusion: that if law has its origins always in commodity exchange and if socialism means the abolition of commodity exchange (its replacement by production for rational use) then it follows that law is always bourgeois, and further, that proletarian or socialist law, whether municipal or international, is a contradiction in terms, an absurd proposition.

Apropos international law Pashukanis argued therefore that

international legal *form* should remain necessarily unchanged, that despite the appearances of the USSR's applying the same norms of international law as the bourgeois states (exchange of diplomats, etc.), this was done *with* the legal form remaining intact. The practical advantages of this position notwithstanding, it was another matter to explain away the position in acceptable Marxist terms—to overlook the Trotskyist implications of Soviet participation in the states-system and its usage of international law.

As we have remarked, it was unfortunate that Pashukanis's arrival at these conclusions was so early since as we have tried to show (Chapter 4) the major feature of the current Soviet doctrine of international relations is that the exterior similarity of forms (and concepts such as state, sovereignty, etc.) does not preclude Soviet foreign policy differing in principle from that of capitalist states. But at the time of his writing such views were untenable, or ill-advised. Pashukanis admitted that international law was a temporary compromise and was becoming *inter-class*, the adaptation to this new function inevitably taking the shape of a series of conflicts and crises (Pashukanis, 1980, 173). But from *inter-class* it is only a short step to *above class*, as Pashukanis himself was aware, and in his *Ocherki* hastened to say that international law when applied between the socialist USSR and capitalist countries was not a compromise but one of the forms in which the struggle between the two systems takes place. He went on to say that international law was not only a means of class war between imperialist states but also a means of class war between two antagonistic worlds. From the fact that both worlds applied the same rules in the blatant absence either of solidarity of ideas or of economic, social, and political unity he deduced that it was not the formalism of legal forms that was important but only the policy that they served. It followed that international law could be used by the Soviet Union as a matter of sheer convenience. And it is these sentiments that pervade Pashukanis's approach to specific questions of international law that enable him to favour such principles as that of *rebus sic stantibus*: the USSR, he argued, must be entitled to abrogate a treaty whenever a change in her interests recommended such action. In other words, Pashukanis totally rejected Korovin's idea of change in international law taking place gradually and, chameleon-like, somehow managing to traverse the spectrum from capitalist to socialist. Instead, international law with the passage of time simply vanishes. Ergo, only rules that suit the USSR should be regarded as binding upon her.

Obviously too, since the obsequies were about to be observed for international law the study of the theoretical aspects of a dying law was of passing interest, receiving temporary respite only in the context of an instrument of Soviet foreign policy. Here, then, in Pashukanis we have the first Soviet advocate of a theory of International Relations, whose argument is to the effect that the only purpose of studying international law is to build theoretical foundations on which to rest the foreign policy of the Soviet Union and to discern which institutions of international law best suit the Soviet purpose.

Pashukanis rejected the definition of international law as 'the totality of norms defining the rights and duties of states in their mutual relations' as devoid of historical and therefore also of class considerations. It was right, agreed Pashukanis, to consider international law 'as a function of some ideal cultural community which mutually connects individual states' so long as we understand that this community 'reflects (conditionally and relatively . . .) the common interests of the commanding and ruling classes of different states with identical class structures' (ibid. 171). Although international law is a product of the struggle between capitalist states Pashukanis was prepared to admit that its origins predated those of the class society. The essential feature of the *ius gentium* was its establishment of universal rules devoid of local peculiarities, which were in any case 'nothing other than a reflection of the general conditions of exchange transactions' (ibid. 176). Even the basic and absolute rights of the state formulated by Grotius were based on private law emanating from commodity exchange. But whilst deriving both municipal and international law from the same roots, Pashukanis was aware of differences between the two. In the absence of a central coercive body in the international arena, the legal basis of the relations between states depends on the balance of forces:

The only real guarantee that the relationships between the bourgeois states (and in the transitional period with states of another class type)

will remain on the basis of equivalent exchange, i.e. on a legal basis
(on the basis of mutual recognition of subjects) is the real balance of
forces. Within the limits set by a given balance of forces separate
questions may be decided by compromise and exchange, i.e. on the basis
of law (ibid. 179).

To the obvious objection to this argument, that international
law consisted largely of rules regulating war, Pashukanis replied
that legal relations did not require a state of peace just as
'exchange did not exclude armed robbery' (ibid. 169). War was
only one source of exchange. And if 'exchanges are concluded,
then forms must also exist for their conclusion'.

The measure of Pashukanis's prophetic talent lies in his
anticipation of the more recent Soviet idea of international law
as a form of inter-class struggle, in his foreshadowing a
(participant determined) typology of international relations, and
in his focusing interest (recently reawakened) in the theoretical
study of International Relations in the USSR. Nevertheless, his
position remained ambivalent on the class nature of international law and, by extension, the class nature of the USSR.
Although the commodity theory of law could be seen to be
consistent with classical Marxism, the needs of the Soviet Union
since its industrialization programme got under way in 1928
required, as we have observed, a doctrine of law answering to
the needs of a strong socialist state—in which there was no room
for an early 'withering away'. Pashukanis's recantation came
too late. His name was linked to Trotsky and Zinoviev and he
was criticized along similar lines, namely for espousing the
argument that the Soviet system was still a capitalist system,
that Soviet legal forms represented the refashioned successors
of bourgeois legal forms, and that the Soviet practice of foreign
policy was subject to bourgeois international law and hence to
the imperialist aspirations of its (bourgeois) practitioners.

Vyshinsky accused Pashukanis additionally of subordinating
law to policy, of a failure to assert the primacy of municipal over
international law and, most particularly, of his failure to
acknowledge the very positive role of the USSR in creating
socialist international law. Once Pashukanis himself was
'withered away', Vyshinsky reigned for long years over the legal
scene as Head of the Institute of Law of the USSR Academy of
Sciences. These were years of crisis and theoretical stagnation

during which the law, rather than being linked to categories of political economy, became simply an instrument of a class, differing from bourgeois law only in its claim to represent the 'true interests' of the people. In this last case it could be argued that such a theoretical construction is no more than a creation of a *Rechtstaat*, for as can be shown, the law is precisely what the Marxist critique of capitalist law insists: an instrument, in this case, of a party dictatorship.

For the entire Stalinist period international law in the Soviet Union was grounded in the Twelve Theses on International Law (*Sovetskoe gosudarstvo*, 1938 (5), 119 ff.), a work ascribed to Vyshinsky and his report to the Second Conference of Soviet legal science held from July 16 to 19, 1938. As it happened Vyshinsky's influence on major systematic codifications of Soviet international law extended into the first post-war years, and Krylov's lectures published in the *Receuil des Cours* (1947 (LXX)) of the Hague Academy, and Kozhevnikov's textbook, *Mezhdunarodnoe Pravo* (1947), whose statement has become legal doctrine serving the needs of the Soviet state are Vyshinsky-inspired. During what we might term the Vyshinsky years the basis for the interpretation of international law resembled Triepel's theory of the primacy of the internal legal order. Vyshinsky totally rejected international law as a historically formulated universal set of principles, taking the view that since international law had evolved in the period of the bourgeois revolution against feudalism it bears the impress of liberal bourgeois thought—essentially the formal equality of states that are independent, sovereign, and national. In the circumstances of capitalist encirclement it was left to the USSR, as her only recourse, to operate under those rules that she explicitly chose to accept whilst rejecting such bourgeois instruments as spheres of influence, capitulations, and secret diplomacy. In the meantime Vyshinsky could salvage something of the Soviet situation by placing emphasis on national self-determination, the equality of states, general disarmament, collective security, and opposition to all forms of aggression. To this position was joined an insistence on the recognition of the Soviet government, on her monopoly of foreign trade, and on the acknowledgement of such other newly-established principles deemed appropriate to a socialist state. As these became accepted by the capitalist states they were to become incorporated as part of international law. The leitmotif of the period, in brief, was Soviet insistence on capitalist recognition of her espousal of different principles of international relations: that in the process of such affirmation international law would be changed goes without saying. Following the signing of the Molotov-Ribbentrop Pact the emphasis was shifted from 'different principles' to 'different goals' of the Soviet state as an important yardstick. The USSR at the time still opposed the codification of international law since it was thought in the early stages that such a newly-fledged Soviet interest would have negligible influence on deliberations and that the bourgeois devised law would be correspondingly advantaged to figure prominently in the codification.

The processes of destalinization after 1956 coupled with the 'de-Vyshinskyization' of international law was not nearly as dramatic as had been the reverse processes of the thirties. The main agencies of change in this later period are neither paramount chiefs nor individual legal luminaries but rather power shifts taking place in the international field itself with the USSR emerging strengthened and fully participating in institutions of the states-system—as Charter member in the case of the United Nations.

It is worth mentioning that in the formulations leading to the new Soviet doctrine of separate socialist international law Stalin himself took a hand with his *Marxism and Linguistics* (1951) wherein the suggestion was made of the powerful if not independent effects of parts of the superstructure on the substructure. The theoretical justification of the 'socialist principles' from which a socialist international law was later to be forged became necessary as a result of the outbreak of the Cold War and the urgent need to integrate East Europe. With several socialist states in existence, however, Kozhevnikov, unlike Korovin in the twenties, could now argue that socialist international law had its own distinct basis. The world was divided into two systems of states. International law was also in a state of transition. Upon that law an emergent socialist international law would encroach increasingly on its way to achieving a total substitution. Boosted by Kozhevnikov and Stalin, Korovin resurfaced in articles published in 1946 and 1951 in which his ideas of the twenties concerning the existence of three systems of international law (capitalist, socialist, and that which regulated the relationship between the systems) were aired. Both Korovin and Kozhevnikov were demoted for overstepping the mark, but soon after Stalin's death Korovin again resumed his thesis, arguing now that the entire debate about whose basis international law reflected was misconceived, a misdirection that led at best to legal nihilism and at worst to a fundamental revision of Marxism. The solution which he now saw rested on an acceptance of the proposition that rules of international law were a part both of the socialist superstructure and of that of its bourgeois counterpart, which, despite some similarities, remained apart because similar legal rules were deployed to serve radically different ends.

But the final acceptance of a socialist international law for the socialist community had to await political events and, in particular, the Soviet invasion of Hungary. In the meantime, following the declaration of the principle of 'peaceful coexistence of states of different socio-economic systems' by the 20th CPSU Congress that put the seal on developments long under way the international jurists were hard pressed to rename the general international law the 'law of peaceful coexistence'. The spirit of peaceful coexistence constituted a plausible enough reason for once again begging the question of the nature of international law in the (officially endorsed) *consensus theory* of international law. Thus Kozhevnikov for example in an early formulation could argue that:

Although international law, like any other branch of law, has a class character and pertains to superstructure, it cannot express the will of the ruling class of any particular state. It is an expression of the agreed will of a number of states in the form of an international agreement or custom which has grown up over a period. The purpose of present-day international law is to promote peaceful co-existence and co-operation between all states regardless of their social systems (Kozhevnikov, *International Law*, 1961, 57).

So too, Tunkin in his Hague Lectures in 1958 argued that whilst socialist and capitalist systems differed as to the identity of the social values that law is to protect, agreement—and therefore a common legal system—is possible (*Co-existence and International Law*, RCDAI, 59). He defined international law as: 'the totality of norms, which were developed on the basis of agreement between the states, which govern their relations in the process of struggle and co-operation between them, expressing the will of the ruling classes, and are reinforced, in case of necessity, by the pressure applied either collectively or by individual states'. And thus, until modification of the consensus theory (on which is based the 'general international law of peaceful co-existence'), by the addition of a separate system of socialist international law applicable to the growing socialist commonwealth of states, the Soviet conception of international law was, for a Marxist-Leninist theory, remarkably Grotian in nature. It was really only the notion of a separate system of socialist international law that restored a semblance of revolutionary radicalism, the reason for its delayed appearance due to the fact that it represented a serious and unprecedented legal departure. In the post-Stalinist climate a much more spirited debate was possible and was conducted even in the heavily politicized precincts of international law. It would be well outside our present scope to follow the turns of these debates but it is of interest to note that in their Soviet version, in so far as the stress on the relative autonomy of state (and law) was concerned, they came curiously close to some of the Western Marxist debates on the nature of the state. As Grzybowski points out, the Soviet Union redefined its own state as a 'state of all the people', a new look at state in fact that was to be reflected also in their approach to the international law of capitalist states. It was now argued that since the class interests of monopolistic capital were tied to war and aggression, and since there existed circumstances where wars were no longer permitted under international law even in capitalist states, the international law of these states had ceased to be subject to the will solely of the ruling class. It was now obliged to correspond to the will of peoples struggling towards peaceful coexistence (Grzybowski, 1970, 11).

The consensus theory of one international legal system was finally modified so as to become a sort of regional systems theory of international law from which it was but a short step to the notion of a separate (regional) system of socialist international law. Tunkin adjusted his general formulations accordingly, and although a 'socialist system of international law' was only just 'emerging' in 1959, in articles published in 1962 and 1970 there is no longer any doubt but that socialist law is 'already here'. As far as the official position is concerned there would appear to be a recognition of the existence of two systems of international law, the socialist law based on principles of (modified) proletarian internationalism, and the general international law of peaceful co-existence from which, since the relationship between the two is based on *lex specialis derogat legis generalis*, the socialist law may borrow.

As we have remarked, most Soviet legal philosophers were 'prematurely' correct in the enunciation of doctrines that at the time were unacceptable. First, the bringing into existence of a group of socialist states after World War II was a prerequisite for the application of a 'socialist international law' to have jurisdiction over a meaningful area. In the second place the Soviet Union had to achieve superpower status before she could declare that the 'general international law of peaceful co-existence' is bereft of those principles that were the legacy of earlier centuries. Such status would also enable her to maintain a higher profile and to play a more enthusiastic role in international organizations and in the formulation/implement-ation of international law. For the concept 'general international law of peaceful coexistence' conveys just that—that the class struggle will be promoted also through the medium of international law: a concept, too (peaceful coexistence), upon which the United Nations is supposed to have been founded. The fact that the establishment of a 'socialist international law' was so gradual did no damage to the Soviet strategy of attempting to legitimize the transformation of these countries into a system of satrapies, excluding them in the drawn out process from the reach of general international law.

The official Chinese position on the nature of international law, it is generally conceded, has not as yet been clarified. However, the record of deployment of international law on the part of the PRC, though not as impressive as that of the Soviets, reveals nevertheless the usefulness of international law to the Chinese, and their preparedness to turn it to account. Although in the fifties and sixties Chinese juridical experts in the main simply reiterated the major Soviet themes in regard to determining the nature of international law, some trenchant formulations on the Chinese part do warrant attention. In 1957, for example, Ch'iu Jih-ch'ing anticipated the Soviet position and argued for two systems of international law, one socialist the other general. The general international law was conceived to apply to relations amongst bourgeois countries and between bourgeois and socialist, whilst the socialist law applied to the relations amongst socialist states (quoted in Chiu, 1966, 253).

We know that international law is the same as municipal law in that they all constitute part of the superstructure. The only difference is that international law as a superstructure does not directly relate to production relations, nor does it directly reflect that base. It must produce a connection and reflect the base through international relations . . . This generally recognized international law possesses neither the character of the bourgeoisie nor that of socialism; it is the type of international law possessing a transitional character. Therefore, it may concurrently constitute part of the superstructure of different countries with various social systems and be used by them (ibid.).

Another Chinese writer, Lin Hsiu, also parted company from his Soviet counterparts with the perception of two systems existing side by side, bourgeois and socialist, and the argument that since there are no rules held in common by socialist and bourgeois countries, therefore there can be no rules binding equally upon both. 'How', he asks, 'can socialist and capitalist countries whose foreign policies are fundamentally opposed, share one system of international law?' Any agreement reached between socialist and capitalist countries is a result of a fierce argument and is a compromise reflecting the state of the power balance between them. The situation is one of 'sleeping in the same bed but dreaming different dreams' (ibid. 253). The argument is persuasive, and, as it happens, is reminiscent of the implications of Pashukanis's doctrine and the Soviet theory of International Relations—the fact that the two interpretations of the same document of international law must be radically different. In the same year (1958) Lin Hsiu's position was attacked by Chou Fu-lun who argued on consensus theory lines that there is one system of international law binding on all countries. By skirting the delicate question of the (class) nature of international law, Chou Fu-lun's thesis could in fact be made to stand up:

International law should not be confused with municipal law. The major unique trait of international law is that its standards are formulated not by a super-legislature, but through agreement reached by the process of struggle, co-operation, compromise and consultation. International law is neither socialist nor bourgeois but reflects the transition from one to the other (quoted in ibid.).

In a meeting of the Shanghai Law Association in February 1958 the majority opposed Lin Hsiu's view, but no agreement as to the two-system (socialist and general) or three-system (socialist, bourgeois, and general) theories could be agreed upon. And there the situation rested. In the fifties and sixties government practice would seem to suggest not only a recognition of the general international law but also an apparent realization that in order to meet the special situation of socialist countries, whose relations were purportedly based on the principles of proletarian internationalism, reference must be made to special principles to correspond. Differences between the Chinese and Soviet cases there undoubtedly were but so long as they shared the Soviet approach to international relations based on the concept of two socio-economic systems, the virtually inescapable tendency was towards a mix of a consensus and a regional doctrine of international law, and with it an emphasis on separate socialist international law—or at least the incorporation of distinctively socialist principles.

The subsequent differences between the Chinese and Soviet attitudes would appear to derive not so much from the Sino-Soviet rift as from the differing perceptions of their standing within the states-system and the consequent degree of damage that might be inflicted upon them through international law and organizations. The PRC, although some considerable distance behind, would seem to be treading a path that the Soviet Union had once travelled. The exaggerated emphasis placed by the Chinese on the concept of sovereignty is one example among many of earlier Soviet attitudes. For the Chinese the question of sovereignty looms large in every issue of international law, whether it is to do with the peaceful settlement of disputes, the observance of treaties, the extension of special privileges and immunities, non-interference, and non-aggression, or offering objection to the concentration of power in international organizations. The perceived erosion of state sovereignty through the recognition of individuals as subjects of international law and determined Chinese opposition to it is another case in point. In fact any move towards 'world government' that smacks even remotely of the PRÇ's subordination to it attracts Chinese resistance.

Since the 'three worlds' theory calls especially for the 'broadest international united front' against the two superpowers, a base is established for a struggle along class lines against either one (or both) of the superpowers, with the Chinese joined with the rest of the world. This latter approach forms the foundation of the unswerving Chinese commitment to international law. And thus, on the basis of the three worlds theory, with its realization of the lengthiness of the process of world revolution and transition to communism, there is every reason to believe that China will continue her endeavours to use both international law and international organizations in her anti-hegemonistic fight. At the same time in her approach to the rest of the world, international law will be employed as a regulatory instrument of co-ordination and co-operation based on China's own principles of 'peaceful coexistence'. Unlike the Soviet version, which excludes from participation the socialist bloc and some Third World countries, Chinese 'peaceful coexistence' applies to all.

The 'new'(?) international law

How valid is the Soviet assertion that international law is either already 'new' or is on the way to becoming renewed—a claim supported by the states of the Third World? Answers given by Western jurists appear to range across a similar ideological – philosophical spectrum to that of explanations of change in world politics offered by Western political science. Thus the jurists can point to the operation of powerful pressures for change and to the attempts at accommodation to such pressures characteristic of the development of international law since Grotius. Not only does Marxism evaporate in such interpretations but the degree of influence on international law by a (self-proclaimed) Marxist superpower also diminishes when placed in the context of a multiplicity of cultures, Hindu,

Jewish, Chinese, Japanese, African, and Soviet. It is seen to constitute a context in which the universal legal order, now already in a growth period, develops by way of the intellectual assimilation of such influences. Some writers would acknowledge a Marxist influence in Soviet approaches to international law to be confined mainly to the (inevitable) Marxist ideological crust, with, on the part of the Soviets, a token recognition of established practice in the introduction of 'one propaganda item a year' (Rosenstock, 1971, 726), and to 'depressing' insistence on 'rigid' anachronistic doctrines such as state sovereignty (ibid. 725). To McWhinney, further along the spectrum, there are 'built-in demands of a priori Marxist dogma and philosophical absolutism' to be seen in the Soviet 'conception of world order' which he (McWhinney) agrees, however, is no more than a 'quite sophisticated, philosophically pluralistic approach that has some elements in common with contemporary Western concepts of pluralistic federalism in municipal or national law' (McWhinney, 1971, 218). McWhinney sees as the chief characteristic of the Soviet approach the search for 'living law' in the complex of accords, arrangements, and *de facto* relations between ideological groupings which McWhinney agrees have always existed but which at the present time are particularly 'profound'. The conclusion to McWhinney is that fortunately states do not have to agree on ideology and do not have to share views about the nature of international law or any of its parts; they only have to reach a consensus on the rules of conduct (ibid. 218).

McWhinney recognizes that there is a logic in the chain of Soviet idiosyncrasies: from the Soviet rejection of 'mondialism', for example, derives a rejection also of the endorsement of tendencies towards the creation of a legally paramount international government, from which follows the denial of the United Nations Charter as a constitution and insistence on regarding it as a treaty. There is, too, such an insistence on the primacy of the Security Council through Great Power veto over the General Assembly, and in the rejection of the World Court to which third-party arbitration is a logical follow-on. McWhinney recognizes that the approaches of the Soviet Union and United States to international law are based on radically different philosophical premises and arrives at the somewhat

startling conclusion that over the years the United States has
come to emulate the Soviet approach in many important regards!
Exemplifying this perceived tendency is the fading of initial
American enthusiasm for the United Nations as a future world
government (a position that has always been part of the Soviet
approach). Then again, the United States has been won over to
the convening of summit meetings *à deux*. Nor does she any
longer 'rush to the World Court' but seems to have accepted
the Soviet position that judicial settlement is only one among
a number of possible ways towards the settlement of disputes—
diplomatic negotiations being deemed the most productive of
these ways (ibid. 229–30). In the implication that there is such
a thing as a 'superpower approach to international law'
McWhinney appears to overlook the fact that the Soviets'
adoption of that approach dates from long before her
achievement of superpower status. There is furthermore an
alternative to McWhinney's reading of events as superpower
'convergence', namely that the United States accepts Soviet-
inspired changes to international law.

Beyond such convergence explanations—as would, it might
be remarked, remove the last trace of Marxism from the Soviet
Union—and further along the interpretative spectrum, there are
those Western jurists whose concern focuses more precisely on
the new *methods* operated by the 'new states' in company most
often with the USSR in the process of bringing change to
international law. Concern, in other words by the 'old majority',
for the brash methods of a 'new majority' comprising over 120
new Third World states which, although in the present legal
structure still hopelessly ineffective (despite apprehensions of
a 'tyranny of the new majority'), nevertheless stand on the basis
of ideological affinity to gain the support of the 'Second World',
and with it also the military strength of a superpower. This 'new
majority', brought into existence with the admission into the
United Nations in the fifties and sixties of numbers of newly-
independent sovereign states, generates a formidable power.
Their influence, channelled by way of documents and
resolutions, though running into the problem of the General
Assembly's impotence, articulates in the resounding voice of
a majority of the world's states, the majority of the world's
populations, with, as sounding-board, the majority of the world's

land areas. Depending of course on one's viewpoint, the vision of a world in cataclysmic transition conjured up by the implementation of some of these documents is indeed profoundly disturbing: after all, the dissatisfaction of which the documents and resolutions are an expression, is targeted directly on the states-system itself, as desirable *leges ferrendae*.

Thus the resolution on the New International Economic Order initiated by the non-aligned countries was adopted in 1974 by the overwhelming majority of 120 in favour against 6 negative votes, with 10 abstentions. Others, thrusting in a similar direction, have come close to unqualified acceptance: one example is the Soviet-initiated attempt at codification of the principles of peaceful coexistence, which represented a blatant attempt to reinforce further her claim to having played a decisive role in the formulation of an 'international law of peaceful co-existence'. On this occasion the majority votes were persuaded that the term 'peaceful coexistence' is not contained in the United Nations Charter and on that basis, with the substitution of a much diluted version, the 'Declaration of Principles of International Law concerning Friendly Relations' was adopted unanimously (1970). That resolution, though reflecting the successful resistance of the Western members to the Soviet attempt at an appropriation of influence, *does* in fact represent an advance in the development of international law along lines favoured by the Second and Third Worlds. There is of course some argument as to whether the Declaration represents a new *ius cogens*, or general principles of law, as is the opinion of the Soviet, East European, and Third World commentators, or wields simply the moral weight of unanimity. Another example of the frontal assault on traditional international law, and a Western resistance that seems increasingly to take on the complexion of a rearguard action, is the draft treaty prepared by UNCLOS (United Nations Conference on the Law of the Sea), adopted and opened for signatures in 1982. This document, permeated by the ideology underlying the New International Economic Order and representative of the arsenal at the revisionists' disposal would 'revolutionise the International Law' (Evriviades, 1982, 201) if in the event it were to become part of that law.

We devote space in the present chapter to a survey of Marxist and Soviet influence such as may be present in the pressures on traditional international law and, in identifying that Soviet/Marxist component, will do so under the rubrics suggested by a Western jurist (Hazard) who admits to a degree of concern regarding the combined (Second and Third World) assault and its effect on international law.

1   *The right of self-determination as a legal obligation*

Using the idea of self-determination generated in the disintegrating multinational empires in the eve of World War I and to which Lenin (certainly not Marx) as much as Woodrow Wilson could lay claim,[1] Lenin saw an opportunity of welcoming oppressed nations into the Marxist ambit as allies—a measure, in other words, to make the most of 'the interests of every oppressed nationality or race, of every persecuted religion, of the disenfranchised sex, etc.' (Lenin, 1963, vol. 4/177). Whereas neither of the two leaders (Wilson and Lenin) was able, or willing, to carry the concept into general application, Lenin showed an inspired grasp of the implications in his search for allies that was to be turned to Soviet account into the future. In a strikingly honest statement he admitted that '. . . we on our part concern ourselves with the self-determination of the *proletariat* in each nation rather than with self-determination of peoples or nations' (Lenin, 1963, 6/454). He seemed, thus, always to have preferred the 'right of the proletariat class to national self-determination and statehood'. Even so, his fellow Marxists on the left disagreed. In this context Rosa Luxemburg's position of hostility would not have recommended her to those of today's Third World Marxists to whom she is a figure of adulation. Luxemburg's opposition was based first of all on the whole validity of the idea of granting 'rights' and 'absolute rights' within the context of dialectics. Promising freedom of oppression as a right, she asserted, was like promising workers that they had the right to eat off gold plates (cf. Davis, 1978, 58). Besides, whatever entity was to be accorded 'rights' it could never be 'nations'; it might at best be the proletariat as a class. Adhering to the doctrine more closely than did Lenin she advocated the inclusion of small nationalities within larger, economically sound imperialist countries, her idea deriving from the conviction that the proletariat, following victory in the capitalist countries, would move outwards from the centre to bring freedom to smaller nations and colonies, under socialist government.

Lenin's 'Theses on National and Colonial Questions', presented to the Comintern at its Second Congress, constituted the bridgehead of Marxism into the Third World, where Marxism, thus modified, has thrived ever since. We have tried to show the crucial and formative influence this work of Lenin's had on, in particular, Chinese and Vietnamese Marxism to mention only two. Lenin's modification was necessary since, as Cabral said later, 'we looked for the proletariat and did not find it'. In the event, Marxism throughout the Third World settled for oppressed nations as a surrogate for the missing proletariat and the Marxist doctrine became the fervent battle cry of the dispossessed. Essentially, therefore, the idea is not Marxist but only a Leninist tactic which through Lenin's careful guidance gradually became the centre-piece of Third World neo-Marxism. When it came to tactical shifts and maximization of advantage, the Soviet Union, as it turned out, had nothing to learn from Lenin and in 1960, in a similar pivotal situation, the USSR 'upstaged' the West by championing a UN resolution calling for an end to colonialism and declaring the principle of self-determination (as already referred to in the UN Charter) to be regarded as a *right* of all peoples. Outmanoeuvred at this psychologically fraught moment the United States abstained, and on the basis of this Resolution[1] the Third World, backed by the Soviet Union, has launched its damaging attacks on imperialism ever since.

The theme (national 'liberation' as a right) figures as largely in Soviet international legal literature as in UN debate in strange contrast to an earlier time when it was colonization that was protected by international law—and colonies (on the gounds of lack of 'civilisation') were excluded from international law (Covenant of the League of Nations, Article 22). The Soviet Union now argues that recognition of this right is already an integral part of the general international law, and is now enshrined in the Declaration of Principles Concerning Friendly

---

[1] The most frequently cited of any UN Resolution. UN General Assembly, 15th Session, Official Records, Supp. No. 16 (A.4684), p. 66.

Relations. The reasons for the refusal of the United States to cast a positive vote in 1960, risking instead the alienation of the Third World need not in the present context detain us. The Soviet Union's support for the promotion of the principle of self-determination to a 'right' would invest with international legality an arms flow that is demonstrably in operation from the USSR and socialist countries to Third World insurgencies.

In terms of the juridical implications, the recognition of such a right would introduce into international law the legal distinction so favoured in Marxism of a 'just' (come to mean legal) war. Support for such anti-colonialist wars or wars of international liberation, or indeed for any great power-designated insurgency (as 'international duty, or 'fraternal assistance' included in the Soviet Constitution), could thus hope to find sanction also in international law. In circumstances where the Soviet notion of 'peaceful coexistence' turns out to mean a peace that is no more than a partial truncated armistice, the right of self-determination would re-open a chapter in the history of war. Taken to a logical conclusion, and short of global nuclear confrontation, virtually the entire field of conflict would depend on as highly subjective and individual an interpretation of 'just' as has frustrated implementation of other relevant articles of the Charter. The waging of war by any expansionist power is thus put on a different footing. The Soviet Union has already utilized the device of legalization of wars in the Third World and of the use of force within the socialist commonwealth. Elsewhere, in a world of nuclear stand-off where traditional expansionist paths are blocked by the destructive power of weaponry, it is one way of transforming the world—in the likeness of a great power. Whilst we do not credit the USSR with exclusive control of these expansionist avenues, her tally of success in the Third World argues the possession of an extensive array of tried and tested instruments, and an already skilled facility in their deployment and legalization. The propagation over the years by the Comintern of the concept of self-determination played a part in shaping the form that the process of decolonization was to take—thus significantly contributing to the building of present tensions within the newly independent states.

2   Pressures for equality with the Great Powers on the part of the new Third World states

The demand for equality finds its main expression in calls for the revision of the Charter of the United Nations, for a redistribution of powers between the General Assembly and Security Council, and/or for changed voting procedures throughout the international organization. The fact that this is one of the areas where the USSR will not go along with Third World demands has given rise to some speculation about the reasons for her reluctance. The disinclination to lend support in this particular area is not on Marxist grounds since equality in general, and for that matter also the equality of states, are not Marxist but liberal principles. In regard to voting procedures, and the possibility of their being revised, the Soviet Union fathered the principle of unanimity in the Security Council and ever since its inception has insisted that this 'right of veto' remains the cornerstone of the international legal order—the guarantee of the equality of the two socio-economic systems. It is also, as it happens, a hedge against the possibility of the Soviets being 'outvoted' in the event of the UN ever becoming reconstituted as a transnational body. The PRC's approach in this regard is noticeably different: committed as she is to the idea of the Third World as the 'motor force' of history she has no alternative but to support Third World states in their claims for a more equitable representation in the voting mechanisms of the organization. In any event here, too, the risk is slight since she may safely assume that the exercise of Soviet and other Great Power vetoes will mean her commitment never being put to the test.

One view of the Soviet refusal to capitalize on the emerging majority in her favour in the United Nations represents the reluctance as evidence of 'terminal value' in Soviet legal doctrine—a failure to overcome in certain areas the inbuilt rigidity of Marxist orthodoxy. Another view takes the refusal as proof that, commensurate with her Great Power status, the USSR has become more responsible—a reading in evidence of which is adduced the Soviet adoption after the second World War of a more positive approach to the United Nations (cf. McWhinney, 1971, 227). There is, of course, not to be overlooked, in this context of the Soviet refusal to subscribe Third World aspirations to the full extent, the bitter past experience of the attempt to manage the international movement of communist parties and states (Chapter 6)—an undoubtedly lingering memory in the consciousness of the leadership. As it is, there is neither urgency nor any particular need to alter a situation in which, when required, the USSR can call on the Third World majority, whilst her Great Power status is sufficient guarantee in itself of her ability to meet any contingency situation arising from a turn in loyalties of this somewhat volatile majority.

3   The pressures of new states to share as equals in the process of codification of customary international law

As once with the USSR all subsequent 'newcomers' to the international legal community are bound sooner or later to claim the right to participate in evolving the rules of the game rather than continuing passive acceptance of old rules drafted before their time. Jenks argues that this is a perfectly understandable expression of what is essentially an anti-Western protest (Jenks, 1958, 74–5), and certainly recognition of international custom is one of the first targets of the newcomers. These, in the shape of the Third World, now adopt what Richard Falk has called a 'strategy of participation', that is to say an insistence on their right to partake in every way in the 'development' of new law, coupled with a refusal to be bound by any law concluded without their participation. Thus the Third World countries insist on participating even in matters in which they have no immediate material interest, and so, at the UNCLOS debates, these countries were liable to advance ambitious ideological demands on nations with an important stake in the outcome (Burke and Brokaw, 1982, 72): Western concessions were traded for signatures in support.

The new states seem to reject the positivist theory based exclusively on customs and treaties as sources of international law. On the contrary they conspicuously address themselves to the naturalist writers who perceive international law as part of a universal moral code (Bello, 1981, 171). Like the Soviet Union and the PRC, the new states reject custom as the source of international law but if pressed would substitute treaty for custom. They therefore demand a progressive codification of customary international law. Custom being by definition impervious to change stands in contrast to law written down in the form of a treaty which is of course subject to change with time. Needless to say, when custom is transferred into written treaty form a reduction in substantive content invariably takes place—to the minimum extent acceptable to all parties. Furthermore new elements are added which might not have figured in customary law, as borne out most recently by the radical changes in the draft codification of the Law of the Sea.

A curious change in Soviet attitudes towards customary law, as also a departure from the hitherto well-established Soviet denial of the law-making function of the General Assembly of the United Nations, has been commented upon by a few observers. Named by Soviet writers 'crystallized custom' and by Western authors 'new custom' (or 'instant custom'), the Soviet Union claims that General Assembly resolutions may be consulted in order to find some indication as to what customary law might have to say on a particular issue. It is in fact one example of the Soviet utilization of the 'new majority' in the United Nations. In this way, as Hazard asserts, the Soviet Union attempts to develop a new *ius cogens* from the resolutions of the General Assembly. A law which predictably is favourable more often than not to Soviet purposes.

4   Adjustments to international law brought about by pressures originating in the economic field

If the substance of the NIEO documents and the UNCLOS draft treaty were to become incorporated into a binding law the operation of such a law would bring about the transformation of the international community and effectively put an end to the states-system as we know it. The 'new states' would have material economic change follow rather than run ahead of certain specified legal changes so as to bring the force of international law to the legitimization of a privileged status to help them overcome the levels of underdevelopment. The drive on the part of these states is in the direction of a general incorporation into international law of the principle of redistributive justice. As an adjunct to the construction of a case for such a basic juridical transformation Marxism is once again an indispensable factor. For it is on the radical liberal (and, more likely, Marxist) theories of imperialism that any claim to establish a *causal connection* between the rich countries' wealth and the new states' immiseration that the Third World must rest such a case. Along these lines the rejection of responsibility of their own regimes for their present predicament becomes possible. The call of these states for institutionalization of 'restitution and reimbursement' to the former colony for damages and lost profits incurred over the centuries of colonial exploitation aims not at a simple instatement of liberal equality of rights, but rather at an equality of conditions from which all their other claims may be seen to derive. Needless to say essential principles on which the states-system at present rests would go by the board; the welfare of each state would cease to be the sole responsibility of the state in question as has been the case under the 'old' idea of state sovereignty and self-help on which so far the system has rested. It would then become the community of states as a whole that would accept responsibility for each of its parts. It might here be observed that the advocates of a 'new' international law of 'co-operation for the benefit of mankind' or (as in UNCLOS) the 'common heritage of mankind', do not call for a combined effort to generate more wealth but for a redistribution of existing assets so as to favour their own states. The demands are clearly based on Kantian ideas that equality is part of justice and remains a goal of the world society, even if in the process the state-system should itself become eclipsed, and such indeed would be the outcome, for these demands obviously negate the 'sovereign equality and reciprocity' of the 'old' international law. The final outcome, a world society with a states-system radically altered (or by-passed), is of course not only Kantian but also certainly Marxist. To those who doubt either the new states' intentions— or have less than complete faith in the attainability of such a goal—the implementation of such demands would provide no more than a fresh boost to the nationalism of some. From there it would lead to a role reversal on the part of the beneficiaries. The states-system, remaining essentially unchanged, would, however, rest on a new, seriously disturbed balance of power.

The claims of the new states do not end there. Additionally, among a number of demands (among which the proposal to place economic pressure legally on a par with physical violence) is that which amounts in effect to no less than the requirement to 'outlaw' international politics. A fanciful single-stroke realization of the Kantian and Marxist vision.

5   The right of individuals to claim international protection against one's own government

The Helsinki Conference in 1975 was regarded as a major step forward in the institutionalization of concern for human rights, and the Soviet Union from the first days made a substantial contribution towards the convening of the conference. Despite these initiatives, however, those invoking such rights and claiming international protection would receive short shrift from that (Soviet) quarter. The Helsinki documents have of course no binding power, but even if such power had been conferred, the likelihood of conforming is remote in a power whose commitment is to an interpretation of peaceful coexistence predicated on ideological inflexibility, and vigilance towards that uncompromising end. The USSR claims that only human rights of groups can be protected by international law as for example racism and sex discrimination. In other words the USSR chooses to abide by article 2(7) of the UN Charter which, together with the Soviet power of veto in the Security Council are seen as the major protective instruments of the socialist states' sovereignty. The euphoric reception in some Western quarters of the text of Helsinki's Final Act was misplaced, for the Soviet Union had already, and without much notice, erected an additional legal barrier in her attempt to strengthen article 2(7) of the Charter when she distanced her bloc from any meaningful interest in the bloc's (human rights and other) domestic affairs: the Soviet Union claims that a new type of international law had already come into existence that regulated relations amongst the socialist countries.

The 'socialist international law' is precisely what it claims to be: a law apart, which in fundamentals contravenes the rules of international law, and which exempts from the reach of general international law a group of countries within Soviet jurisdiction, which in the last (practical) analysis enables the USSR to interfere, intervene (or invade) at will (and with impunity) in the affairs of the countries along its borders. In

characteristic circumlocutory manner the USSR enshrines tr
concepts of socialist international law in her Constitution wher
(art. 30) it is stated that the USSR is a component part of th
world socialist system and of the socialist commonwealth o
nations—whose relations are governed by the principles o
socialist internationalism.

Socialist international law is based allegedly on a new concep
of state sovereignty, any resemblance of which to the tradition.
variety remains purely terminological. Tunkin argues in fac
that this concept bears little resemblance even to the 'limite
sovereignty' of the 'Brezhnev doctrine' (the latter occupying n
place in official Soviet legal theory). 'Fraternal aid' (the argumer
runs), far from 'limiting' sovereignty, aims at precisely th
opposite, at assuring , that is, the preservation of sovereign
and the national independence of the socialist states. Th
flexibility of the Soviet doctrine of sovereignty is seemingl
endless, leading on the one hand to the recognition of insurgen
as 'sovereign' and, at one and the same time, to a denial of suc
a right to dissidents in countries of her bloc in which the rigl
of people to sovereignty has purportedly already bee
consummated and merged with the sovereignty of the state. I
this context the Marxist – Leninist doctrine lends a plasticit
to the concept and justification for the gradual absorption of
number of countries' sovereignties into a *de facto* federatio
to which the integrative process well under way within th
framework of Comecon (Lavigne, 1983), the Warsaw Pact, an
other exclusively socialist international organizations be,
testimony (Szawlowski, 1976). Such incorporation involves
simple redefinition of the absorbed sovereignties which thu
become a variety of sovereignty to be found not in the glossar
of international law but in that of constitutional law. The Sovi
authors could of course argue that the idea of state sovereignt
is un-Marxist and that sovereignty always rests with 'peopl
or 'nation' as possessed of, and defined by, certain class feature
Marxism is indeed of immense ideological and semantic valu
for *inter alia* in its reservoir of classical Marxist statemen
historical bounds have been set on the states-system an
international law, both of which are allegedly on the way t
being superseded. Even partially rehabilitated Pashukanis di
not doubt that the 'proletarian states, not having merge

formally into one federation or union, must present in their mutual relationships an image of such a close economic, political, and military unity that the measures of "modern" international law become inapplicable to them' (Pashukanis, 1980, 173).

What then is the answer to the question whether international law has changed/is changing and that such changes derive from Marxist or Marxist-inspired Soviet roots? Western international jurists seem to be very divided. McWhinney sees a possibility of adapting to the pressures for change, whilst Hazard on the other hand feels that international law is already in a transitional state. Hazard in other words agrees with the Soviet and Third World analyses but far from expressing their feelings of elation at the prospect he awaits 'with a fear of chaos and despair' (Hazard, op. cit. 2, 20). The student of International Relations might of course dismiss such intimations with the thought that international law is not real law and performs only a negligible role in the regulation of complex political and economic processes. A second thought might suggest however that areas of dysfunction perceived to exist in the present legal arrangement by the Russians since 1917, joined now by a formidable number of other newcomers may be taken as manifestations of dysfunction in the states-system as a whole.

There are at least four possible interpretations of the pressures for change in international law from the point of view of the rationale and provenance of these pressures: first of all, that they are made simply on behalf of members of the system aspiring at their (further) advancement in the states-system hierarchy, either individually or (temporarily) as a collective. The ideological dressing-up of such claims (whether radical, liberal, or Marxist) is therefore of little consequence since such claims are made only in promotion of the national interest/advancement. Second, the view that such claims are made with an eye to the creation of a 'world state' in the manner of which the USSR has not infrequently been accused. The third interpretation sees such claims as made with the purpose of restructuring not only international law, nor for such restructuring so as to advantage any state(s) in particular, but rather as part of a drive towards the socio-economic restructuring of the world as a whole, away from the present system, on a path unknown.

A fourth view represents none of the first three options as *cul de sacs* but as staging posts along the road—a road that can be followed either consciously or inadvertently by a force already in existence or one that is still to emerge. Such a road must also of course lead to the reformation of both the socio-economic and legal structuring of the world. It is a road that might well be taking mankind towards an unknown destination, a world of unfamiliar social formations and modes of production where rules as yet inconceivably different from those of the present would apply—a world in other words in accordance with Marxist projections, or otherwise.

The relevance of a serious study of Marxism to the context of International Relations lies precisely in this direction. Whilst the 'national interests' of the socialist and the Third World countries are clearly seen to be advanced by their reference to Marxism, and whilst there is of course a distinct possibility that these countries see no further than their own respective 'national interest'—since the more propitious milieu for all of these claimants might well be the anarchical world in which they as states have thrived—it is not to say, even as their claims are advanced, that certain irreversible processes may already have been set in motion. The nature and name of the destination towards which we might already be in transit might not be of much consequence. Not one of the numbers of Marxists seems confident of a knowledge of the outcome of such a transition. But the proclivity to urge transitional processes, the keen awareness of participating in such processes, and the capacity to recognize and ride the wave have been distinguishing features of Marxist approaches—and a hallmark of Marxist participation in world politics. In retrospect Marxism, although initially not boasting an explicit doctrine of international relations, has in fact been handling international relations extremely well. It has therefore a persuasive claim to being one of those forces that have shaped world politics of the twentieth century and in its demonstrated flexibility will no doubt be called upon even into the future.

Part III

International relations as mainly a theoretical problem

9 Gramsci: The Substructure Undermined

In the aftermath of the successful Bolshevik Revolution and revelation of the failure of the proletariat as the historical revolutionary agency (recognized as such by all of European Marxism) there stood at this parting of the ways three major Marxist figures: Lukács, a Hungarian (1885–1971) Karl Korsch, a German (1886–1961), and an Italian Antonio Gramsci (1891–1937). All three could claim their Marxist roots to be in the old guard, but, as it happened, all three were to become leading figures in the opening of a new chapter in Marxism, as in fact (it also turned out) the future of the concept (international relations) was in their hands, to be shaped by their writing in the next decades. There emerged from their work in the early twenties something of a codification of Hegelian Marxism. The writings of the three pointed the sharp contrast with and offered an alternative to the 'economism' of the Second International or to the Marxist variant practised by Soviet Marxism – Leninism wherein superstructure reflects substructure and states become mere instruments of the ruling class, their actions deriving from the needs of the capitalist accumulation process. This conceptual handcuffing of state to substructure suited the USSR whose state and foreign policy were thus *ipso facto* legitimized. The connection did not, however, appear to match developments in capitalism taking place in the post-war years, and thus a gap in classical Marxism was brought to the fore, namely the lack of theories to explain various aspects of superstructure—portrayed traditionally as mere epiphenomena. It is indeed something of a problem. For Marxism (as Raymond Williams puts it) without some concept of determination is in effect worthless whilst at the same time a Marxism with many of the concepts of determination it has had is quite radically disabled (Williams, R., 1977, 83). Gramsci illustrated the problem, relevant also to the conceptualization of a states-system, on the example of a Church:

The existence and conflicts of the two Churches do depend on their

economic base and on their historical developments but the specifi
positions of the Holy Ghost were set forth as an area of differentiatio
by the two Churches to strengthen their internal cohesion. They coul
have changed positions and it would not have mattered so long as th
conflict was maintained. This is the real problem to be analysed an
not the casuistry on each side.[1]

Thus Gramsci (throughout his work) is concerned with 'freeing
superstructure, making it clear that the causes of historica
change were to be sought in the superstructure of society rathe
than in the base. The latter was so much an 'ultima ratio' a
to be almost indistinguishable for political purposes.

Even before Gramsci, Lukács, and Korsch had 'freed' th
superstructure from economic determination when they re
turned to the concept of Hegelian totality in which a singl
'essence' or dominant principle comes to pervade the societa
whole. Each part of the social structure becomes, of course, a
expression of the whole, of the defining spirit. 'It is not primac
of economic motives in historical explanation that constitute
the decisive difference between Marxism and bourgeoi
thought, but the point of view of totality. The category o
totality, the all pervasive supremacy of the whole over the part
is the essence of the method which Marx took over from Hege
and brilliantly transformed into the foundation of a wholly nev
science' (Lukács, 1971, 27). Karl Korsch said pretty much th
same thing when he spoke of the 'totality of the historico-socia
process' and when he said that Marxism was a 'theory of *socia
development* seen and comprehended as a living totality; or
more precisely, it is a theory of *social revolution* comprehende
and practised as living totality' (Korsch, 1970, 52).

The theme of totality pervades Lukács's work: in his essay
on Lenin he points to Lenin's ability to perceive *Totalität* as a
indication of his greatness. Otherwise he sees little of originalit
in a contribution (Lenin's) that borrows mainly from hi
predecessors. Lenin's contribution to the theory of imperialisn
lay precisely in his capacity to integrate the theoretical part
into one whole, whilst, by the same token, Luxemburg als
comes in for Lukács's praise for her talent for analysis at 'global
level. Thus Lukács reinterprets the somewhat vague, well-wor
axiom of the notion of 'social being determining consciousness

[1] A. Gramsci, 'Il Materialismo Storico e la Filosofia di Benedetto Croce
p. 76, quoted in Davidson, 1962, 32.

and diverges thereby from the 'economist' idea that content of consciousness is linked with the economic structure in a directly reflective relationship. There is no direct, unqualified, and causal link between the economy (or even particular aspects of it) on the one hand and ideology on the other (cf. Lukács, quoted in Kolakowski, 1981, 268). But neither is there, 'in the last analysis, any autonomous science of law, of political economy, of history, etc.; there is only one science, historical and dialectical, unique and unitary, of the development of society as a whole' (ibid.). In such a conception, paradoxically enough, conceptualization of a separate problem such as international relations becomes absurd, and international relations as such, whilst formally freed in the superstructure, disappears again within Lukács's reading of the 'totality', with his reinterpretation of the dialectic, and with his major thesis of the proletariat being at one and the same time a subject and object of history. His ideas however were soon to serve as an inspirational springboard for other Marxists and were duly to reappear as an influence also on international relations.

Gramsci's work has aroused a great deal of attention, some seeing in him a Marxist genius of no less a stature than Lenin himself (cf. Miliband), some on the other hand disputing his scholarship or originality (cf. Anderson, 1976–7). The cryptic and fragmentary nature of his writing in the long years of imprisonment (published posthumously as *Selections from the Prison Notebooks of Antonio Gramsci*) imparts a considerable degree of ambivalence if not confusion to the legacy. It might of course be remarked that such ambivalence in the case of Marx himself served as a powerful protective shield and something of a surety of posterity's recognition—a guarantee of that 'ewig' for which Gramsci wrote in the knowledge (correct as it turned out) that he would not leave prison alive, or if he did that his days would be numbered. Gramsci's 'problematique' is certainly not international relations, and yet, although it might well be because his writing often takes the form of fragments, there are references and concepts with which he repopulated historical materialism that beg for extension into the sphere of international relations—as indeed were such references extended and applied for example to law (Genovese, 1974) in the 1970s when Gramsci became overnight a Marxist fad.

Palmiro Togliatti's call for polycentrism, as opposed to the Soviet-dominated 'proletarian internationalism' (Chapter 6), undoubtedly had roots in Gramsci's work. For Gramsci is certainly not ambivalent in his criticism of the Comintern, and of Stalin as well as of Trotsky. To Gramsci, the 'national' emphasis is necessary to the proletarian movement. It derives from the fact that his central concept, hegemony, expresses itself nationally and that the proletariat is based in national matrices. The internationalism practised by the Comintern was thus necessarily wrong, and led to passivity or 'napoleonism'. Trotsky's idea of world revolution, for example, was, according to Gramsci, yet another example of mechanistic Marxism and completely faulty as a strategy. 'To be sure', he says, 'the line of development is towards internationalism, but the point of departure is "national"—and it is from this point of departure that one must begin. Yet the perspective is international and cannot be otherwise' (Gramsci, 1971, 240). Gramsci's rejection of the Soviet-led Comintern's policies was obvious in his repeated stress on a combination of the international with national considerations, in fact implying on the contrary that the Comintern was *not* a leading agency because it had not provided such a combination in its interpretation. 'The accusations of nationalism are inept if they refer to the nucleus of the question' (ibid.) and the 'non-national concepts (i.e. ones that cannot be referred to each individual country) are erroneous'. Such 'non-national concepts' led to passivity in the case of the Second International when 'nobody believed that they ought to make a start' and 'waited for everybody to move together'. Later on this led to what he calls 'napoleonism', 'masked by the general theory of permanent revolution', by which is meant the expectation of the revolution's spreading from Russia in the way that Napoleon's armies carried certain of the ideas and achievements of the French Revolution beyond the borders of France. 'The international situation should be considered in its national aspect' (ibid. 40) is Gramsci's verdict. Proletarian internationalism in this rendition is of necessity fragmented into its state compartments which are very real and which do not lend themselves to uniformity and subordination. But what is this international situation that is thus refracted into national strategies for every individual state?

Unlike Lenin, who thought that within the framework of imperialism proletarian leaders can be bribed and deflected from the revolutionary path, Gramsci believed that the deviationist tendency is in fact on the part of a whole populace, 'confused' not by monetary inducements but by the operation of political and cultural structures that evolved in capitalist societies. In capitalist society (he says), the dominant economic class no doubt exercises sheer coercive forces through the state and government apparatus: but this alone cannot explain the astonishing and unwavering control over society. The exercise of such a formidable control is made possible in these Western capitalist societies by the dominant class establishing what he refers to as 'hegemony' in the social, cultural, and moral spheres. This means there is the possibility of ruling with the consent of the oppressed classes, the iron fist of the state being kept in reserve and rarely in evidence. Thus Gramsci adds to the usual meaning of hegemony in international relations as political rule or domination, or (in a Marxist situation) the hegemony of the proletariat over other classes (cf. Anderson, 1976–7, 17 ff.). The coaxing of public consent is through the media (schools, churches, and intellectuals working hand in glove with the ruling class), agencies, in other words, that customarily form part of the political socialization process. From this point Gramsci is led to a rejection of the Bolshevik method of seizing power in Tsarist Russia as totally inappropriate to a 'West' characterized by the presence of this hegemony within civil society. He arrives at the conclusion that in order to combat the hegemony the proletariat has to develop a 'counter-hegemony'. Led by the Party, which like Machiavelli's Centaur, half-beast, half-man, has the dual capability of fighting the bourgeoisie on both fronts—that of civil society, and the other, of state. But where is the relevance in all of this to International Relations?

Gramsci highlights a difference between 'West' and 'East' which as Anderson irreverently points out is merely the highlighting of parliamentary bourgeois democracy in the West and feudal autocracy in Tsarist Russia respectively (Anderson, 1976–7, 55). Whilst in the East 'state is everything', in the West it is only an 'outer ditch' of the inner fortress of civil society which, since it is so robust and structured (not, as in the East, primordial and gelatinous) can withstand a more intense bombardment. To these differences correspond various proletarian strategies: the 'war of manœuvre' in the East—which was successful in the case of the Bolshevik seizure of power, and the 'war of position' in the West. Although his allegoric fortresses are obviously *introverted* since they are built to turn aside the 'internal' enemy within each society, all of the paraphernalia of 'ditches and fortresses' can hardly be denied a usefulness and a deployment also in the operation of external relations amongst states.

For Gramsci the states-system is obviously fragmented into those areas with complex social structures on the one hand and immature social structures on the other: nothing unusual one would think for a Marxist who is committed to treating state as an epiphenomenon of classes with the resulting, almost inevitable, conclusion that there are 'types' of international relations to correspond with the 'types' of states. The variation in such structures would suggest the degree of relative ease (or difficulty) the particular state would experience in the penetration of other societies. But Gramsci jettisons the connection between the domestic structure of a state and its external behaviour—a rejection that is both indirectly implied in his general emphasis on superstructural phenomena and the autonomy of such phenomena—and is also quite explicitly made clear when (once again unusual in a Marxist) he answers the rhetorical question regarding the 'organic relations between the domestic and foreign policies of a State'. In other words, he asks, 'is it domestic policies which determine foreign policy, or vice versa?' What more should a student of International Relations wish by way of answer in his search for Marxist theories of International Relations? Gramsci answers his own question by subdividing states into categories and by reference to special conditions—'In this case too, it will be necessary to distinguish: between great powers, with relative international autonomy, and other powers; also, between different forms of government, a government like that of Napoleon III had two policies apparently (reactionary internally, and liberal abroad)'. Of importance also would seem to be the 'conditions in a State before and after a war':

It is obvious that, in an alliance, what counts are the conditions in which a State finds itself at the moment of peace. Therefore it might happen that whoever has exercised hegemony during the war ends up by losing it as a result of the enfeeblement suffered in the course of the struggle, and is forced to see a 'subordinate' who has been more skilful or 'luckier' become hegemonic. This occurs in 'world wars' when the geographic situation compels a State to throw all its resources into the crucible: it wins through its alliances, but victory finds it prostrate, etc. This is why in the concept of 'great power' it is necessary to take many elements into account, and especially those which are 'permanent'—i.e. especially 'economic and financial potential' and population (ibid. 264).

Gramsci's understanding of international relations is obviously not reducible to simple class considerations. In a different context he once again brings up the question of international relations: 'Do international relations precede or follow (logically) fundamental social relations', that is to say the 'degree of development of productive forces', 'relations of political force and those between parties (hegemonic systems within the State), immediate (or potentially military) political relations?' And again the answer is qualified:

There can be no doubt that they follow. Any organic innovation in the social structure, through its technical-military expressions, modifies organically absolute and relative relations in the international field too. Even the geographical position of a national State does not precede but follows (logically) structural changes, although it also reacts back upon them to a certain extent (to the extent precisely to which super-structures react upon structure, politics on economics, etc.). However, international relations react both passively and actively on political relations (of hegemony among the parties). The more the immediate economic life of a nation is subordinated to international relations, the more a particular party will come to represent this situation and to exploit it, with the aim of preventing rival parties gaining the upper hand . . . one may conclude that often the so-called 'foreigner's party' is not really one which is commonly so termed, but precisely the most nationalistic party—which in reality, represents not so much the vital forces of its own country, as that country's subordination and economic enslavement to the hegemonic nations or to certain of their number (ibid. 176–7).

From a cursory perusal of the *Prison Notebooks* alone there seems no doubt that Gramsci is prepared to regard the states-system as a virtually autonomous organism which interacts with the circumstances of the nation in a most complicated fashion. There is thus a strong temptation to stretch his innovative categories and apply them to the society of states. That society is obviously hierarchically structured with great and lesser powers whose respective strength derives from a variety of sources not usually recognized by a Marxist. At the same time the society is heterogeneous in regard to its component parts: some states are 'civil societies' based on internal hegemonic rule (the West), some are simple 'states' internally based on coercion (the East). Taken as internal fortresses, the variety of their defensive fortifications are enormously varied. So must also be their international relations: 'international relations intertwine with the relations of nation-states, creating new, unique, and historically concrete combinations. A particular ideology, for instance, born in a highly developed country, is disseminated in less developed countries, impinging on the local interplay of combinations' (ibid. 182).

Gramsci's use of the term 'hegemonic nation' appears to be more consistent with its more traditional usage to describe the relation of state rather than with the new meaning he confers upon it in its domestic sense. If an extension of Gramscian concepts to the international system were possible—and he seems often to be tantalizingly close to bridging the conceptual gap himself—there would derive one immediate advantage for international relations in so far as it would multiply that rather dull range of choice in types of international relations which for the first Marxists consisted of 'imperialism', 'inter-imperialist rivalry', and contradictions, 'ultraimperialism' and more in the same vein. In his 'Notes on Italian History' and the question of the unification of the rich North and the poor South (Mezzogiorno) dealt with therein Gramsci himself speaks of a 'territorial version' of the 'town-country' relationship and admits that 'the North concretely was an "octopus" which enriched itself at the expense of the South, and that its economic-industrial increment was in direct proportion to the impoverishment of the economy and the agriculture of the South'. Thus he sees between his North and South the application of 'Jacobinism', or the subordination of the 'countryside to the city in an organic relationship'—which is to say the organization of peasant consent. Also tugging at our mind and portending its apprehensions there is Gramsci's concept of caesarism: or a situation in which the forces in conflict balance each other in such a way that a continuation of the conflict can only terminate in their mutual destruction. When the 'progressive force A struggles with the reactionary force B, not only may A defeat B or B defeat A, but it may happen that neither A nor B defeats the other—that they bleed each other mutually and then a third force C, intervenes from outside, subjugating what is left of both A and B' (ibid. 219). Whilst Gramsci uses this relationship to describe a power relationship within a society, it does not take too great a mental leap to see in it a conceptual portent of the East–West nuclear stand-off situation —of an international relationship in fact whose ground rules are not at all dissimilar to those of the Gramscian analysis.

The distinction between a 'hegemonic' as opposed to an ordinary 'coercive' type international relations certainly tempts elaboration and seems to invite the application of the theory to the contemporary international cosmology that Gramsci appears to have foreshadowed. One is drawn inevitably to a comparison of the different methods and characteristics of the relations with their respective 'peripheries' of both of Gramsci's contemporary West and East with the East–West relations of the present system—that is, the relations between the capitalist countries with their ex-colonies on the one hand and the Soviet relations with her bloc on the other. Additionally, there is the caesarist relationship that exists between the present-day East and West. In addition to these different relations between East, West, North, and South there is a further temptation: to think of the states-system as an 'international civil society' in the Gramscian sense, the impermeability of whose states-system (capitalism's international superstructure) to change is illustrated by reference to the agonizingly slow progress made by the establishment of international law and other hegemonic instruments.

If this conceptual extension were to be validated then Gramsci's counsel in regard to the war of manoeuvre and 'counter-hegemony' would have to be seen as equally prescient in so far as they apply to the present-day situation. The only agency capable of restructuring the states-system would indeed then appear to be the Machiavellian Centaur, a mix of coercion and consent, of authority and hegemony, violence and civilization. The dissemination of a counter-ideology—the attempts of a 'hegemonic' use of international law to create abroad international consensus have all been tactics deployed both by the USSR, the United States, and the new states for a number of years—tactics, moreover, which have enjoyed a certain measure of success. The Soviet Union, by appearing (unwittingly) to base her rule on less direct coercion than on hegemony both internally and externally, would seem to have taken a leaf from Gramsci's book (cf. the post-Stalinist campaign for the inculcation of values). The indications are that that form of hegemonic rule over Eastern Europe is not practicable and that the alternative (reliance on coercion) will continue to be applied in these regions. However, the establishment of a hegemonic relation with other Marxist states in the Third World seems to hold some vindication for the Gramscian concept.

After Bernstein, Gramsci would appear to be the first Marxist to have a keen awareness of international relations as a concept, inattention to which could render any attempt at a domestic 'national' analysis futile. By paying such attention however Gramsci, unlike Bernstein, does not cease to be a Marxist. Even if it is only through the element of ambivalence in his writing—leading possibly to a gratified wish on the part of his reader—Gramsci does appear to have widened, and smoothed the path (if not opened several possible alternative avenues) by which International Relations may 'arrive' in Marxism. There is, too, some intimation of the states-system when Gramsci corrects Marx's dictum that history is the history of the class struggle when he is prepared to declare that history in the case of the ruling classes is at best 'essentially the history of States and groups of States' (ibid. 52).

We turn now to the Marxist generation that followed and for which Gramsci's work supplied some valuable guidelines.

10 Marxists: The Professors

When Fernando Claudin says that 'Marxism that was imprisoned by states and parties has died' (Claudin, 1979, 142), he reduces the content of five of our Chapters (4–8) at one stroke into curios for the collectors of theories of international relations. Many other of his fellow Marxists would agree with Claudin and consign the Soviet, Chinese, Cuban, Vietnamese, Yugoslav and Trotskyists, etc. to the role of historical imposters, some or most of the time, with no right to invoke Marx's name. Nor, it appears, by the way, do students of International Relations have a use for these theories since they are mere 'conflations of politics and theory' to be accorded at best the status of one of many regional 'inputs' in the decision-making process. As far as Claudin is concerned only in the foregoing Chapter on Gramsci, Lukács and Korsch, and now in the present do we at last broach the subject of contemporary Marxist explanations of international relations. The true Marxists, again according to Claudin, are those 'outside of or on the fringes of the mass parties'. Those to whom he refers go under the (also disputed) names of 'Western Marxists' or 'Neo-Marxists'.[1] We cannot afford to indulge ourselves in Claudin's particularist approach. Simply put, his reference group consists of no politicians, let alone diplomats, of no individual, group, or movement actively working towards a destination. The group he selects is one of Professors who essentially teach and write in universities and research institutes. With any connection to political movements more often than not coincidental, the term 'engagé' is bandied about among themselves to describe most

[1] The terms 'Western Marxism' and neo-Marxism' were used by Merleau-Ponty and Foster-Carter respectively to distinguish (in the case of 'Western Marxism') Lukács, Korsch, Trotsky from Leninism and Soviet Marxism, and 'neo-Marxists', such as Baran, Sweezy, Magdoff, Jalée, Emmanuel, Amin, Bettelheim, Alavi, Jenkins, Buchanan, Green, Hansman, Arrighi, Frank, Horowitz, Caldwell, Shanin, Gerassi, Debray, Mao, Ho, Kim Il Sung, Castro, Guevara, Fanon, from 'palaeo-Marxists'. (Foster-Carter, 1973, 7.)

often a person or persons who are in fact *disengaged* from the action.

The works of Gramsci, Lukács, and Korsch form a bridge to that (Western Marxist) variety that became almost exclusively theoretical; and yet despite whose stress on theory inexplicably have for a long period shied clear of the connection between international relations and Marxism. The Institut für Sozialforschung (the Frankfurt School), the bastion of Western (ethnically largely Jewish) Marxists, founded in 1923, moved progressively away from those international relations topics, and even from those adjacent that have been used by us in previous Chapters here to help us form an opinion of their predecessors' 'contextual' theories of international relations. Particularly after Horkheimer replaced an Austro-Marxist Grünberg in the directorial office of the Institute, a substantial reorientation was undertaken. The selected direction was away from what was then already called historical materialism, towards the development of 'social philosophy', as officially announced in Horkheimer's inaugural speech in 1930. Whilst in the twenties some members of the Institute did show an interest in international economic problems (for example Pollock in a pioneer analysis of the Soviet economy in 1929) a close scrutiny of the Institute's output would be hard pressed to discover a 'theory of international relations'. Perhaps it is as well, since given the prevailing orientation such a theory would have rivalled the gloomiest of power realist statements. Economic substructure as central to social analysis was cast into serious doubt if not rejected outright, as was the revolutionary potential of the working class, and class struggle as a motor force of history (Jay, 1973, 295). Marcuse, Adorno, and Horkheimer were loath to believe that socialism was a necessary outgrowth of capitalism whilst Horkheimer argued that twentieth-century politics asserted autonomy beyond anything Marx had predicted (ibid. 53).

Explanations for this distancing from the concerns of historical materialism—so central to Marxism—vary. The word 'Marxism' itself came in for de-emphasis, to disappear from the name of the Institute and to be expunged also from association with the theory itself (which became not 'Marxist' but 'critical' theory). One searches in vain for a generally agreed explanation not only of the complete lack of acknowledgement of an international political connection, but also of such omissions or changes as went to the heart of Marxism itself. It is possible that the changes were made in order to distract the attention of an unsympathetic (to Marxists) post-World War I Germany and, later, for the same reason and also so as not to embarrass the host when the entire Institute sought refuge in Columbia University from Hitler's pursuit of both Jews and Marxists. Another possible reason that has been offered for the otherwise inexplicable changes made by the School was to distract attention from the connection with the KGB (of lesser figures in the Institute) that to the German authorities might have suggested Soviet sympathies and the Institute as fellow traveller (Feuer, 1982, and Jay, 1982). But whatever reasons motivated the change of approach it certainly reflected disappointment and pessimism: both with the revolutionary failure in Europe and later also with Soviet (domestic) practices that followed a brief (early) period of co-operation between the Institute and Ryazanov's Moscow-based Marx–Engels Institute in connection with such matters as the publication of Marx's works.

The point to be made is that somewhere along the line the Marxism of the Frankfurt School became something else and, as McInness put it, like other social and religious movements it came to have a double doctrine: one for the ignorant and one for the educated (McInness, 1972, 10). We could hardly better the description today, for, as we said earlier of Soviet Marxism's conjuring up a land of (conceptual) Faerie here (albeit in a very different sense), we have its counterpart: a country populated by equally abstract concepts, by esoteric fancies and neological forms whose meanings take on at best seductive shape but that shimmer, dematerialize, and vanish—to those without a substantial philosophical background. The climate is introspective, the mood decadent. Just as 'critical theory' lost the traditional optimistic component of Marxism, so it rejected also Engels's contribution to the joint (Marx–Engels) partnership. Particularly after the publication in 1932 of the hitherto little known *Paris Manuscripts* of the young Marx (1844) the preoccupation of the School was with the philosophical and methodological questions arising in Marxism. Marxism was thereby delivered into the hands of the philosophers despite the fact that (as has been frequently pointed out) the strength of Marx quite clearly lay elsewhere, namely in the explanation of the economic laws of motion, the investigation of capitalism as a mode of production, and the analysis of the strategy of class struggle.

Perhaps the neglect of such Marxist themes might be adduced as an additional reason for the lack of understanding of an interaction with the discipline of International Relations—itself at that time in its important formative years. When the first 'Grand Debate' in the studies of International Relations took place between idealists and realists, when E. H. Carr, one of the first Professors of International Relations at Aberystwyth in Britain wrote his *Twenty Years Crisis* (1946), and the American Hans Morgenthau published his *Politics Among Nations* (1948) there was, as it turns out, no important contemporary Marxist work with which these writers might have joined polemical battle. These considerations, taken in conjunction with the Marxist intellectual atrophy induced by Stalin's totalitarian dictatorship (the unseemly spectacle of the main political bastion of Marxism working its way up through the hierarchy of the states-system!), and the reorientation of 'Western' Marxism by the Frankfurt School, cause us to see Marxism, as Garaudy once put it, like a sleeping beauty, waiting for the kiss.

The Awakening

Although she had to compose herself patiently for some time, several such kisses were eventually forthcoming and in the fifties and sixties a sequence of events conspired to breathe life back into the sleeping form. There arrived then the destalinization process in the USSR and its effect in this case on the Western and Third World communist parties. There came the massive decolonization process that changed virtually overnight the political map of the world, and the size, coherence and nature of the international system. With the appearance of the New Left as a movement and intellectually the emergence of such Marxists as Althusser, Colletti, the 'Socialisme ou Barbarie' group among others, Marxism once again moved on to centre stage. Internationally speaking it was pointed out that wars such as those in Vietnam and the Congo rather than being regarded as disconnected events should be placed within the long perspective of international relations, and seen against European attempts since the sixteenth century to dominate non-European areas. Significant changes in the nature of capitalism were under way, such as its unprecedented centralization in large transnational organizations, the emergence of new forms of imperialism, the growth of state power and bureaucratic administration to accompany the development of interventionist states, and, similarly remarked, were the changes in class structure, as in the political orientation of different classes.

The important issues of international politics, the East-West conflict in particular, hitherto sadly neglected in Marxist theories, finally become a focus of Marxist attention, and when the reintensification of the nuclear arms race in the 'New Cold War' led in the first years of the eighties to a rebirth of peace movements across the globe, Marxists clearly could not afford either politically or intellectually to be left out. As a consequence, and as compared with the period between the two world wars, we have been witness to a rebirth in Marxism. In its renaissance it is a Marxism that is once again internationalist in character with representatives of virtually all nationalities ready and anxious to participate. There emerges from the ideological ferment an extremely heterogeneous Marxism, methodologically, ideologically, and politically divided. It is an eclectic Marxism that is often flavoured/diluted by such strong ingredients borrowed from other philosophical systems as to cause many of its advocates to refuse to acknowledge themselves as Marxist. The term 'the Left' is sometimes used, or 'socialism' (with the Soviet system referred to as 'actually existing socialism' to distinguish that variety from true socialism). In these circumstances Marxists are often indistinguishable from radical liberals, and as far as developing a coherent explanatory model of the world is concerned they tend to admit that Marxism is 'in crisis' (Amin *et al.* 1982, 238). They converge on the subject of International Relations not out of choice but out of a driving need to come to grips with a serious problem that is simply there. Understandably in light of the foregoing they come to International Relations from different directions, either coming the full distance or meeting the subject part-way.

With rare exceptions the separate focus of International

Relations is still rejected out of hand as essentially ill conceived, the subject considered to be neither sufficiently autonomous for detached analysis, nor freed from the broader context of economic and social forces. For, as always for Marxists, international events are not enactments of simple (or for that matter of complex) parlour war-games, but have a profound meaning in the context of the socio-economic transformation of the world. Committed as they are to political economy as a method, the Marxists attempt to show how networks of social relations—international relations included among numbers of other—are generated by underlying (economic) structures. It is then the underlying structure that becomes for them the primary subject of investigation in the analysis, so there is no simple explanation of one international occurrence in isolation. Rather than the single event placed within a context (however large) of other international events to provide theoretical conclusions, the event is taken instead against the highly involved complex of (updated) historical materialism. Indeed, in order to answer any question about international relations prior answers must be arrived at to such questions as: what is the nature of the world as a whole, in other words within the context of the historical process, is that 'whole' capitalist, a mix of capitalist and pre-capitalist, or capitalist, pre-capitalist, and socialist (or at least post-revolutionary)? The answers will turn on such first principles as the definition of the mode of production itself and its manifestation in the individual social formation.

Methodological preliminaries

Methodologically speaking, and most significant for our present concerns, is the rejection arrived at (by whatever route) by most of these Marxists, of the simple basic scheme of base–superstructure and the idea of the superstructure's being determined by the base, on lines similar to those suggested by their generally recognized immediate predecessors Lukács, Korsch, and Gramsci. For the USSR, for the PRC, and for the others we surveyed in Part II 'mechanistic determination' is of course indispensable for the 'instant legitimacy' it provides for the respective regimes. In sharp contrast their Western counterparts reject this approach and one after the other jettison economic determinism. As Bobbio says of Gramsci, for example, a Marxist remains a Marxist so long as he accepts a *dichotomy* between structure and superstructure and recognizes that the economy always is determinant 'in the last instance' (Mouffe, 1979, 3). Thus, as in the cases of Gramsci and Lukács it is permissible to go as far as recognizing the primacy of ideological superstructure over economic substructure, which in Gramsci's case becomes the primacy of civil society (based on consensus) over political society (based on force). Likewise with Lukács, it is no longer only the economic factor but, in the context of the Hegelian totality, is a single 'essence' or dominant principle that comes to pervade the societal whole, where each part of the social structure becomes an expression of the whole of the defining spirit. In contrast to the idea of 'totality' in Lukács and in Korsch, the dismissal of that approach in favour of 'over-determining' or 'complexly determining' the totality, there is an alternative approach most cogently argued in the work of the French Marxists, and in particular by Althusser (Althusser, 1969, and [with Balibar] 1970). To distinguish it from the *totality* approach this approach is referred to here as *structured totality* (a term used, for example, in Burawoy, 1978) in which a single part (the economic) determines the *relations* among all parts. In this approach the economy, by virtue of its functional require-ments, defines the contributions of the different parts of society and so the relations amongst those parts. The relations between the parts are established on the basis of their several distinctive contributions to the working of the whole. The 'function' of each part defines its form or structure, and in so doing endows it with an autonomy and logic of its own. The parallel is not absolute, but the major and primary concern and starting-point of the first stream (totality approach) was the developmental problems of the Third World, whereas the starting-point of the other (structured totality) was primarily with the various aspects of capitalism in the advanced capitalist countries. What effect do these different methodologies have on the concep-tualization of international relations? The answer is—a con-siderable one for the two methodologies lead to different views of the world as a whole. There is either the perception of the world as *one* single world system in which each nation and state is subordinated to one pervasive dynamic of the system, as the followers of Wallerstein maintain, or, the alternative to that whole world view, as the world as a *structured totality* in which different nations exhibit a *political* and economic independence and a world economy is constituted by various combinations of capitalist, non-capitalist, and, to some authors, also post-capitalist societies. It is the answer arrived at by, for example, Ernest Mandel (1975), Genovese (1971), by Krippendorff (1982), and by Amin (1980). The distinction is in turn predicated on a different definition in each case of capitalism itself. Does capitalism refer to the particular relations entered into by people as they transform nature, that is to say does capitalism refer to a mode of production? Or does capitalism refer to the particular relations people enter into as they exchange the products of their labour—when it becomes in other words a mode of exchange?

The proponents of the dependency and world-system approaches were forced into taking the later position in recognition of the fact that the orthodox definition of capitalism—based on three factors (commodity production, the relations between wage labour and capital, and pressures brought to accumulate and introduce new methods of production)—simply does not have relevance to the situation of Third World countries. Capitalism in these circumstances can only be defined as a world system in terms of *production for exchange* on the world market regardless of whether wage labour is involved or not. But is this the same capitalism that Karl Marx was talking about? There are, as a matter of fact, further changes to capitalism (and Marxism) that flow from this approach. Whilst capitalism in its orthodox Marxist meaning was supposed to perform a positive role and 'develop' the areas it touched, this approach modifies that older thesis when it turns out as part of its understanding that it is by no means a general development that capitalism promotes, but rather the development of some at the expense of the 'underdevelopment' of others. In fact the terms core, semi-periphery, periphery, metropolis, satellites are a substitute for the classical Marxist stages to suggest different political and economic roles which individual states or geographic areas can play within the overall system. 'Underdevelopment', no longer synonymous with the earlier Marxist 'undeveloped', means in this reading incorporation into the world system in a subordinated position. It means that a country cannot be defined as 'underdeveloped' except in so far as it relates to its being part of, and by reference to, a whole. Development and underdevelopment are opposite processes, each resulting from the other. On the other hand what happens if, as critics of Wallerstein and Frank have suggested (cf. Laclau, 1971), we stick to the orthodox definition of capitalism: then it would appear that because the level of wage labour in the Third World countries is very low, capitalism is not a world-wide economic system and that the world is based on a coexistence of different modes of production. Such a coexistence is to be found not only within the world at large but also within a single society. This conclusion is also un-Marxian but in a rather different sense: the conceptualization is driven to acceptance of the possibility of seeing the world in a state of long-drawn-out transition, instead of the development of societies proceeding in stages.

Marxism and International Relations: the literary engagement[2]

As a reflection of the increasing importance (perceived threat) of international relations a trickle of Marxist works on the subject began in the seventies in which the development of explicit theories of international relations was attempted. A similar response by students of International Relations resulted in attempts to bring the Marxist writing within the framework of their discipline, and there is every indication that the initial interest aroused in both cases has a developing potential and that there is the likelihood of the literary interchange becoming a steady flow.

In this connection Robin Jenkins's *Exploitation: The World Power Structure and the Inequality of Nations* (1970) issued a challenge from the Marxist side to Western studies of International Relations finding, in terms of the explanatory capacities of each, Marxism to be distinctly superior although somewhat restrictive in its (explanatory) range. Jenkins found that it would require a major theoretical innovation to break away 'from the irrelevance of the atomistic theory produced by academic

[2] The following section is obviously highly selective and reflects the authors' preferences.

international relations' but at the same time he conceded that there was a need to develop 'the Marxist theory of capital in such a way that it relates to the modern activities of states' (Jenkins, 1970, XV, 208, 211). Generalizing the findings of the dependency school, he himself portrayed the world as an octopus with eight unequal exploitative tentacles, with the Chinese and Soviet tentacle as yet disconnected from the octopus's head (the United States).

Published a year later in the West another Marxist attempt to write a theory of international relations was that of a Romanian Sylviu Brucan (*The Dissolution of Power: A Sociology of International Relations*, 1971). In contrast to Jenkins, Brucan saw a serious lacuna in Marxism and declared the conceptual distinction between the economic infrastructure and the superstructure, so central to Marxism, unworkable in the study of international relations. The trouble according to Brucan lay in the failure to apply Stalin's notion of language as not fitting into that dichotomy to other characteristics of nation such as territory and ethnic origin—these, like language, similarly unaffected by class divisions. From that proposition derives the major thesis of the book, that international relations are a see-saw of class relations and national relations (Brucan, 1971, 50, 82), and, since the new socialist (Soviet) subsystem has not yet become a decisive influence upon world politics as a whole, he proceeds to review the essentially unchanged international system not so much in Marxist terms but in those of the discipline of International Relations. In his later work, *The Dialectic of World Politics* (1978), Brucan is troubled by the same problem that Soviet international jurists for decades had tried to resolve, namely that there is to be found neither a base nor a superstructure as a unitary whole in the international field. He is again driven to the conclusion that Marx's theory runs into difficulties in its application. In circumstances where the relations between superstructure and substructure work vertically within national societies, and not horizontally from one nation to another, he concluded that 'the primary role of the economic factor in International Relations must always be viewed in its dialectical relationship with political, social, military and ideological factors' (Brucan, 1978, 11, 18). An even more sceptical conclusion is reached in R. N. Berki's seminal article of 1971: namely that international relations create serious, possibly intractable, problems for Marxism. Berki's article is probably the best known (most frequently quoted) piece in the community not of Marxists but of students of International Relations. Inadvertently however this article may have shut off further lines of enquiry in so far as it strengthened the conviction of International Relations experts that Marxism provides no alternative intellectual model for their subject. Marxist writers themselves incline to more optimistic conclusions. For example, German Marxist E. Krippendorff's *International Relations as a Social Science* which was first published in German in 1975 (translated into English only in 1982) was written with a much deeper knowledge of the Western International Relations discipline than is possessed by Brucan. Unhampered by the excessively respectful approach of the latter, Krippendorff dismisses that discipline as a deliberate bourgeois attempt to confuse and create 'false consciousness' (Krippendorff, 1982). The study of international relations according to Krippendorff is necessarily located in the more general framework of the world-wide development of productive forces (imperialism). Unusually for a Marxist, however, Krippendorff believes in the usefulness of maintaining the narrow analytical focus of the (International Relations) discipline because of the unimaginable perils and pitfalls that bestrew mankind's path through the nuclear age. 'Seen in this way the subject of International Relations is a systematological dysfunctionalism, a macro-pathological reproduction system. . . . The conflicts in the international system, full of violence and catastrophes, from the Middle East to Central and South Africa, are today apparently inter-state conflicts, but are actually explicit class conflicts' (ibid. 43–5). The dysfunctionalism of power, whose essential function is to preserve the extreme inequalities, which itself is no longer justified in the face of production capacities already achieved, manifests itself macro-politically in the state organization of an international system dominated by the few 'Great Powers' (ibid. 44).

In a uniquely comprehensive work, *State and Class: A Sociology of International Affairs*, 1979, R. Pettman, whilst not himself attempting a Marxist theory of international relations, brings to the attention of students of International Relations (mainly) dependency-inspired writing. Pettman however concludes that a methodological and intellectual synthesis of the two approaches (the one confronting global politics in terms of the 'horizontally arranged hierarchies that run across geographic boundaries' with the approaches of International Relations studies explaining the same topic in terms of the 'flow of diplomatic traffic and wealth springs of foreign policy') is impossible. On this subject we have in our own work (Kubálková and Cruickshank, 1977, 1980, 1981) attempted to reconstruct selected Marxist theories as theories of international relations and have advocated the opening of another 'grand debate'—between International Relations and the Marxists.

Paralleling these works but not so specifically focused on the perspective of International Relations studies there developed in the late 1960s and 1970s a radical liberal/Marxist school of dependency (or *dependencia* as reminder of its Latin American origin) which whilst offering a theory of development at one and the same time embodied at least a partial theory of international relations (between centre–periphery states). In the sixties there were such major influences as Gunder Frank (1966, 67), Furtado, Cardoso and Faletto to mention a few among many others writing against a background of Latin American experiences, whilst the chief influence of the seventies was that of an Egyptian, Samir Amin, and his prolific writing on the subject (Amin, 1974, 1976, 1977, 1980). Amin took for development the notion of a fellow Marxist, that of unequal exchange (Emmanuel, 1972), through which he worked at the establishment of a direct line to Marx's concept of surplus value. Amin, joined with, and, reinforced by the parallel efforts of Immanuel Wallerstein (with main support forthcoming from the latter's *The Modern World-System*, 1974a), drove that initial idea of dependency one stage further.

Literally hundreds of books and articles have been written on the world-system approach, whose central thesis (shared with dependency) is the division into centre and periphery states with a similar asymmetrical division reproduced inside the states of the periphery. Treating the whole world as a totality the approach represents a fully-fledged rewriting of historical materialism along lines we touched on briefly above (the whole world as a totality). The states-system, although coming in for frequent mention, is considered not to constitute a separate analytical level. The result is not only disappointing to Marxists (in projecting a circulationist thesis as well as with the substitution of nations for classes etc.), but is equally unacceptable to students of International Relations. However, the relegation of the states-system and denial of its autonomy does not appear to be absolute. In a joint work by four leading proponents of the school (Amin, Arrighi, Frank, and Wallerstein), *Dynamics of the Global Crisis*, 1982, the authors recapitulate their previous positions when they imply that International Relations mistakenly focus upon a superficial (political) aspect of what is no more than a historical episode in which the states-system happened to be a part of the political structure of the world (37, 40, 41). However Samir Amin, for one, suggests that in order to 'further the materialist historical analysis of our era . . . historical materialism cannot be reduced to simply recognizing modes of production and social classes'. Instead, he says, questions have to be answered concerning nations, their relation to classes, state, states-system, the strategic aims, outlook, and nature of the USSR, of the Third World, and so on. The lack of autonomy of the states-system cannot be absolute if he concludes his list of (largely unanswered) questions by asking 'how does world politics function, what are the real conflicts, how valid are the various geopolitical analyses'! (Amin *et al.*, 1982, 170).

The theory of international relations as contained in the world system falls some way short of recounting the whole story of the Marxist interest in international relations. In addition to the prolific continuous theoretical writings of the leading contemporary Trotskyists (above all Ernest Mandel) which happens in the Trotskyist tradition always by definition to be also a theory of international relations there arrived in the 1980s another incursion into the concerns of International Relations by Marxists when in the first years of the decade some Marxists began to address themselves to the long-neglected issues of the Cold War and the relations between the USSR and the USA. E. P. Thompson's article 'Exterminism, the last stage of civilization', published in the *New Left Review* in 1980 led to the publication in 1982 of a volume containing a broad Marxist and non-Marxist left debate on the issues raised by Thompson and thus *tout court* on international politics.

Conceptualizing the states-system: world-system

Our purpose here is not to summarize what has become a vast literature on the subject: we make reference only to André Gunder Frank's, Wallerstein's, and Amin's attempts at conceptualizing the states-system.

The whole-world capitalist system consisted for *André Gunder Frank* of a chain of metropolises and satellites. The former were seen to be developing and on the ascendant, the latter reduced to a state of dependence. International relations in such a cosmology did not fare well, for in the hierarchical structure thus erected, and which enabled monopolistic powers to transfer surplus, interstate relations were only part of a larger context of such transfer mechanisms. Since Frank defined exploitation as expropriation of the surplus, it could in that conceptualization be seen as obtaining not only between countries and regions but between entities larger and smaller than these, not excluding individuals. The classes also quietly disappeared from an analysis in which 'international system' was a mere link in the chain. In his early formulations nations or states within this context hardly figured. Understandably, Frank put the word 'nation' in inverted commas to imply the spuriousness of the (national) unit. Whilst 'nations' might appear to have 'policies', they were in fact doing no more than enacting in their international intercourse the capitalist dynamic. A separate focus on states to explain international relations, either through their characteristics or by reference to their domestic structures, is discarded by Frank as analytically unsound.

Where for Frank the chain of metropolises is simply incorporated in interstate relations as one of its sections, to *Immanuel Wallerstein* the large parts of the world referred to as core and periphery are made up entirely of countries. But like Frank (Lukács and Althusser), Wallerstein insists that any social system must be seen as a totality. Nation-states are not closed systems, nor are they autonomous analytical units, but rather parts of a larger 'totality'. At this point a caveat is in order for the student of International Relations, for Wallerstein, who would at first sight appear to come very close to the Western discipline of International Relations, merely creates the illusion of doing so. In seeming to acknowledge the states-system as an

219 Marxists: The Professors

important political structure within the single-world concept and a system made necessary by the requirements of a capitalist world economy, international relations suddenly appear once again to occupy an important place in the theory. The terminology is misleading, for instead of the progression that gained currency in studies of International Relations ('states–system–international society–world society') as we defined them in our Introduction, and into which Wallerstein's two types of world-system ('world empire', 'world economy') would seem to fit, there is in fact no resemblance between the two sets of concepts—except perhaps in so far as in neither set does the term 'world' have to mean 'world-wide', simply sufficiently encompassing. Wallerstein's 'world empire' is in fact a sort of political world state with a central authority. It would seem that 'world empire' cannot be capitalist, for it is precisely the peculiar nature that capitalism assumes that transforms the 'world empire' into a 'world economy'. In Wallerstein's words: 'an empire cannot be conceived of as an entrepreneur as can a state in a world-economy. For an empire pretends to be the whole. It cannot enrich its economy by draining from other economies, since it is the only economy' (1974, 60). 'That is why the secret of capitalism was in the establishment of the division of labour within the framework of a world–economy that was *not* an empire rather than within the framework of a single national state' (ibid. 127). The term world-system is a neologism by which it is intended to refer to a broader category than does either states-system or (any particular) mode of production. 'Capitalism and a world-economy (that is, a single division of labour but multiple politics and cultures) are obverse sides of the same coin. One does not cause the other. We are merely defining the same indivisible phenomenon by different characteristics' (1974b, 391). Capitalism can and does embrace various forms of production: in fact capitalism is based on the existence of these various forms, but the world-economy remains capitalist.

Wallerstein's model consists of a web of interconnecting categories of political, economic, and 'cultural units': the acephalous world economy with one division of labour and three zones of economic activity (core, semi-periphery, and periphery) between which there exists a mutiplicity of imbalances and unequal exchange. The political organization thus becomes so interwoven with the constantly forming and re-forming numbers of ethno-national groupings as to complicate the manifestation of the main class formation. The origins of the distinction between the three areas of the division of labour (core, periphery, and semi-periphery) are explained in technological terms: Western Europe specialized in more skilled activities of well-paid wage labourers. The resulting political structure consisted of relatively strong states capable of manipulating markets. In contrast, in the periphery areas less specialized, less skilled activities led to the emergence of weak states readily brought into subordination by the core. Once in position the distinction between core and periphery is auto-regenerative: core countries have a range of methods for perpetuating their primacy over the periphery ranging from monopolistic restrictions and protectionism to their elimination by conquest. The semi-periphery acts as a 'cordon sanitaire' in preventing the otherwise inescapable onset of mutually destructive conflict between the core and periphery. The semi-periphery is also something of a halfway house: countries may proceed into the semi-periphery and from there to the core. A degradation from the core by way of the semi-periphery is also possible.

International relations, or rather states-system, are important in this schema for a number of reasons, above all because the main notion in the conceptualization of capitalism is that of the surplus transfer *between countries*. The division of labour that defines this system is 'not merely functional—that is, occupational—but geographical . . . [and is] a function of the social organisation of work, one which magnifies and legitimises the ability of some groups within the system to exploit the labour of others, that is, to receive a larger share of the surplus' (1974a, 349). The 'exploiter' and 'exploited' are not classes but countries, and capitalism is that system which brings this relation of exploitation about.

For *Samir Amin* international relations would appear to enjoy a greater autonomy. His major contribution, summarized in the title of his two most important books, is the analysis of the 'accumulation on the world scale' and his identification of the 'law of unequal development'. By adding these important theories he in fact built a hedge against such criticisms to which Frank, Wallerstein, and even Emmanuel laid themselves open.

To Amin the world economy is also divided into centre and peripheral social formations and he too built on the dependency theory:

In the system of capitalist imperialism, the centers are economically dominant, the peripheries are dominated. The capitalist system, furthermore, is the first global economic system. The central-dominant economies are autocentered, that is, complete; the peripheral dominated economies are extroverted, incomplete and hence backward. Economic domination blocks them, stops them from catching up. In this sense, the cause of backwardness is external, although it is internalized through the class alliances that reproduce it (Amin, 1980, 16–17.)

Correcting and developing Emmanuel's thesis of 'unequal exchange', both Amin and Emmanuel stand out amongst this group when they manage to establish in their definition of capitalism a linkage between production and exchange. It is a link, by the way, which seems to derive from the existence of an international system: the capital and commodities having world-wide mobility whilst labour, locked into the compartments of states, does not. Thus commodities have a single value. Capital tends to the average rate of return whilst in the circumstances of the segmented labour market (into states) there are unequal rates of surplus value. This particular discrepancy is supposed to explain the roots of exploitation and links the unequal exchange theory of Amin and Emmanuel to Marx's surplus value.

He explains the centre–periphery division by reference to the different historical circumstances in which the introduction of capitalism was effected. Unequal specialization is thus both a cause and a consequence of unequal development. But Amin's major contribution is in the magnitude of the picture he draws—in effect redrawing historical materialism in its entirety. The impression one has from reading Amin is that he treats Marx as if the latter provided us with only a few (albeit important) pieces of the puzzle, and, failing to lay his hands on the missing pieces, proceeded to assemble the picture (wrongly) from those at his disposal. Hence Marx had to invent the concept of Asiatic mode of production in order to validate his major, otherwise untenable, Marxian thesis. In this way Amin explains the logical leaps and discontinuities in the Marxian argument which

(among other perceived flaws) Amin, in his revised version c
historical materialism, corrects.

Essentially Amin redesigns the sequence of stages throug
which the world passes and he, too, manages partially t
'emancipate' the superstructural phenomena from their mech
anistic determination by economic forces when he speaks of th
'double dialectic of forces and relations of production'. He argue
that in some modes of production the relations might b
modified so as to have superstructure play a leading role—wit
the implication that states in certain social formations may pla
a dominant role. He invents an all-encompassing mode of prod
uction which he calls 'tributary' to embrace both the Asiati
mode of production and the feudal mode of production. Th
main modes of production are separated by 'transitions', whic
makes for the present world consisting of capitalism (alway
divided into centre and periphery capitalism) coexistent wit
transitional formations, a suggestion that takes him away fror
Wallerstein's insistence on the homogeneity of one (capitalis
world. There can be two types of such transitional formations
the Soviet variant of statism which can develop only in th
capitalist periphery or semi-periphery, and the state collectivi
mode of production—a transitional option for both countries c
the centre and of the periphery. The main contradiction c
capitalism—and world economy at large—is that which exist
between centre and periphery which capitalism cannot resolv
The world is heading towards one of three possible outcome
the continued dominance of imperialist capitalism, the est
blishment of nationalistic state capitalism along Soviet line
or the emergence in the periphery of real socialism in glob
competition with imperialist capitalism and state capita
ism.

Historical materialism to Amin provides a universall
applicable set of concepts without which narrative history, an
presumably also an account of international relations, is capabl
of only immediate explanations. History is, in the final analysi
the history of class struggle, but (Amin carries on Marx's famou
dictum) classes are contained in a specific society—bounded b
state or nations. In fact class struggle in the centre is no longe
a motive force of history (ibid. 188) but is to be found instea
in the struggle of the peripheral nations, with the peasantr

ranking as the most revolutionary class. Then comes his assertion: that these societies do not constitute (as at present they do) a
system and can no longer be studied (as they may at present) at the
societal level, but instead at the level of the global system. It is a
conclusion Amin shares with Wallerstein. To Amin, international
relations do matter: in order to analyse the systemic contradictions of the world these contradictions have to be placed in the
framework of the real international political 'conjecture' of the
period. Amin acknowledges that the 'confrontations which
occupy centre stage are those between states, east and west, north
and south' (ibid. 242), but whilst explaining the North–South confrontation (capitalist centre versus periphery, which is the main
world-system's contradiction) he does not explain the East–West
interstate confrontation. The Soviet Union is 'not socialist'; it is
'in transition', and from some of Amin's phrases appears to be
superior to the capitalist system in which the class struggle is seen
to be stagnant. One is given to wonder whether this 'statist mode
of production' of the Soviet variety is that 'necessary stage' after
capitalism through which the world is to pass. He does say elsewhere that the Soviet model does not lead to communism, which
he regards as the certain destination of mankind.

The world as a 'structured totality', theories of social formations and of state

Except perhaps for the term 'mode of production' the Marxist
approach, antithetical to that of world-system, has found no
such instantly popular name. It is to be remarked of course that
the Marxists we refer to now are in at best only loose agreement
with each other, and indeed in most cases, beyond acceptance
of the basics of the approach, the differences amongst the authors
range widely. Our intention here is to do again no more than
trace this orientation as an alternative avenue of Marxist thinking on international relations.

The writing on the subject shares some common features that
separate this orientation from that of the world-system authors.
First of all, they reject the world-systemists' changed definition
of capitalism, Laclau's critique of Frank (Laclau, 1971, reprinted
1977), having in itself become a classic statement of this position: '. . . for Marx—as it is obvious to anyone who has even

a superficial acquaintance with his work—capitalism was a mode
of *production*. The fundamental economic relationship of
capitalism is constituted by the free labourer's sale of his labour
power, whose necessary precondition is the loss by the direct
producer of ownership of the means of production' (Laclau, 1977,
23). Laclau's argument relies on an emphasis on the distinction
between 'modes of production' on the one hand and 'economic
systems' on the other, according to which 'mode of production'
is 'an integrated complex of social productive forces and relations
linked to a determinate type of ownership of the means of
production' (ibid. 34) and 'economic system' is 'the mutual
relations between the different sectors of the economy, or between
different production units, whether on a regional, national or
world scale' (ibid. 35). In other words economic system can
include among its constituent elements different modes of
production. A similar distinction is made by Althusser and Balibar
(1970), Foster-Carter (1978) between mode of production on the
one hand and social formation on the other just as (they point out)
it is in a neglected passage of Marx himself. According to Balibar
for example, mode of production is an abstract, timeless concept
which one cannot ever find in real life in pure form. Mode of
production in its pure form is defined by a particular relation
connecting two classes in class (as opposed to classless) modes of
production. Social formation is also a conceptual construct but of
a more concrete kind. Whilst Althusser and Balibar insisted that
in each social formation there is always one predominant mode
of production except in the transitional stages, P. P. Rey's (and
Laclau's) innovation is expressed in the view that the social
formation (for Rey) and economic system (for Laclau) may contain
several modes of production. The resulting departure from
classical Marxism is obvious. For classical Marxists modes of
production were conceived of as successive (and progressive)
stages. The process of transition, even in classical Marxism, was
recognized as a complex process in the course of which an old
mode of production continues to dominate in the time it takes for
the new mode to come to maturity and take over. Over a
considerable period of time the reverse is true and the new mode
of production dominates whilst the old continues in existence
before disappearing. The contemporary Marxists—among them
Arrighi and Perry Anderson, the French structuralists Althusser

and Balibar, and French anthropologists such as Rey, Terray, and Meillasoux—modify radically many of the classical Marxist ideas. Anderson (1974) questions for instance the idea of one mode of production being born out of another and gives as example the feudal mode of production that arose from the catastrophic collision and fusion of two dissolving modes (primitive Germanic and ancient Roman), Balibar argues (Althusser and Balibar, 1970) that the new mode of production is not necessarily built inside but may be outside the old mode of production. Rey expresses the view that the processes of transition take place over so long a period of time that transitions are effectively the normal state of affairs. Thus the idea of progress as well as staged sequence is lost. Hindess and Hirst argue in fact that there is no logical or teleological way of ordering these possibilities: that all there is left is radical indeterminacy (Hindess and Hirst, 1975).

What are the implications in these conceptualizations for international relations? The level of analysis is back from the one world (of the world-system approach) to the level of its constituent parts. As Brenner puts it in his critique of Wallerstein (Brenner, 1977), different parts of the world economy have their own dynamic and tendencies that derive from the modes of production installed there. Whilst they are by no means independent of each other, the analysis should start once again from the workings of distinct modes of production and only then proceed to an analysis of their interactions with one another. We are back in other words to the classical Marxist notion of the domestic structure of societies determining their external behaviour. Many authors (e.g. Krippendorff) support this thesis—Mandel in his uneven development thesis, for example, argues that the world is made up of a variety of modest of production united by capitalist modes of exchange. In fact Amin's own work borders on this same position—of perceiving a unity of world system on the one hand and at the same time recognizing variety in coexisting modes of production within it. But although we said that the world-system approach of the Wallerstein variety led to a denial of the autonomy of international relations, international (or state) system in the world-system conceptualization was still relatively much more important than it is in this 'structured totality' approach. For

the latter group international relations are less important because it is the internal features—in this case of the Third World
societies—that are to be blamed for the slow development, and
the 'underdevelopment" (more often than not the major 'problematique') is *not* a result of external factors. Many of these
authors (e.g. Rey, 1973, 16) reject totally the idea of 'underdevelopment' and return to Marx and Luxemburg in their belief
that although capitalism has an inherent proclivity to expand
at the expense of pre-capitalist societies, capitalism cannot be
blamed for the Third World societies' immiseration. One could
obviously complete the picture provided by these theories and
assemble the theories of external behaviour of individual social
formations in order to arrive at a composite picture of international system as a whole. Most authors would designate the
overall state of the international system as transitory, based on
a conflict of 'articulating modes of production'(?) within social
formations as well as between them. The latter (states-system)
does not, however, play an important part, or, alternatively, not
enough attention is paid to the problem. One of the reasons
would appear to be that most of these social formations (once
again the primary analytical units) are regarded as being in a
stage of 'transition'. In such an indeterminate state the principle
of domestic structure as determinant of foreign policy crumbles.
We should perhaps repeat here our earlier word of caution: that
none of these authors is explaining international relations, and
by forcing a statement on the subject from the content of their
writing we may do some an injustice. Yet for many of them,
like it or not, international relations at certain points assume
an extremely important role. Perry Anderson, for example,
shows that as the international system emerged from the feudal
mode of production it took a most active part in accommodating
and fostering the development of the new (capitalist) mode of
production. As Anderson puts it in a conclusion that could come
from the pens of the world-system authors:

Laws and States, dismissed as secondary and insubstantial, reemerge
with a vengeance, as the apparent authors of the most momentous break
in modern history. In other words, once the whole structure of
sovereignty and legality is *disassociated* from the economy of universal
feudalism, the shadow paradoxically governs the world: for it becomes

the only principle capable of explaining the differential development of the whole [capitalist] mode of production.

And later:

the feudal mode of production, itself wholly 'pre-national' in character, objectively prepared the possibility of a multinational state system in the epoch of its subsequent transition to capitalism (Anderson, 1974, 403, 412).

In contrast to the world-system approach, in which nationalism, although recognized (as ethno-national consciousness), performs no special or decisive role, in the context of structured totality approaches based on the coexisting multiplicity of modes of production and interdependence of such modes, nationalism can be conceptualized as providing a powerful basis for resistance to subordination propelled by economic forces. Tom Nairn resurrects the explanation of nationalism as a consequence of the uneven development of capitalism implied in theories of imperialism. The rising but still weak bourgeoisie in this interpretation contrive a development of capitalism frequently in the circumstances of attempts at subordination (by the bourgeoisie of other states). As we have remarked (Chapter 3) nationalism for the early theorists of imperialism enabled the bourgeoisie to mobilize the only available defence: the people (cf. Nairn, 1977).

But as far as the world view of 'structured totality' is concerned, except for fleeting moments when international relations are acknowledged as playing a part, the 'articulation of neighbouring social formations' (a Marxist code word for international relations?) does not arouse much enthusiasm in the Marxists.

The indeterminacy in regard to the conceptualization of the states-system is shared also by Marxist theories of state and of class as in, for example, the fashionable thesis of the 'relative autonomy of the state' vis-à-vis the classes. For instance Poulantzas denies the one-to-one correspondence between the needs of capitalist accumulation and the policies of the state, whilst acknowledging that the state remains biased towards the goals of the 'hegemonic fraction' of the bourgeoisies, i.e. in order to meet the needs of capitalist accumulation. State to Poulantzas is a 'relation', or more precisely 'the condensate of a relation of power between struggling classes . . . conceiving of the capitalist State as a relation as being structurally shot through and constituted with and by class contradictions . . . [which means] . . . that the state that is destined to reproduce class divisions cannot be a monolithic, fissureless bloc, but is itself, by virtue of its very structure (the state is a relation), divided . . .' (Poulantzas, 1976, 74–5). But what exactly is the connection between the hegemonic fraction of the bourgeoisies, the economy, and the state that Poulantzas assumes does create the consistent historical bias of the state in favour of the fraction? As some critics argue, it leaves us either with a leap of faith or sophisticated economism. Although Miliband's 'relative auto-nomy' of the state is differently conceived, it leads us into the same impasse. International relations would be relations not of those 'relations' as understood by Poulantzas but as 'relations between (relatively autonomous) state apparatuses'. But again we come against the problem of identifying that factor that would determine the nature of the relationship. Although both Miliband and Poulantzas recognize that there is something there beyond the state, perfunctory recognition of an old Marxian axiom[3] is not enough.

The types of international relations?

In the circumstances of great intellectual as well as political disagreement among Marxists can one descry first of all any common features that they share in the interpretation of what Amin calls the 'political conjecture of the period' and, second,

---

[3] 'Here, perhaps even more than in other fields, the purposes which governments proclaim their wish to serve are often made to appear remote from specific economic concerns, let alone capitalist interests. It is the national interest, national security, national independence, honour, greatness etc. that is their concern. But this naturally includes a sound, healthy, thriving economic system; . . . [and] thus, by the same mechanism which operates in regard to home affairs, the governments of capitalist countries have generally found that their larger national purposes required the servicing of capitalist interests; and the crucial place which these interests occupy in the life of their country has always caused governments to make their defence against foreign capitalist interests, and against the foreign states which protect *them*, a prime consideration in their conduct of external affairs' (Miliband, 1969, 83–4).

what theories are implied in this more specific understanding of international affairs?

It is beyond our present scope even to attempt to throw light on divergencies in the analysis of the evolution of the states-system—the starting-point for many Marxists, among them Krippendorff, Amin, Wallerstein. Instead we focus on the 'current' epoch, and essentially on the period since World War II, a period on which Marxists disagree with each other at virtually every step of the interpretation. But the main contours would seem to be as follows. After World War II there arose a new stage of imperialism and, irrespective of whether or not it was accompanied by structural changes in the capitalist system, a new phenomenon came into existence, namely US hegemony across the entire imperialist system. Conceptually this implies either a new (US hegemonic) type of state or at least a new, previously unknown type of state behaviour unfamiliar to her capitalist bedfellows. The multinational companies, whose existence is claimed to represent a recent vindication of the accuracy of virtually all Marxist and Leninist theses (uneven development, concentration and centralization of capital, and its internationalization) are seen in this interpretation, despite the issuance of a smokescreen of 'transnationalism', to distract attention from their real (United States) home and base as an American fifth column/foreign legion. In those early stages of the US hegemony the USSR was still in a state of confinement, which had resulted, so the argument runs, from highly success-ful US policies designed to create an atmosphere of what Joyce Kolko refers to as the 'so-called "Cold War" ' (J. Kolko, 1974). From the mid-sixties onward however US hegemony came under attack from nearly every quarter. The strongest challenge (coupled with the US fiasco in Vietnam and other failed Third World policies) issued from the successful national liberation movements of the Third World. That, together with the challenge of growing European and Japanese capital, exposed American weakness, creating a vacuum which, without the expenditure of any great effort, was filled by the USSR.

In the seventies, according to most of these interpretations, the American ploy of 'détente' was engineered, whose purpose since has been to make up for the lost territories of the Third World and to incorporate into the American orbit also the vast markets of East Europe and of the USSR. The USSR became a lifebuoy sustaining a shattered US hegemony. Apart from—most notably—the Chinese version which at this point portrays the USSR as a chief villain representing a new variant of (social) imperialism, most Marxists concentrated on studying the effect of the successful US 'transideological enterprise' (A. G. Frank) of co-opting the 'East' economically, with once again the invaluable aid of multinational companies. The USSR in such renditions is conceived of as a superpower as it were by default (a 'giant with clay feet' [Amin *et al.*, 1982, 8]) whilst on her own she lacks in particular the economic drive to match the other superpower's hegemony.

An inescapable impression gained from most such Marxist writings is that if there is any implied real determinant of the states-system as well as of the foreign policies of individual states it is—the dynamism of the US hegemony. The portrayal of the world subscribed to by most Marxists in the West and in the Third World is that of a world consisting of hierarchical structures of exploitation, hegemony, and subordination with the states, like the toys of children shuffled hither and thither by US imperialism. It is not a world state but effectively if differs from one in hardly any respect. In such a reading there is in other words no room for a states-system, with its anarchical structure, sovereignty, international law, diplomacy, and preoccupation with East–West conflict, arms race, and so on—these until the early eighties constituting the most conspicuously absent topics in Western and Third World Marxism. Until the recent debate created by the concept of 'exterminism' there has been, curiously enough, no adequate theory of cold war. Unlike the North–South conflict central to most Marxist analyses and laden with economic substance, the East and the West—the degree depending on the individual author—would appear to have been little more than the two parties joined in an ultra-imperialist collusive relationship or locked in inter-imperialist rivalry. Such a conclusion is in itself in contravention of the tenets of Marxist analysis. For unless an equation can be reasonably established between the social formations in the West and in the East, the East–West relationship is trivialized to the status of a giant parlour game, devoid (to an unpardonable extent in Marxist analyses) of economic substance—or worse still, engagement in a nuclear arms race without heed to the consequences.

Certainly the analysis of the USSR upon which any analysis of the East–West conflict is predicated extends Marxist resourcefulness to the full.

An exploration of the anatomy of the USSR raises again complex questions about the nature of the world economy, its structure and coherence, up to and including the possibility of social formations based on different modes of production, coexisting side by side. For although the problem of coexisting elements of different modes of production *within* a social formation has attracted considerable attention, not all the writers on the subject have pushed it to the logical conclusion of coexisting social formations based on such mixes of modes of production. The Trotskyists and world-system approaches have generally argued *against* such a possibility. There were, however, other Marxists who concluded that although the USSR is *not* capitalist, nevertheless the possibility of its becoming so could not be ruled out. After these 'preliminary' questions, there are others with important political implications: the question of the definition of capitalism, the nature of class and class struggle; matching these elements against the Soviet experience; the nature of the communist party, of central planning and its relation to a market economy, etc., etc.

It is then no wonder that *dependencia* authors often tried to ignore the USSR and conceptualize the core and periphery as 'two halves', thus leaving out another substantial dimension—to make the surprised discovery that their analysis does not apply to Soviet relations with her communist periphery. Nor did they come to grips with the argument that it is in fact the North-west–Northeast dimension of the conflict that threatens global peace and the future of mankind, *as well as* continuing to exacerbate the so-called North-South conflict. If the plight of the South is to do with the shortage of wealth alone then it could hardly be clearer that the Northeast–Northwest conflict absorbs that amount and more in annual expenditure towards escalation of an irrational arms race. As Peter Wiles points out: 'There is no North–South tension, for the "North" is divided practically into two and the "South" into many: simply the Northeast has moved South, and the Cold War covers the globe'

(Wiles, 1982, 363). We will now—consistently with the pattern adopted in earlier chapters—turn in greater detail to the 'types' of international relations, inter-capitalist first of all as well as that of the Cold War (old and 'the new') as a separate category or indeed a subtype of inter-capitalist relations.

Relations amongst capitalist states

When we try to strip Marxist writing on the ever-popular theme of 'crisis of capitalism' of its economic overburden, we soon discover that, as far as types of inter-capitalist relations are concerned, not much advance has been made in this area since Lenin and his generation: relations amongst capitalist states are regarded as being based either on Kautsky's old thesis of 'ultra-imperialism' or on Bukharin's and Lenin's thesis of 'inter-capitalist rivalry'. Some Marxists add a new category—that of superimperialism or hegemony, a category specially created for the USA. Poulantzas, for one, acknowledged this fact when precisely along these lines he divided the entire field of writers on the subject of 'metropolitan capitalism' into two categories. In the first category, Paul Sweezy, Harry Magdoff, Martin Nicolaus, Pierre Jalée, etc. are representative of what Poulantzas calls a modern left-wing version of Kautskyite theory of 'ultra-imperialism'.[4] The writers of the first group, whilst agreeing on the dominant role of the United States in the capitalist world as a whole, tend to underestimate the inter-imperialist contradictions that stem from the continuing uneven development of capitalism, and see the sole line of cleavage within the imperialist bloc as that between metropolises and dominated formations. Within that context the relations among the imperialist metropolises themselves are conceived of as characterized by pacification and an integration under the uncontested dominance of and exploitation by American capital. In fact the relationship is analogous to that of neo-colonialism—as, for example, that existing between Canada and the United States. The dominant theme, then, is the virtual disappearance of national state power within the American superpower or

[4] cf. Baran and Sweezy, 1966; Magdoff, 1969; Jalée, 1970 and 1968. Also Robin Murray, 'The Internationalisation of Capital and the Nation State', *New Left Review*, 67, 1971.

the disappearance of that (state) power under the domination of American or 'international monopoly capital freed from its state "fetters" ' (Poulantzas, 1975, 38, 39).

In the second category of writers there are two subgroups: the first consists (according to Poulantzas) of those who continue to regard the main type of relations amongst capitalist states as deriving from the traditionally postulated inter-imperialist contradictions, and who see 'independent' states as still struggling for hegemony with one another. The tendency towards internationalization affects only market relations and the 'national bourgeoisies' and 'national states' remain disconnected from each other (cf. Ernest Mandel, Michael Kidron, Bill Warren, Bob Rowthorn, J. Valier). Here also the only structural cleavage in the imperialist chain is that between the metropolises and the dominated formations.[5] The second subgroup (made up largely of the theorists of the French Communist Party) see a modification of the capitalist mode of production into national 'state monopoly capitalism', simply juxtaposed and added together. The EEC and the steps taken towards European unification are seen as the expression of an increased domination by American capital, domination which however adds only one new supernumerary function to the 'national functions' of these states.

Poulantzas extends the neo-Marxist dependency analysis when he suggests that the relationship between the centre and periphery (as described by neo-Marxists) had in fact a profound influence (largely overlooked by Marxists) on the centre (or core) countries themselves. In a 'metropolitan' version of dependency Poulantzas argues that whilst the line of demarcation and cleavage between the metropolises and the dominated formations is becoming sharper and deeper a structure of domination and dependency is being established also within the imperialist chain, i.e. amongst the capitalist states. This structure is by no means ultra–imperialist and is different from the centre – periphery relations. Poulantzas argues that it is in fact a different type of relation, hegemony (elsewhere also called super-imperialism),

[5] E. Mandel, *Europe versus America*, NLB, 1970; Michael Kidron, *Western Capitalism Since the War*, 1968; Bill Warren, 'How International is Capital?', in *New Left Review*, 68, 1971; Bob Hawthorn, 'Imperialism in the Seventies: Unity or Rivalry', *New Left Review*, 69, 1971; J. Valier, 'Imperialisme et revolution permanente', in *Critiques de l'economie politique*, Nos. 4–5, 1971.

characteristic of United States imperialism and typical of her special capitalist needs. The United States and other imperialist states are locked in a struggle over the domination and exploitation of the periphery, whilst in the course of the struggle the latter are subjected to a sort of 'structural dependence' under United States hegemony. The hegemony is based on subtle economic mechanisms (ibid. 44 ff.) to do with the new international division of labour concocted by the United States, the international centralization of money capital (in American hands either directly applied, or heavily disguised as 'autonomous' European ownership). This process goes hand in hand with the expansion of ideological conditions as embodied in a 'series of practices, know-how, customs and rituals which extend to the economic domain as well' (ibid.).

Although Poulantzas does not say so, he seems to correlate what we identified earlier as the world-system (dependency) approaches with the interpretation of relations amongst metropolitan countries based on ultra-imperialism, in the manner of Kautsky. On the other hand he correlates the 'structured totality' approach with the inter-imperialist rivalries of Lenin and Bukharin; and as far as he himself is concerned (again without mention of the fact), he applies a variant of Gramsci's idea of hegemony when he conceptualizes a modern admixture of overt imperialist relations (amongst capitalist states) with their attendant cultural, ideological, etc. functions of confusing, and inducing acceptance of American hegemony. The essence of these distinctions is in the degree of resistance offered to the march of United States imperialism. The ultra-imperialist thesis sees the countries pacified, and integrating on the basis of their own consent. The inter-capitalist contradictions thesis sees lesser capitalist states either effectively negated, or eclipsed (above all through the agency of the multinational corporations). The hegemony thesis sees them cajoled as well as tricked into subordination. All three relations are based on a mix of economic, political, and ideological methods the precise proportions of the constituent components not always being made clear.

The analysis of the 'Cold War'[6]

One has to wonder, however, to what extent would the three types of inter-capitalist relations have to be altered to allow for the accommodation in the same system of states of the USSR. For if the Eastern theorists are correct in their description, and if it were to be accepted that upwards of twenty countries (including one superpower, one great power, and a number of important regional powers) were in their foreign policies enacting a Marxist revolutionary design (the degree of success achieved so far is of no consequence) then surely the whole interpretation of the present epoch would be different, and less focused on the rise and decline of American hegemony? Indeed questions that otherwise seem to go unasked—or appear to be sedulously avoided—would require to be answered: for example to what extent is the Western theorists' ultra-imperialism (or at least the assumed reduction of contradictions characteristic of the 1970s) a product not of theoretical but of political considerations stemming from distrust/fear of the Soviet Union on the part of the USA? For our part we wonder what is the nature of the theoretical block that produces such pronounced inattention to the analysis of inter-imperialist war? Is it because of the 'hope' that in the nuclear stand-off situation there can be no such war? Or does United States-Soviet political understanding on the subject preclude the possibility?

As we noted earlier, there has never been an adequate theory of the Cold War by Marxists. The US 'revisionist' historians, vaguely connected through the New Left to Marxism (e.g. William Appleman Williams, Gabriel Kolko, Gar Alperovitz, David Horowitz, Ronald Steel, *et al.*) came closest to a comprehensive theory of the East–West conflict with the rather unexpected result of attracting Soviet gratitude. One Soviet historian noted, '[o]ften people find that their arguments coincide with the Soviet point of view. Without a question, this is correct—the "revisionists", somewhat tardily, have agreed

[6] It is of some interest that the term Cold War was used for the first time by Bernstein in the *Neue Zeit* in 1893: 'This continued arming, compelling the others to keep up with Germany is itself a kind of warfare. I do not know whether this expression has been used previously but one could say it is a cold war [ein Kalter Krieg]. There is no shooting, but there is bleeding' i.e. in the sense of squandering wealth needed for social reform (quoted in Fletcher, 1981, 420).

with Soviet historians regarding who bears the responsibility for the cold war and who is to blame that the reasonable possibilities in American–Soviet relations were not realized' (Sivachev and Yakovlev, 1979, 214),[7] W. A. Williams in his bulky *chef-d'œuvre*, *The Tragedy of American Diplomacy*, devotes a few pages in this history of the Cold War to the role of the Soviet Union. Of which, seeming to merit Sivachev's plaudits he writes:

> . . . the sources of Russian conduct are the drives to conquer poverty and achieve basic security in the world of nation states. From these efforts developed, on the one hand, the practices and traditions of centralized power to force savings, allocate investment, and maintain security . . . and the ambivalence of a foreign policy at once militarily and suspiciously defensive, yet characterized by a missionary desire to help other men save themselves (Williams, 1959, 191).

Essentially all US 'revisionist' historians agreed that it was the dictates of US imperialism that had caused the East to 'react' and escalate. Concurring in this regard fully with the Soviet analysis of the Cold War then and now, they place the blame on only one source of evil: capitalism and its chief exponent, the USA. Whilst, however, the Soviet analysts accord the East–West conflict a most significant and central socio-economic content, the Western Marxists and the 'revisionist' historians of the Cold War do not.

The reasons for this curious attitude are not difficult to find. The very existence of the Soviet Union has baffled Marxists and since the twenties has represented something of an intellectual challenge to them and to non-Marxists alike—with Otto Bauer one of the first Marxist sovietologists.[8] It is characteristic, of course, that whilst political movements on the left have always been obliged to define very clearly their position on the USSR as an inevitable referent to their existence, Western professors have felt no such pressing need—a politically convenient omission commented upon by no less a figure than George Lukács. Thus neither the wide disagreement that exists amongst

---

[7] See also O. L. Stepanova, 'Istoriki "revizionisty" o vneshnej politike SShA' [The 'revisionist' historians on the foreign policy of the US], *Voprosy istorii*, No. 3, 1973, pp. 105, 107.

[8] cf. Otto Bauer, *Kapitalismus und Sozialismus nach dem Weltkrieg*, 1931, *Zwischen Zwei Weltkriegen?* 1936, *Der Neue Kurs in Sowjetrussland*, 1921, *Bolshewismus oder Sozialdemokratie*, 1920.

students of the Soviet social formation—nor the 'Marxist sovietology' itself—is new. Several authors have tried to list the possible Marxist interpretations of the USSR (cf. Chase-Dunn, 1982; Carlo, 1974; Beliss, 1979). It is our impression that the different positions vary more significantly on the *internal* functioning of the Soviet-type social formation than on the explanation of her foreign policies. The difference, particularly between positions 2–4 (below) on her foreign policies are ambivalent, and most of them would seem to fit with the same degree of compatibility into the persisting Marxist reading of the present 'historical conjecture', as we summarized it earlier on. The final, fifth position which sees both the USSR as well as the USA involved in the 'exterminist' race abandons largely the Marxist framework in favour of a determinism by the state-system.

1. The USSR as a *socialist* formation (the Soviets' own claim to this effect is supported by a few Western Marxists, cf. Albert Szymanski, 1979, 1981).
2. The USSR as a *deformed workers' state* i.e. with deformations confined to her superstructure. The USSR 'degenerated' from an original proletarian democracy whilst her Eastern bloc countries, China, North Korea, Cuba, and Vietnam were 'deformed' from the outset (the position characteristic of the Trotskyist movement).
3. The USSR as a *post-revolutionary society*, neither socialist, nor capitalist, but a new class formation (Sweezy, 1980; Bahro, 1978; Tictin, 1973).
4. The USSR as a *state-capitalist formation* (Bettelheim, the PRC, Binns, Mattick, Wallerstein, Arrighi, but also Schachtman, Burnham, Rizzi).
5. Both the USSR and the USA with any differences in socio-economic foundations obliterated as victims of *exterminism* (Thompson, 1980, 1982).

To comment briefly on these positions: Szymanski shares the thesis with the Trotskyists that the USSR has a socialist socio-economic foundation and thus he is able to postulate that there is no 'structural compulsion' for her to behave imperialistically. Szymanski concedes that the USSR has been known to dominate nations politically but describes that domination of East

Europe—not yet of the Third World—as not imperialist but only hegemonistic. He admits that as a result of such behaviour the USSR exploited other nations' workers and secured for herself special economic gains (Szymanski, 1979, 103, 179).

The Trotskyist position (2) regards the USSR as a bureaucratically deformed workers' state somewhere between capitalism and socialism. The state is dominated *not by a class* but by a social layer which usurped the fruits of the October Revolution when the expected world revolution did not eventuate. Consistent with our rendition of the Soviet ideology (Chapter 4) the Trotskyists see the role of Marxism–Leninism and of the professed goal of communism as the most important integrative mechanism and the sole factor legitimizing the rule of the bureaucratic caste. Where Trotsky in his *Revolution Betrayed* (and in other pieces according to his followers) erred was in his underestimation of the longevity of the Soviet regime whose collapse followed by a restoration of capitalism he regarded as imminent, *unless* forestalled by the overthrow of the bureaucracy in a working-class uprising, and world revolution. Of interest to us here is whether, in the event of the economic substructure's being regarded as superior to the capitalist, it follows that Soviet foreign policy is also directed to the pursuit of superior non-capitalist goals? Between Trotsky and later proponents of his position there is, however, a significant difference. Trotsky himself quite unequivocally and explicitly abandoned the foreign policy–domestic structure axiom. In 1935 in his article 'The Workers' State and the Question of Thermidor and Bonapartism' he discussed the dual role of the Soviet bureaucracy: on the one hand, the defence of the economic base of the workers' state against world imperialism and international reaction, and on the other, a conservative outlook (characteristic of all bureaucracies) and a need to maintain the 'balance of power' in the international arena in which the advance of world revolutuion and the independent activity of the international proletariat would in any event threaten its own position. It is an interesting twist to the argument and one that leads Trotsky to the conclusion that whilst the bureaucracy was obliged to arrive at a 'working compromise' with imperialism if its rule was to remain secure, it would in so doing have simultaneously undermined the stability of the economic base upon which that rule was predicated (Beliss, op. cit. 66).

In a paragraph that foreshadowed much of the modern dependency argument Trotsky argued:

The pressure of imperialism on the Soviet Union has as its aim the alteration of the very nature of the Soviet society. The struggle—today peaceful, tomorrow military—concerns the forms of property. In its capacity of a transmitting mechanism in this struggle, the bureaucracy leans now on the proletariat against imperialism, now on imperialism against the proletariat, in order to increase its own power. At the same time it mercilessly exploits its role as distributor of the meagre necessities of life in order to safeguard its own well-being and power. By this token the rule of the proletariat assumes an abridged, curbed, distorted character. One can with full justification say that the proletariat, *ruling* in one backward and isolated country, still remains an *oppressed* class. The source of oppression is world imperialism; the mechanism of transmission of the oppression—the bureaucracy. If in these words 'a ruling and at the same time an oppressed class' there is a contradiction, then it flows not from the mistakes of thought but from the contradiction in the very situation of the U.S.S.R. (Trotsky, 1970, 94.)

Notwithstanding many arguments as to detail most Trotskyists in the past viewed the Soviet Union's foreign policy—Stalinism above all—as being on a counter-revolutionary par with fascism, but more recently, when forced to choose between the USA and USSR, the preference has been for the latter (cf. Thompson *et al.*, 1982, *passim*). And thus Ernest Mandel can come to the somewhat startling conclusion that by building and stockpiling nuclear weapons the USSR has saved humanity thus far from a nuclear holocaust! (Mandel, 1983, 28).

The third option also allows the view of the USSR as a 'lesser evil'. Neither socialist nor capitalist (a feature shared with the Trotskyists), the USSR is post-revolutionary but (unlike the Trotskyist) it is a new *class* society in which the state is used by a combined bureaucrat–technocrat class to exploit the workers. There are many variations of detail: Rizzi for instance described the proletariat in the USSR as outright slaves and capitalism everywhere necessarily leading towards this new mode, or on the other hand Carlo saw the USSR as only a future model, which could be transplanted, for underdeveloped countries as indeed it was in East Europe, through a military occupation, in these areas, however, its functioning was impaired, it soon entered into serious crisis and remained artificial and shortlived (Carlo, 1974, 70 ff.). But for foreign policy this approach too is ambivalent. Most of these authors tend to see the Soviet foreign policies as superior and preferable to those of capitalist states, a view often shared with the world-system authors. For them, too, the world-economy is capitalist, and parts are by definition capitalist also. Wallerstein's argument, recalling that of Trotsky, explains that the 'various groups' which arise 'out of the structural contradictions of the capitalist world-economy' and which 'seem to take organizational forms as movements, as parties, and sometimes as regimes' precisely when they become regimes, are 'caught in the dilemma of becoming part of the machinery of the capitalist world-economy they are presuming to change'. The implications of Wallerstein's approach are twofold. First, whilst other supporters of the 'state capitalism' thesis do not rule out the possibility that other countries might in the future be more successful in revolutions to come, Wallerstein like Trotsky dismisses, a priori, any such possibility, for, as he says, 'inevitably they "betray" in part their stated goals'. It is not much consolation to future revolutionaries to learn that the movements that gave birth to such regimes represent 'real forces' and that they 'contribute to the long-run process of social transformation' (Wallerstein, 1975, 26) particularly in the light of his prognosis that the capitalist world-economy has another 300 years to run! Second, the East–West confrontation once again is reduced in importance. Wallerstein said at the beginning of *détente* that it simply meant the Soviet Union's abandoning its designs in the world system: 'the relations of the hegemonic powers are only one of the many issues that confront the world-system' (Wallerstein, 1975, 17).

The view of the USSR as capitalist and negative in her foreign policy gained currency amongst Marxists particularly when the PRC herself adopted that interpretation in her thesis of the USSR as a social–imperialist superpower. Meticulously elaborated, the theoretical foundation was developed in the course of observation of the USSR over a number of decades, and in a series of books by the French Marxist economist Charles Bettelheim.

Bettelheim's views attracted criticism from fellow Marxists (see Introduction to Bettelheim by Barry Hindess, *Economic Calculations and Forms of Property*, London, 1976) that removed any possibility of general acceptance by Marxists of the interpretation in spite of its theoretical erudition. Bettelheim based his diagnosis on the capitalist nature of Soviet enterprise (based on the separation of workers from the means of production, and the separation of the means of production from each other) thereby differing from proponents of the (state capitalist) thesis such as Cliff and Binns who, more interestingly from our point of view, introduce a more elaborate international nexus. For example Peter Binns saw the capitalism of the USSR as a function of military competition and arms production. Tony Cliff in an earlier work had concluded that it was military competition that led to an accumulation of capital which caused social differentiation and the rise of a new class: thus value and accumulation in that system are not, as they are elsewhere, internally determined but (reminiscent of Bahro) externally determined, and the entire system of the USSR, East Europe, China, North Korea, Cuba, Vietnam, etc. is thus conceived to revolve around a defence system. For these authors, therefore, the East–West conflict is essentially yet another offshoot of inter-capitalist contradictions and imperialist rivalries. It is a similar argument to that explored in Paul Mattick's *Marx and Keynes* (London, 1971).

E. P. Thompson, leader of European Nuclear Disarmament and distinguished British historian of the left, moving further along the explanatory spectrum of the USSR and of the Cold War, explicitly rejects those traditional Marxist attitudes (our 1–3 and partly 4) which in their sympathetic approach to the USSR suggested that as there is no profit motive in the USSR the 'fault' for the arms race lies only with the West. The dozen or so authors responding in that volume, and later to Thompson's challenge, essentially restate their respective positions, located somewhere along our continuum of positions. How, Thompson asks, do we know that the culpability is not also shared by the USSR? Can states and bureaucracies not have motives for arming? (Thompson, 1982, 7). Although Raymond Williams sees 'exterminism' as a result of technological determinism the concept can be interpreted as also a result of *determinism by the states-system*, that in fact enabled such technological developments in the first place. Thompson argues along lines anticipated by all 'revisionists' of the Second International, but particularly by Liebknecht, that militarism has a dynamism all of its own when he says that 'nuclear weapons and their attendant support-system seem to grow of their own accord, as if possessed by an independent will' (ibid. 5). His term 'relative autonomy' is reminiscent of all those Marxists and Marxist 'revisionists' trying to break out of the Procrustean bed of economic determinism. But for Marxists Thompson of course goes too far. We are here, he says, at a point beyond class analysis: 'exterminism' is not a 'class issue'; it is a human issue. Certain 'revolutionary posturing and rhetoric can in fact inflame exterminist ideology and are thus luxuries mankind should do without' (ibid. 28). Exterminism is to him obviously a product largely of interstate politics, of the seemingly invincible states-system which, with its peculiar illogic, exacerbated all the inequalities on which it is based, produced militarism that has led to the development of the monster superpowers. This bipolarism, that 'fulcrum upon which power turns', is to Thompson a field of force which further engenders armies, diplomacies, and ideologies, which imposes client relationships upon lesser powers and exports militarism into the periphery. In this reading, then, it is of little moment whether one superpower is driven by 'imperialism' and the other is 'post-revolutionary', 'socialist', or 'deformed socialist'. It no longer matters whose posture is defined as 'overwhelmingly defensive' or 'basically defensive' for the fact remains that mankind is in acute danger of annihilation. 'It means rather little to peer into the entrails of two differing modes of production, searching for auguries as to the future, if we are so inattentive as to overlook what these modes produce, namely the means of war' (ibid. 4).

Thompson echoes Engels's fears of fatally destructive weapons, Luxemburg's 'catastrophism', and, like Liebknecht and Luxemburg, despairing, finds solace in the peace movement. But he acknowledges substantial differences between his concept and that of imperialism: where imperialism is an unequal relation of an exploitation of a victim, exterminism simply confronts itself. It confronts an equal. It is a non-dialectical contradiction, a state of absolute antagonism, a deadly symmetry of overkill on both sides, in which both powers grow through confrontation, and which can only be resolved by mutual confrontation (ibid. 24). Thompson's concept is in fact a pathological caricature of the Soviets' own notion of the class struggle, that is to say peaceful coexistence, with substantial affinity also to the Chinese portrayal of the 'First World'. It is a mix of a version of convergence theory, arms race theory, and imperialist rivalry, all three pressed *ad absurdum*, wherein the two irreconcilable superpowers are made to look alike by their position within the states-system. Exterminism is not a new mode of production. In fact the ideologies of both the East and the West distil addiction to exterminism, which in turn triggers war preparations, legitimizes the privileged status of the armourers, and polices internal dissent (ibid. 20).

Relations between the USSR and other countries with 'actually existing socialism'

Related to the confusion in regard to the clear definition of the USSR are the problems Marxists would seem to have in explaining the relations of the USSR and the other 'socialist' states.

The dependency and world-system authors in particular, in those rare moments of extending their analysis in that direction, have been baffled by the relationship of the USSR with her 'dependencies'. Chase-Dunn, for example, notes the peculiar 'reversal of the usual pattern of uneven development' that obtains between the USSR 'centre' and her East European 'periphery' in contrast to the very different development in the Third World 'periphery'. In fact none of the *dependencia* argument on relations between centre and periphery seems to apply here. The countries that have the lowest level of development at the beginning of their incorporation into the Soviet 'periphery' are the ones that grow fastest. The most industrialized countries, Czechoslovakia and the German Democratic Republic, experience the slowest growth rates (Chase-Dunn, 1982, 45). Overall, the USSR (centre) has been known increasingly to have to subsidize her 'dependencies' (Lavigne, 1983). It has in fact been argued that economically speaking both the 'centre' and the 'periphery' have *in the long run* been damaged by the prolonged intimate relationship: East European countries have been forced into 'systematic

244 International Relations as Mainly a Theoretical Problem

undertrading' (that is to say limiting their trade relative to production), a process which is believed to retard technological change. On the other hand the USSR does not always benefit from her relations with the CMEA, and in a (controversial) assessment it has been claimed by a Western economist that the full resource costs of Soviet exports to her CMEA partners may in at least some periods have been greater than the full resource costs that it would have incurred in providing directly by her own productive efforts the goods received in exchange. As an economic 'quid' for a political 'quo' (Hanson, in Dawisha and Hanson, 1981, 94–5) it has been conceded that the USSR uses aid and economic co-operation generally as a political mechanism 'to play the interstate game' (Chase-Dunn, 1982, 45) for the USSR 'failed to escape the geo-political logic of the interstate system' (Chase-Dunn, ibid. 45, 41). The primacy of the 'interstate game' it has been argued by various Marxists is demonstrated also in the Sino-Soviet split, by the bloody contentions amongst socialist states in South-East Asia as well as the 'transideological enterprise' (Frank, 1980, 178–262) in the recent return of socialist states to commodity production for the world market, and their extensive dealings with capitalist multinational corporations.

Whilst the world-system approach by definition denies the possibility of countries being truly socialist (since the extant world-system is based on a *capitalist* world-economy) Ernest Mandel argues in the Trotskyist tradition that the fate of these 'deformed workers' states' left in a state of limbo fully depends on the future course of world revolution. As far as their relations are concerned, since these 'deformed workers' states' are ruled by bureaucracies which spuriously usurped the fruits of success-ful proletarian revolutions, their relations are in fact the rela-tions of a multitude of states all practising 'socialism in one country' which subordinate everything else to the needs of national development of individual countries leading necessa-rily to nationalism and national–messianism. And, Mandel argues, it is precisely because the ruling bureaucracies are not ruling *classes* with no necessary social role to play, that it is only through the maintenance of their power monopoly that they can defend their privileges. The Sino-Soviet conflict in this read-ing owes its existence to the objective impossibility for the Soviet and the Chinese bureaucracies to maintain a common political–ideological orientation internally or, more particularly, in foreign affairs. But whilst the conflict amongst capitalist and 'deformed workers' states', as well as the conflict amongst the capitalist countries, is inevitable, the conflicts amongst ruling bureaucracies in the 'deformed workers states' by no means derive inevitably from their socio-economic structure (which remains essentially socialist). Thus Mandel can argue that these conflicts are 'political and ideological' since there is nothing in their economic structures impelling their ruling groups to expand in the manner characteristic of capitalist states: to 'conquer' for example inner Mongolia so as to exploit its wealth nor any interest on China's part in 'conquering the wealth of Siberia' (Mandel, 1979, 188–9).

From this brief survey what emerges most clearly is that once again Marxists are 'hopelessly divided' in their attempts to overcome the doctrinaire obstacles inherited from Marx and Engels: we have referred to Marx's unfounded optimism over mankind's progress towards its universalization and his failure to see the role of international relations and particularly of the states-system in that process. Marx's axiom of the dependency of external function of state on the domestic economic dictates of capital accumulation, particularly in its absolute form, goes some way to show Marx's short-sightedness in this regard. His formula does not lead easily to a conceptualization of the states-system, a system whose very existence may significantly influence not only the foreign policy of each state but also have bearing on their domestic economic life. Furthermore Marx reduced the explanation of violence to class roots and in so doing precluded (did not seem to consider seriously) the possibility of conflict and violence amongst neighbouring communities ever over-shadowing the evils of class confrontation. We have of course referred to Engels's fears of mankind's capacity for self-destruction, but these amount to little more than hunches, having no real foundation in historical materialism: such apprehension could not really be explained adequately in terms of an irreconcilable hostility amongst capitalist states motivated and fuelled by an in-built competitive drive for profit.

And thus, beyond the individual states, there was for Marx and Engels, either nothing at all, an empty space, a void, or at best (as

Anderson put it) a 'shadow'. Where the shadow to them was small, insignificant, and evanescent, their heirs had to cope with a states-system (shadow) that instead of 'withering away' assumed such increasing proportions as itself to become globe-encircling. Bukharin in particular remarked on the 'shadow' resembling in its action more a coat—or indeed a straitjacket, as it significantly moulded capitalism to itself. But no Marxist, other than the 'renegades' (who become ex-Marxists in the process), ever seems to have fully appreciated just how serious or indeed permanent a constraint on the march of history the states-system can prove to be. It is one additional regard in which the Marxists diverge sharply from the Kantian tradition, a tradition with which they indeed converge in arguing, for example, that the states-system not only enables but encourages interstate conflict. With the passage of time Marxists seem to be becoming aware of the discrepancy. Particularly with the freeing of the superstructure from the bondage of the substructure which in different guises of dogma is common to virtually all contemporary Marxists, the way is clear for the integration of the notion of the 'shadow paradoxically governing the world' as a permanent (not merely temporary and casual) part of historical materialism. The awareness to which we refer is to be seen in Marxist reference to state-building and geo-military aggrandizement as being possessed of a logic apart and distinct from the logic of the capitalist accumulation process. It is to be seen also in the acknowledgement of the USSR's having become caught up in the power political game. But how are the two separate logics to be related or brought together? The world-system approach for one seems not to recognize two logics but only one when in a merger of both the states-system is regarded as no more than the world-economy's skin. The case of those prepared to treat the states-system as having a degree of autonomy is more perplexing: what, we may well ask, are those 'rules of power politics' possessed of the magical powers of a *deus ex machina* referred to whenever they run into theoretical difficulties? Are we to assume their accept-ance of those rules that were elaborated essentially in the establishment of the state-centrist power-realist case which is philosophically, methodologically, and politically alien to their own: which is indeed antithetical to their own Marxist premisses in such crucial areas as advocacy (and indeed feasibility) of change as well as the general orientation of mankind's onward path?

These are formidable problems for Marxists and will have to be resolved. For, as Bottomore put it (Bottomore and Goode, eds., 1983, 10–11), any sociological theory (and that of course applies not only to Marxism) which does not define as a central problem the conflict between inordinately powerful states armed with nuclear weapons is wholly unrealistic. As we intimated in our introductory remarks, the very relevance of Marxism is now in the balance as in a context of capacities for destruction unimagined by Marx or later Marxists, the significance of all traditional Marxist themes is reduced by comparison with the looming issue of survival and extinction of the human race itself. But the obstacles are likewise enormous. These are not only theoretical in nature but, it would appear to us, also ideological and political. For, in retrospect, Marxist theories (and classical theories of imperialism and the Soviet theory of international relations come to mind) managed a modicum of integration of the analytical levels of class and of states-system when, and only when, they found a way of vesting the major issues of international politics with class content. So long as the Western and Third World Marxists are inhibited (presumably also politically) from seeing in the USSR a superior or at least post-capitalist socio-economic formation and consistently with that position from regarding Soviet foreign policy as playing not only the states-system game but also advancing the world historical process along the lines of historical materialism (as she herself claims), they are abandoning the only possibility of vesting the superpower conflict with class substance. They must then as a consequence insist on looking at the North–South conflict as the sole expression of the global class conflict, and, unintegrated as the class forces in the world are, the Marxists tend to fall upon the horn of international politics and that of world relations of production. Thus they are bound by their own analysis to subordinate the nuclear conflict between superpowers to their (chief) concern for the world capitalist accumulation process. In other words, in their global class analysis they run into the problem that classes are not internationally integrated (except when they become amalgamated in states) and conversely that the major inter-state conflicts in the world today appear to them to be lacking in socio-economic (class) content. Their unequivocally sympathetic attitude towards the USSR might be, however, politically, as well as intellectually, untenable. So their attitude towards the world peace movement would have to be redefined in these terms. Yet many Marxists seem to be actually moving in that direction: apart from Mandel's statements there is Samir Amin's realization that communism will remove only economic alienation but will leave us with an 'anthropological alienation'. From this, then, one might conclude that progress to Samir Amin is not absolute but relative, and after the removal of one set of societal ills (capitalism), another, similarly objectionable (and unforeseen in classical Marxism), is there to take its place, and so on in endless sequence. The Marxists' definitional relation to the USSR, however, appears to be pivotal since upon it rests the integrity and clarity of their explanations of international relations. Those amongst them however who do see the superpower nuclear confrontation as a conflict of competing social formations come close to—at least in rough outline—the much abused and rejected Soviet theory of international relations!

Despite the almost self-negating differences among Marxists across the world, and notwithstanding their many problems, the students of International Relations should feel an obligation to look to and correct their annals, and essentially to acknowledge for their discipline not a threefold but fourfold tradition. None of the recognized traditions (Hobbesian, Kantian, or Grotian) were renowned either for the political or intellectual unity of their proponents, let alone for their lasting theoretical accomplishment in explaining the iniquitous features of international relations or for that matter for charting their future course. The Marxist theories of international relations, those that we have covered in this book and those which are no doubt still to be added will strengthen significantly the claims of the growing international political economy sub-school. They will continue to challenge that rendition of international relations we boast in the West and that we have learned to accept from journalists, statesmen—and the International Relations discipline—as axiomatic. The challenge is in itself valuable, for it may well be that the world is indeed governed not by one but by several 'shadows'.

Postscript to the Paperback Edition[1]

The fact that a fourth (Marxist) philosophical tradition of International Relations has not been formally added to the other three does not necessarily contradict the proposition we have made in the Preface that there now is a Marxist approach within the discipline of International Relations. It may simply indicate the problems of understanding the Marxist approach as well as distinguishing it from the other three philosophical traditions. All of the recent developments in Marxist thought would indeed appear to 'fit' into the Grotian tradition, a tradition which we described as 'antithetical' to Marx (p. 20). As in the earlier case of a Marxist overlap with the Hobbesian and Kantian tradition, however, it is essential to our interpretation to consider the possibility that the coincidence with the Grotian is left ambivalent and may well be a temporary

[1] The selection of literature on which we base our comments here can be found in the *Bibliographical Supplement* on pp. 287–8. We refer *first*, to the Western 'critical' or Marxist approach to International Relations of such authors as H. Alker, R. Ashley, R. W. Cox, John Maclean, Fred Halliday, and M. Hoffman, although the work of R. B. J. Walker, A. Linklater, F. Ajami, Mittelman, H. Targ, and of many others is equally relevant. *Second*, we comment on the Soviet 'New Thinking' on International Relations whose most comprehensive statement in our view can be found in the Political Report of M. Gorbachev to the 27th CPSU Congress and in the New Edition of the Programme of the CPSU. Its points have been elaborated (or indeed anticipated) in the voluminous writing of A. Bovin, F. M. Burlatsky, I. T. Frolov, M. S. Gorbachev, Anatolii Gromyko, A. V. Kortunov, Y. Plimak, E. M. Primakov, G. K. Shakhnazarov, A. N. Yakovlev, V. Zagladin, and many others. By Soviet 'New Thinking' we propose to understand ten points: 1, the identification with the global problems of mankind (nuclear catastrophe, ecological disaster, poverty, and so on); 2, the concept of the interdependence of survival of mankind in a world regarded as 'one' interrelated totality; 3, the renunciation of war, with 4, the concept of peace presented as the highest of humanity's values; 5, the security of all states regarded as global, indivisible, and 6, attainable not by military but by political means on the basis not of 'balance of power' but of 'balance of interests'; 7, the level of military confrontation in all areas to be reduced; 8, the level of military arsenals to be based on such 'reasonable sufficiency' as to repulse aggression, with 9, an essential flexibility in International Relations; 10, the one interrelated and interdependent world perceived as such is none the less the world of coexisting socialism and capitalism with their coexistence as socio-economic systems to be divorced from their coexistence and relations as states. Thus 'peaceful coexistence of states of different socio-economic systems' is no longer described as formerly, that is as a 'form of class struggle' (see p. 93). The mode of thought continuing to distinguish socialism from capitalism is Marxist historical materialism based on dialectics. *Third*, our comments refer also to Deng's view that the world has now reached a stage of 'peace and development' (Deng Xiaoping, 12 May 1987, reprinted in *Beijing Review*, 11–17 January 1988): as distinct from the earlier version of the Three World Theory, *détente* between the two superpowers is now deemed desirable and feasible with the avoidance of war between them become also possible (cf. p. 101).

expedient, a preferred state of affairs with other goals—no matter how remotely in sight, or already designated.

And thus Soviet 'New Thinking' would appear to converge with the Grotian approach even further than did its predecessor (the theory of peaceful coexistence (p. 20)) in its new declaration of the world's having achieved the stage described in the literature of International Relations as 'world society' based on the discovery of shared ('global', 'all human') values that spring from the binding effect and integrative (traumatizing) impulse of the volatile mix of nuclear armed states in mutual contact. This is obviously the Soviet meaning of 'interdependence'—the survival of humanity in a nuclear world. Any further advance on the traditional Marxist goal (communist 'world society') is in fact declared to be radically contingent upon the *co-operative* relations of states. The traditional Soviet goal of 'peace' as a socio-economic restructuring of the world (peace *postively* defined) is now predicated on the achievement of 'peace' (Deng's 'tranquility') *negatively* defined as merely *an absence of war*. It is clear that in theory at least the ultimate goal, the other 'world society', might not necessarily be abandoned.

The convergence on the Grotian tradition is paralleled by developments in Western Marxism. Richard Ashley, for example, explicitly subscribes to the Grotian tradition through his identification with the approach of Karl Deutsch, one of its chief protagonists and obviously Ashley's 'point of contact' with the International Relations discipline. As with Deutsch, Ashley and his colleagues would wish to produce a viable alternative both to the 'state centric' and to the 'state-as-actor' power realist model of which they are critical. In the Marxist approach the multitude of uniform (and indivisible) states of the power realist is always seen as part of a context, either domestic or global, or both. The resulting Marxist 'structured totality' (albeit 'holistic') images of the world are similar indeed to Deutsch's vision of a pluralistic world of limited regional 'pluralistic security communities'. Ashley's proposal, however, to develop further Deutsch's 'communitarian perspective' goes much further than both Grotius or Deutsch. Ashley envisages a 'communitarian tradition' based on an understanding of the world as a 'discursive plurality of social reality', which is to say the 'evolution of social reality through the creative yet constrained interaction of multiple, mutually interpenetrating vantage points on and within reality',[2] but among the 'communitarian thinkers' he includes not only Deutsch but also Habermas, Foucault, Bourdieu (and Alker) (Ashley, 1983, 533–4).

The Marxist or Marxist derived approach has been widely recognized in the literature of International Relations under a confusing variety of names[3] with neither the discipline's classificatory devices (such as the 'three traditions')[4] nor the protagonists of the approach offering much by way of assistance towards its understanding. As a matter of fact almost without an exception the left writers deny their Marxism. Essentially they object to the treatment of Marxism as a *generic term* along the same lines as a wine-maker would object to the 'historical and geographical elevation' of a particular wine ('sparkling, produced in Champagne') into a generic term (champagne). And just as the wine-maker might call for a return to the more general and more 'accurate' (pre-champagne) designation of his product as 'sparkling wine', so many left International Relations writers do not wish to be subordinate in category to Marxism, and proceed to fortify their position by calling for a return to other generic descriptions that in their view preceded Marx. By way

[2] Alker in plainer language speaks of four 'contending but partial world order systems' namely capitalist power balancing, Soviet socialism, corporatist authoritarian, and collective self-reliance, based (as he puts it), on 'more or less state-centered modes of production'. The more commonly postulated number of the major constituent parts of the world, mutually interpenetrating and interdependent, is three. Halliday, reminding us of the Soviet or Chinese tripartite imagery of the world, refers to capitalist, and pre- and post-capitalist 'coexisting structures'.

[3] Seldom called 'Marxist' or explicitly connected to Marxism, the approach is either referred to by the name of one of the Marxist theories to which the approach is reduced (as dependency or World System) or it goes under a variety of labels designed to reflect its main feature such as 'revolutionary', 'revisionist', 'non-determinist', 'structuralist', 'post-structuralist', 'dialectical', 'radical dialectical', 'non-materialist dialectical', 'historical materialist', 'critical', 'informed by hermeneutics and language philosophy', or 'post-Marxist'. It may, indeed, be given no specific identity, passing simply as a 'third approach' to International Relations.

[4] It is worth remarking that as argued elsewhere (Kubálková and Cruickshank, 1986) the other standard form in the discipline of International Relations for the classification of theories of International Relations, namely Waltz's 'three images' is equally unhelpful. The Marxist writers seek to build and develop a 'fourth image' not anticipated by Waltz, and one that transcends Waltz's second image (which was designed with Marxism in mind) and his third image by adding both to the domestic structure of the society and to the states system as a source of international conflict (Waltz's second and third images respectively). This 'fourth' image postulates as a source of conflict a range of differently defined entities based within and beyond states, such as social forces, classes, ideas, and ideologies.

of evidence they invoke (pre-Marxist) 'specific cases' that either 'better' exemplify the genus or are the 'genuine' originators of the approach that in their view is erroneously called 'Marxism'. They argue, for example, that dialectics, pre-dating Marx, draws not only on Hegel but on Heraclitus, Plato, and Aristotle. The approach of historical materialism (although the term itself is known to have its origin with Lenin's contemporary, the Russian Marxist Plekhanov), has a 'pre-Marxian' origin— allegedly in the eighteenth-century work of the Neapolitan Vico. And thus the left International Relations writers place themselves in a 'vichian' (or 'Vicoian') tradition or in a 'dialectical' approach, with Marxism and Marx himself becoming a specific, concrete, historically unique instance; and with their peculiar preoccupation with economic determinism Marx and his work become circumscribed in (European) place and fixed in (nineteenth-century) time. The argument only reduces the originality of Marx. It not only does not remove him from the lineage but has a strengthening effect on contemporary Marxism in the same way in which a voguish reference by power realists to Thucydides (400 BC) neither reduces nor removes the validity of the writing of the twentieth-century 'father' of power realism, Hans Morgenthau. Nevertheless, the argument produces a repudiation of one type of connection, but as it happens one which in the context of International Relations must be seen as crucial, namely the denial of any connection to or relation with the Marxism of the Soviet superpower whose attempts as it were to register the champagne trademark continue to be seen as an unsuccessful imposture. It remains to be seen whether Gorbachev's promises to liberate Soviet thought, and to 'creatively develop' historical materialism and dialectics in particular, will in any way change the Western perceptions of the Marxist genealogy of the Soviet Union.

In quest of a suitable and acceptable name for the approach we argued for the use of the term 'critical' (Kubálková and Cruickshank, 1986) to conform with the adoption in a number of social sciences of the German distinction between the 'conventional' (traditional) disciplines and their 'critical' Marxist derived wings. A broadly based category of academics on the left, all inclining towards the 'critical' share (at a minimum): a rejection of the epistemological and methodoogical foundations of 'conventional' (read traditional, or bourgeois') social sciences on the fringes of which the critical wing has evolved; an antipathy towards positivism (a 'source of reification and an endorsement of the status quo'); a heightened sensitivity to change and an awareness of conflict as well as of the transitory, impermanent nature of the (capitalist) present. Their common goal is to all intents and purposes the 'radically reconstituted idea of "revolution" as "human emancipation" deemed achievable by enlightening human subjects about the nature of the constraints upon them and by attempting to uncover the possibilities of autonomy dormant within their forms of life' (Linklater, 1986, 308). Since the International Relations discipline's emerging 'non-conventional' wing seems to subscribe wholly and wholeheartedly to these dicta and to partake in the intellectual tradition of other critical social sciences, the designation of that wing as 'critical' would seem only sensible, drawing as it would the discipline's perception of its Left into line with that of other social sciences rather than confusing Marxism with an economic determinist straw man.

Whilst only one of the proposed appellations for the 'third approach' (the 'radical dialectical' of Alker and Biersteker, 1984) encompasses every Marxist—or more correctly all who share the concept of dialectics (including also the Soviet Marxist-Leninist together with all others named in this book)—the embrace of the critical approach would not be so encompassing. To speak of the Western and the Soviet Marxists in the same breath still arouses scholarly protest; and yet when critical Marxist writers attack Western International Relations scholarship as being invariably unscholarly, ideological, always 'for a purpose' (Cox, 1981, 128), indeed constitutive of International Relations power relations (Ashley, 1981, 217 and Maclean, 1984, 132), and then proceed to its detailed scrutiny, the dismissal by the same authors of another ideology (the Soviet) without such ado, indeed without a second glance, betrays an unscholarly inconsistency.

Certainly, between the Soviet and Western Marxists there exist large differences—just as there exist rather significant parallels. The differences derive from the two separate intellectual lineages and the shared parts of the genealogy (Table 1) would not go beyond Marx and in some cases Lenin.

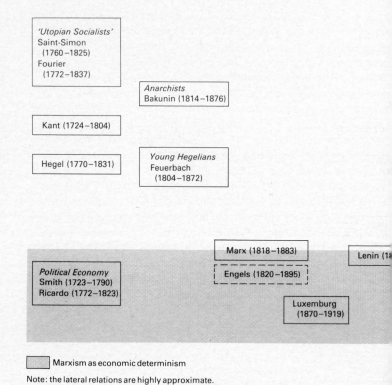

Marxism as economic determinism

Note: the lateral relations are highly approximate.

Table 1. *Marxism and International Relations:*
The Menu of Sources

Lévi-Strauss (1908–)		*Structuralism*	
		Structural Functionalism Merton (1910–)	
		Radical Sociology	
Sartre (1905–1980)			
		Existential Sociology	
eud (1856–1939)		*Structural Marxism* Althusser (1918–) Poulantzas (1936–1979)	*Post-Structuralism* Foucault (1926–1984) Bourdieu (1930–)
Marxism 885–1971)	*Critical School* Horkheimer (1895–1973) Adorno (1903–1969) Marcuse (1898–1981)		
			Habermas (1929–)
			E. P. Thompson (1924–)
i (1891–1937)			Anderson (1938–)
c Determinism (1854–1938)		*'Revisionist' historians* W. A. Williams (1921–) Alperovitz (1936–) G. Kolko (1932–)	*Economic Marxism* Sweezy (1910–) Baran (1910–1964) Braverman (1920–1976)
			World-System Wallerstein (1930–)
tsky (1879–1940)	*Fourth International*	Hobsbawm (1917–)	
		Mandel (1923–)	
			Misc. Western theories of IR WOMP (R. Falk) 'communitarian perspective' (K. Deutsch) the critics of the US strategic doctrine
			the peace movement
			the ecology environment movement

Table 1 is therefore designed to show mainly the wide range of intellectual sources of the Western critical approach.[5]

Looking at Table 1 it is to be remarked how underrepresented in its influence on the 'third approach' is the economic determinist (shaded) 'band', a result consistent, and in line with, the development of left thought in this century. The major source of inspiration is definitely Hegelian Marxism, a tradition that began with the work of Lukács, Korsch, and Gramsci (Chapter 9) that has held sway over continental (Western) Europe and that only recently has found its way to Britain and the United States, there displacing or reducing the Trotskyist influence.

We list in Table 1, adjacent to the German critical Frankfurt School, the work of French structuralists Althusser and Poulantzas only for the sake of completeness. Anti-Hegelian in its thrust, and of the rejected 'scientific' variety, their structuralism has been demolished by E. P. Thompson and others along lines that so impressed Richard Ashley as to provide the blueprint for his attack on the International Relations discipline's own structural realism or 'neorealism' (Ashley, 1984). With the tragic departure from the scene of the main protagonists of the approach (after Poulantzas's suicide and Althusser's institutionalization in a mental asylum) we are left mainly with the neologisms that they popularized such as 'problematique', 'conjecture' and many others.

The French post-structuralists Foucault and Bourdieu are two of the main influences. Not only post-structuralist but allegedly also 'post-Marxist', their conclusions are nevertheless strikingly similar to those of an equally popular German critical sociologist, and self-confessed Marxist, Jürgen

---

[5] Those who might question the inclusion of some obvious non-Marxists we refer to the Left's own intellectual historiography which amply documents the fact that the influence of Croce on Gramsci, of Weber on Lukács, of Freud, Schopenhauer, Nietzsche, Dilthey, and Bergson on the Frankfurt School, of the French School of Annales on Wallerstein, and of the various structuralists on Marxist French structuralists and post structuralists has been as potent an influence as has been the Marxian. The indication of our Table are not only consistent with Perry Anderson's magisterial accounting of the Left's intellectual history (Anderson, 1976 and *In the Tracks of Historical Materialism* Verso, London, 1983) but with a similarly construed pedigree of left sociology (G. Ritzer *Sociological Theory*, Alfred A. Knopff, New York, 1983). Table 1 shows the contemporary divisions and currents as they can be traced (along approximately horizontal lines) in a manner consistent with Burawoy's analysis ('Introduction: The Resurgence of Marxism in American Sociology', *American Journal of Sociology*, Vol. 83, Supplement, 1982) of the effect of Marxist currents on American sociology.

Habermas. The concerns of post-structuralist study would indeed seem to be distant from Marxism let alone from International Relations. With their interest in literary theory and criticism, in semiology (the theory of signs), and in hermeneutics (interpretation of texts), it is their *methodology* that has been found extraordinarily appealing and even inspirational right across the spectrum of the Western left. When economic determinism is apparently no longer regarded as the sole or main source of the Marxist/Left contribution, when the search for classes and class formations as the influence on, and explanation of, state behaviour and of the states-system is neither obsessive nor compulsory, it is apparently to the field of theories of knowledge that 'critical' methodology draws our attention as the source of the contribution. Finally, we co-list in Table 1 structural functionalism because of its influence on both French Marxism and 'post-Marxism' as well as on dependency theory.

Virtually all left writers listed in Table 1 have 'auditioned' for an International Relations role. They all in point of fact tend to be drawn upon randomly from 'all over the place', often by the same author and regardless of the differences between them. Engels is one of a few important exceptions of a Marxist whose mention is sedulously avoided. Lenin's intellectual guidelines too are tapped, but ever so discreetly.[6] Conspicuously absent too is any direct acknowledgement of Marx apart from that made by John MacLean, Ajami, Mittelman, and Targ.

Apart from the often quite inordinate enthusiasm for Habermas and the French post-structuralists, the most powerful and potentially fruitful influence has been that of Gramsci.[7] R. W. Cox (1981, 1983, 1987) and under his influence also John Maclean (1981) endeavoured a decade after the discovery of Gramsci in other social sciences to show as relevant to the study of International Relations and Organizations Gramsci's concepts, particularly that of hegemony and

[6] Alker (1981), for example, uses Lenin's concept of dialectics, and Ashley (1981) in his theory of 'lateral pressure', although he claims to draw on non-Marxist sources, quite clearly parallels Lenin's theory of intercapitalist contradictions.

[7] Significantly too Gramsci needs no rehabilitation in the USSR; his work is recognized as a tactical extension of Lenin's ideas, and his collected works are presently being published in the USSR.

historical bloc.[8] Last but not least there are the less philosophically oriented Trotskyists, one of the alleged influences on Wallerstein. Fred Halliday's theory of the New Second Cold War (1983) draws on both the 'revisionist' Cold War historians, and he continues the Trotskyist tradition from his Chair at the London School of Economics.

In the relatively short span of their existence the critical theorists have proven themselves in the polemical attack in International Relations to be in their element, an aptitude which, as the history of other social sciences attests, characterizes the critical wing's early stages of development. It is for this role that the left armoury appears to equip them best.[9] The major targets are the compartmentalized knowledge of the 'bourgeois' social sciences, political conservatism, positivism, the empirico-analytical epistemology of International Relations, the focus on statist structures and inability of the discipline to handle change, and the inadequate analysis of conflict. There is denunciation of the discipline's state centrism and more recently its economism, as well as of the structuralism of neorealism. International Relations, it is claimed, has failed in its special responsibility to account for the increasing globalization of social relations. It is unnecessary here to survey the defence of the 'neorealists' to the various charges.[10]

[8] According to Cox's extension of Gramsci, hegemony in International Relations is an order within a world economy expressed in the (dominant mode of production supporting) universal norms, international institutions, and mechanisms for the behaviour of states and other actors. The hegemony is based on a consensus of those who believe themselves in fact to be pursuing their 'national interests', instead of which their own exploitation is continuous, with no coercive political methods necessary. Instrumental in the creation and inculcation of the 'hegemonic' consensus is Gramsci's 'historical bloc' which consists of the 'bourgeois intellectuals' (including obviously the International Relations community responsible for the dissemination of its miscellaneous myths). Conversely, in the only available (revolutionary) 'anti-hegemonic' strategy, it is the left intellectuals, the 'new historical bloc', whose task is to undermine and to replace the 'hegemonic' consensus.

[9] There is not only an inconsistency but also a manifest expedience in the use of sources by critical International Relations theorists and in the manipulation of their mentors. Using the post-structuralists they do not reach their conclusions—as for example the Nietzschean anarchism that is found in the later Foucault. So too Ashley having drawn so extensively on Foucault and/or Habermas supplements his overkill attack on the conventional discipline with a concluding sentence more in keeping with the argument of pre-Foucaultean Marxists: 'In the end, the only kind of criticism that would possibly do away with realism is a global revolutionary change that would put an end to the current order of domination without establishing a new one in its place' (Ashley, 1981, 234).

[10] J. Herz, 'Comment', *International Studies Quarterly*, Vol. 25, No. 2, 1981; R. Gilpin, 'The Richness of the Tradition of Political Realism', *International Organization*, Vol. 38, No. 2, Spring 1984; K. Waltz, 'A Response to my Critics', in R. Keohane, 1986.

The difference between 'critical' International Relations writing and the 'New Thinking' are sufficiently clear. The attitude of Soviet 'New Thinking' to the Western International Relations discipline is significantly much less harsh. By 'old' thinking (or that for which the 'new' is replacement) is meant not only Soviet thinking of the pre-Gorbachev era but primarily Western power realism in its many variants. There is nothing new in the Soviet rejection of the 'bourgeois' mainstream: the striking departure however from earlier Soviet practice as well as from Western critical writing is in the acknowledgement in 'New Thinking' of non-Marxist intellectual sources equally critical of the mainstream. Thus, Soviet writers have no hesitation in attributing their term 'New Thinking' to an Einstein initiative after the Second World War, and in particular to the Einstein–Russell Manifesto of 1955 that inaugurated the Pugwash peace movement of Western scientists. True enough, there are conceptual parallels with a number of Western Marxists (among them E. P. Thompson's 'exterminism' and the writing of the END group), but Soviet writing also parallels the much broader lines of the Western critique of power realism and particularly of the US strategic doctrine.

Beyond the critique the strength and purpose of the *critical approach* (as evidenced so far at least) unlike that of Soviet writers had not been in the presentation of a 'new' approach but in its destructionist attack on virtually all areas of an International Relations discipline from which Soviet 'New Thinking' with an apparently more liberal cast would seek to learn and even incorporate.[11] In other words, the critical

---

[11] There is, for example, the concept of interdependence which figures largely in 'New Thinking', that is at one and the same time a butt of criticism for the 'critical' writers by reason of its constituting an 'ideological intervention' and thereby hampering the development of a genuine Marxist approach (Maclean, 1984). Even the voguish International Political Economy which has taken under its wing various Marxist approaches ahead of the International Relations discipline surprisingly comes in for attack from the critical quarter. It is worth noting that International Political Economy is an area whose terminology Soviet 'New Thinking' freely deploys. This difference in attitude is at its most striking in regard to NIEO, and with reference to International Organization, the North–South conflict and, in particular, in relation to the work of WOMP. Where each of these, and for a variety of reasons, comes in for rough handling by the critical writers all of these topics meet with Soviet approbation. The parallels between 'New Thinking' and the writing of Willy Brandt are openly acknowledged just as they undeniably exist between 'New Thinking' and the work of WOMP, the ideologically disparate but essentially idealist, normatively oriented group associated with the work of Richard Falk and Samuel Kim. 'New Thinking' is in fact developing into a normative theory of the

writers appear to be much more radical ('less liberal') in their commentaries on their fellow International Relations writers than are the 'New Thinkers'. The main target of both however, is the same: realism in all of its forms and the state system that realism accepts as the 'political superstructure' of the world. And it is precisely the globalization of social relations, a phenomenon which, as both 'critical' writers and Soviet 'New Thinkers' agree, power realism cannot handle that leads to the Soviet concepts of 'global', 'all-human' problems—concepts now become the battle slogans.

With that said, the major argument against the Soviet's 'New Thinking' *as a new theory of International Relations* might well be that as an intellectual exercise it is an eclectic mix of liberal, radical, and Marxist normative thought—it could indeed be seen as yet another Messianic ideological response to an exaggerated description of the predicament of mankind in the nuclear age.[12] Soviet 'New Thinking' lends itself also, however, to the alternative interpretation, as the foundation of a new Soviet (Gramscian) *anti-hegemonistic* strategic blueprint for the future foreign policy direction of a weakening superpower. The anti-hegemonic strategy is consistent with a high diplomatic profile which indeed is an essential part of its working, one that projects an innovative

same cosmopolitan stamp. Again, though utterly demolished in writing such as that of Ashley, the world modelling approach has gained considerable popularity since the seventies in the Soviet Union.

[12] Soviet leaders declare their main source to be the work of Lenin, and yet the picture of the world that they now envisage is significantly post-Leninist in its implied rejection of the major tenets of the theory of imperialism, the rearrangement of the time frame of Leninist historical materialism, and desynchronization of certain anticipated developments, postponing some and advancing others. The longevity of capitalism and the possibility of its enduring into the future is now acknowledged, hence the coexistence of socialism and capitalism will span an entire epoch. The nuclear danger activates 'ahead of schedule' Marxist universalism, with the Soviet Union now speaking on behalf not only of states of the socialist socio-economic system but on behalf of humanity as a whole. Entities seen by both Bukharin and Lenin as bound together (the capitalist mode of production and the states system) are now disconnected. War, no longer the Clausewitzian/Leninist 'continuation of policy by other means', is deemed to derive not from capitalism but from capitalist states. It is in their separation that is to be read the meaning of the otherwise puzzling excision of the 'form of class struggle' from the concept of 'peaceful coexistence of the states of different socio-economic systems' Capitalism itself can be handled *in a co-operative relation* (and through the deployment of International Law and International Organizations) so long as it is a capitalism disarmed: a disarmed capitalism which will make available the technology necessary for a communist society. According to Soviet theory the next, final stage of the historically given struggle between capitalism and socialism will be won only in the absence of armed states as a form of the political organization of humanity.

flexible, well-informed, and altruistic image, the obverse side in fact of the traditional image of 'Soviet threat', playing down (without abandoning) the coercive mechanism of military might. It demands the achievement of an intellectual ascendancy and points in the direction of a new reliance on other superstructural elements such as international law, international organizations, and propaganda. Stress is laid on the importance of these as, through the gradual assumption of the intellectual front-running, the economy-technology powered appeal of capitalism may be supplanted in the individual mind with the only 'revolutionary' option that is realistically available to the Soviet Union in the eighties and (it must be presumed) beyond. 'New Thinking' is to be a joint venture of Soviet and Western intellectuals, in other words of the new 'historical bloc' of 'humanity in the nuclear age'. On the bloc's shoulders, then, is to rest the task of creating a new consensus that will undermine the instruments of hegemony, including that of the states system.

Western Sovietologists and critics of Soviet Marxism-Leninism echo the attitude of Western critical Marxists when they argue the end of the road for Marxism in Soviet 'New Thinking' as a result of the 'demise' of its 'class approach'. Which raises the question as to whether account should then not be taken of the Western Marxist postulate that the meaning of Marxism even in the West has so changed as to bear only a tenuous resemblance to the classical form. In reference to their own Marxism, Western Marxists themselves contend that arising from the more orthodox definition of Marxism that places emphasis on 'class structure and conflict as the key to social organization and historical change' (Giddens) all that is called for is a definitional broadening so as to place a more liberalized emphasis on 'class struggle as the principal force behind the development of freedom and history' (Olin Wright). Already in the critical theory of the Frankfurt School, applied now also to International Relations, the stress on class struggle (and with it the very idea of a 'revolution') had subsided in favour of emphasis on 'emancipation' and 'freedom', with Western Marxism gradually broadening into a 'theory of historical change and progress' (Linklater, 1986, 307).

The presence of the new 'critical' wing within the discipline of International Relations brings with it a number of side effects that merit attention regardless of the claims and counter claims as to its designation and Marxist credentials. We refer to the *novel emphasis on the exploration of ideas, of ideologies, and indeed of world views in the study of International Relations* that curiously enough are highlighted simultaneously in both Western and non-Western Marxist approaches. The exposure to these concerns might be as beneficial as were the insights reaped by the discipline from the economic concerns of the earlier Marxist theories.

Bibliography

Adelman, I. and Morris, C. T., 1973, *Economic Growth and Social Equity in Developing Countries*. Stanford University Press.

Althusser, L., 1969, *For Marx* (trans. from French). New York: Pantheon.

—— and Balibar, E., 1970, *Reading Capital* (trans. by B. Brewster). London: New Left Books.

Amin, S., 1974, *Accumulation on a World Scale*. London: Monthly Review Press.

—— 1976, *Unequal Development*. Sussex: Harvester Press.

—— 1977, *Imperialism and Unequal Development*. New York: Monthly Review Press.

—— 1980, *Class and Nation; Historically and in the Current Crisis*. London: Monthly Review Press.

—— Arrighi, G., Frank, A. G., and Wallerstein, I., 1982, *Dynamics of Global Crisis*. New York and London: Monthly Review Press.

Anderson, P., 1974, *Lineages of the Absolutist State*. London: New Left Books

—— 1976, *Considerations on Western Marxism*. London: New Left Books.

—— 1976–7, 'The Antinomies of Antonio Gramsci'. *New Left Review*, No. 100.

—— 1978, *Passages from Antiquity to Feudalism*. London: Verso.

Andropov, Iu, 1983, 'Uchenie Karla Marksa i Nekotorye Voprosy socialisticheshogo Stroitelstva v SSSR. *Kommunist*, No. 3, Feb.

Aron, R., 1962, *Peace and War: A Theory of International Relations*. London: Weidenfeld and Nicolson.

Aspaturian, V. V., 1971, *Power and Process in Soviet Foreign Policy*. Boston: Little, Brown.

Avineri, S., 1968, *Karl Marx on Colonialism and Modernisation: His Despatches and Other Writings on China, India, Mexico, the Middle East and North Africa*. New York: Doubleday.

—— 1970, *The Social and Political Thought of Karl Marx*. Cambridge: CUP.

Badia, G., 1967, *Le Spartakisme. Les dernières années de Rosa Luxemburg et de Karl Liebknecht 1914–1919*. Paris: L'Arche.

Bahro, R., 1978, *The Alternative in Eastern Europe*. London: New Left Books.

Bailey, S. D., 1978, 'The UN Security Council: Evolving Practice'. *World Today*, 54 (3), Mar.

Balbus, I. D., 1977, 'Commodity Form and Legal Form: An Essay on the "Relative Autonomy" of the Law'. *Law and Society*, 11, Winter.

Baran, P. A., 1973, *The Political Economy of Growth*. Harmondsworth: Penguin.

—— and Sweezy, P. M., 1966, *Monopoly Capital*. New York: Monthly Review Press.

Barratt Brown, M., 1963, *After Imperialism*. London: Heinemann.

—— 1971, *The Economics of Imperialism*. Harmondsworth: Penguin.

Bauer, O., 1907, *Die Nationalitätenfrage und die Sozialdemokratie*. Vienna: Wiener Volksbuchhandlung.

Beirne, P. and Sharlet, R. (eds.), 1980, *Pashukanis: Selected Writings on Marxism and Law*. London: Academic Press.

Bellis, P., 1979, *Marxism and the U.S.S.R. The Theory of Proletarian Dictatorship and the Marxist Analysis of Soviet Society*. London: Macmillan.

Bello, E. G., 1981, 'The Pursuit of Rights and Justice in International Law by the Developing Nations'. *Verfassung und Recht in Übersee*, 14 (2).

Bergesen, A., 1982, 'The Emerging Science of the World System'. *International Social Science Journal*, XXIV (1).

Berki, R. N., 1971, 'On Marxian Thought and the Problem of International Relations'. *World Politics*, Oct.

Bettelheim, C., 1974, *Cultural Revolution and Industrial Organization in China; Changes in Management and the Division of Labour*. New York: Monthly Review Press.

—— 1975, *Economic Calculation and Forms of Property*. New York: Monthly Review Press.

Binns, P., and Hallas, D., 1976, 'The Soviet Union—State Capitalist or Socialist?'. *International Socialism*, No. 91, Sept.

Bloom, S. F., 1941, *The World of Nations: a Study of the National Implications in the Work of Karl Marx*. New York: Columbia University Press.

Bober, M. M., 1962, *Karl Marx's Interpretation of History*. Cambridge, Mass.: Harvard University Press.

Borkenau, F., 1938, *The Communist International*. London: Faber and Faber.

Bottomore, T., 1978, *Austro-Marxism*. Oxford: Clarendon Press.

—— (ed.), 1981, *Modern Interpretations of Marx*. Oxford: Basil Blackwell.

—— and Goode, T. (eds.) 1983, *Readings in Marxist Sociology*. Oxford: Clarendon Press

Brenner, R., 1977, 'The Origins of Capitalist Development: A Critique of Neo-Smithian Marxism'. *New Left Review*, No. 104, July, Aug.

Brewer, A., 1981, *Marxist Theories of Imperialism*. London: Routledge and Kegan Paul.

Brezhnev, L., 1969, 'Brezhnev discusses Czechoslovakia at Polish Congress'. *The Current Digest of the Soviet Press*, XX (46).

—— 1978, *Leninskim Kursom*, 6 Vols. Moscow: Politizdat.

—— 1979, *Our Course: Peace and Socialism*. Moscow: Novosti.

Brinkley, G. A., 1972, 'Khrushchev Remembered: On the History of Soviet Statehood'. *Soviet Studies*, Vol. 24.

Brucan, S., 1971, *The Dissolution of Power: A Sociology of International Relations*. New York: Knopf Publishers.

—— 1978, *The Dialectic of World Politics*. New York: The Free Press.

Bukharin, N., 1966, *Imperialism and World Economy*. New York: H. Fertig.

Bull, H., 1977, *The Anarchical Society: A Study of Order in World Politics*. London: Macmillan.

Burawoy, M., 1978, 'Contemporary Currents in Marxist Theory'. *American Sociologist*, 13 (1), Feb.

Burke, J. P., Crocker, L. and Legters, L. H. (eds.), 1981, *Marxism and the Good Society*. Cambridge: CUP.

Burke, W. S. and Brokaw, F. S., 1982, 'Law at Sea'. *Policy Review*, 20, Spring.

Butler, W. E., 1971, ' "Socialist International Law" or "Socialist Principles of International Relations"?' *American Journal of International Law*, 65.

—— 1974, 'Some Reflections on the Periodisation of Soviet Approaches to International Law', in Barry, D. P. (ed.), *Contemporary Soviet Law*. The Hague: Martinus Nijhoff.

—— 1978, *The Soviet Legal System. Legislation and Documentation*. New York: Ocean Publications.

Cabral, A., 1969, *Unity and Struggle: Speeches and Writing*. London: Monthly Review Press.

Cain, M. and Hunt, A., 1979, *Marx and Engels on Law*. London/New York/San Francisco: Academic Press.

Caporaso, J. A., 1980, 'Dependency Theory: Continuities and Discontinuities in Development Studies'. *International Organization*, 34 (4), Autumn.

Carlo, A., 1974, 'The Socio-economic Nature of the USSR'. *Telos*, No. 21, Fall.

Carr, E. H., 1934, *Karl Marx, A Study in Fanaticism*. London: Dent.

—— 1946, *Twenty Years Crisis*. London: Macmillan.

—— 1950, *History of Soviet Russia*. London: Macmillan.

—— 1950–3, *The Bolshevik Revolution*, 3 Vols. London: Macmillan.

Carsten, F. L., 1974, 'Freedom and Revolution: Rosa Luxemburg' in Labedz, L., (ed.), *Revisionism*, New York: Books for Libraries Press.

Chabal, P., 1981, 'The Social and Political Thought of Amilcar Cabral: A Reassessment'. *Journal of Modern African Studies*, 19 (1).

Chai, T. R., 1979, 'Chinese Policy toward the Third World and the Superpowers in the UN General Assembly 1971–1977: A Voting Analysis'. *International Organization*, 33 (3), Summer.

—— 1980, 'Chinese Politics in the General Assembly'. *Public Opinion Quarterly*, 44 (1), Spring.

'Chairman Mao's Theory of the Differentiation of the Three Worlds is a Major Contribution to Marxism – Leninism'. *Peking Review*, Nov. 1977, No. 45.

Charles, M., 1980, *The Soviet Union and Africa: The History of Involvement.* Lanham, Md: Univ. Press of America.

Chase-Dunn, C. K. (ed.), 1982, *Socialist States in the World System*. Beverly Hills: Sage.

Chiu, H., 1966, 'Communist China's Attitude towards International Law'. *The American Journal of International Law*, Vol. 60.

—— 1976, 'Mainland China and International Law: A General Observation'. *Issues and Studies*, XII (6), June.

—— and Leng, S.-C. (eds.), 1972, *Law in Chinese Foreign Policy: Communist China*. New York: Oceana Publications.

Clark, G., and Sohn, L. B., 1960, *World Peace Through World Law*. Cambridge, Mass.: Harvard University Press.

Clarkson, S., 1978, *The Soviet Theory of Development*. Toronto: University of Toronto Press.

Claudin, F., 1979, 'Some Reflections on the Crisis in Marxism'. *Socialist Review*, No. 45.

Cliff, T., 1968, 'The Theory of Bureaucratic Collectivism—A Critique'. *International Socialism*, No. 32.

Cohen, B., 1973, *The Question of Imperialism*. New York: Basic Books.

Cohen, J. A., 1972, *China's Practice of International Law. Some Case Studies*. Cambridge, Mass.: Harvard University Press.

—— and Chiu, H., 1974, *People's China and International Law: A Documentary Study*, Vol. I. Princeton, NJ: Princeton University Press.

Corrigan, P., Ramsay, H., and Sayer, D., 1978, *Socialist Construction and Marxist Theory: Bolshevism and its Critique*. London: Macmillan.

Cox, R. W., 1979, 'Ideologies and the New International Economic Order: Reflections on some Recent Literature'. *International Organization*, 33 (2), Spring.

Dallin, A., 1962, *The Soviet Union at the U.N*. Conn.: Methuen.

Davidson, A., 1968, *Antonio Gramsci, The Man, his Ideas*. Sydney: Australian Left Review Publications.

Davidson, B., 1979, 'Cabral on the African Revolution'. *Monthly Review*, 31.

Davis, H. B., 1967, *Nationalism and Socialism*. New York: Monthly Review Press.

—— 1979, *Towards a Marxist Theory of Nationalism*. New York and London: Monthly Review Press.

Dawisha, K., and Hanson, P. (eds.), 1981, *Soviet-East European Dilemmas*. London: Heinemann.

Day, R. B., 1976, 'The Theory of the Long Cycle: Koldratiev, Trotsky, Mandel'. *New Left Review*, No. 99, Sept. –Oct.

Debray, R., 1967, *Revolution in the Revolution? Armed Struggle and Political Struggle in Latin America*. New York and London: Monthly Review Press.

—— 1974, *La Critique des Armes*. Paris VIe: Éditions du Seuil.

'Declaration on principles of international law concerning friendly relations and co-operation among states in accordance with the Charter of the U.N.' [text]. *American Journal of International Law*, 65, Jan. 1971.

de George, R., 1970, *Patterns of Soviet Thought*. Ann Arbor, Mich.: University of Michigan Press.

Degras, J. (ed.), 1948, *Calendar of Soviet Documents on Foreign Policy 1917–1941*. London: Royal Institute of International Affairs.

—— 1951–53, *Soviet Documents on Foreign Policy, 1917–1941*. London: OUP.

—— 1956, *The Communist International 1919–1943, Documents*, Vol. 1. London: OUP.

—— 1960, *The Communist International 1919–1943, Documents*, Vol. 2. London: OUP.

—— 1971, *The Communist International 1919–1943, Documents*, Vol. 3. London: Frank Cass.

d'Encausse, H. C. and Schram, S. R., 1969, *Marxism and Asia*. Harmondsworth: Penguin.

Deutscher, I., 1949, *Stalin: A Political Biography*. New York: OUP.

—— 1970, *Russia, China and the West 1953–1966*. Harmondsworth: Penguin.

—— 1971, *Marxism in Our Time*. Berkeley: Ramparts Press.

Devlin, K., 1979, 'Eurocommunism: between East and West'. *International Security*, 3 (4), Spring.

Djilas, M., 1966, *The New Class: an Analysis of the Communist System*. London: Unwin.

Documents Adopted by the International Conference of Communist and Workers' Parties. Moscow: Novosti Press Agency Publishing House, 1969.

Dominguez, J. I. (ed.), 1982, *Cuba: Internal and International Affairs*. Beverly Hills and London: Sage.

Dos Santos, T., 1970, 'The Structure of Dependence'. *American Economic Review, Papers and Proceedings*, 60 (2), May.

Duiker, W. J., 1977, 'Ideology and Nation-building in the Democratic Republic of Vietnam'. *Asian Survey*, 17 (5), May.

—— 1981, *The Communist Road to Power in Vietnam*. Boulder, Col.: Westview Press.

Duncan, W. R. (ed.), 1970, *Social Policy in Developing Countries*. Waltham, Mass.: Finn-Blaisdell.

—— 1980, *Soviet Policy in the Third World*. New York: Pergamon.

Dunn, S. P., 1979, 'The Position of the Primitive—Communal Social Order in the Soviet-Marxist Theory of History', in Diamond, S. (ed.), *Toward a Marxist Anthropology*. Hague: Mouton.

Elliot, P., and Schlesinger, P., 1979, 'On the Stratification of Political Knowledge: Studying "Eurocommunism"': An Unfolding Ideology'. *Sociological Review*, 27 (1), Feb.

Elliott, C. F. and Linden, C. A. (eds.), 1980, *Marxism in the Contemporary West*. Boulder, Col.: Westview.

Emmanuel, A., 1972, *Unequal Exchange: A Study in the Imperialism of Trade*. London: New Left Books.

Engels, F., 1943, *Herr Eugen Dühring's Revolution in Science (i.e. Anti-Dühring)*. London: Lawrence and Wishart.

—— 1963, *Principles of Communism*, in D. Ryazanoff (ed.), *The Communist Manifesto of K. Marx and F. Engels*, New York, Russell and Russell.

Engleborghs-Bertels, M., 1981, 'Les conceptions chinoises en matière de relations internationales'. *Études internationales*, 12 (2), June.

Erickson, R. J., 1972, *International Law and the Revolutionary State*. New York: Oceana, Leyden, Sitjhoff.

Evans, P., 1979, *Dependent Development: The Alliance of Multinational, State and Local Capital in Brazil*. Princeton, NJ: Princeton University Press.

Evriviades, E. L., 1982, 'The Third World's Approach to the Deep Seabed'. *Ocean Development and International Law*, 11 (3–4).

Falk, R. A., 1965, 'Coexistence Law Bows Out'. *The American Journal of International Law*, 59.

Fanon, F., 1967, *The Wretched of the Earth*. Harmondsworth: Penguin.

Farina, N., 1976, 'China's attitude towards the development of International Law of Armed Conflict'. *Comunita Inernazionale*, 31 (3).

Feeney, W. R., 1977, 'Sino-Soviet Competition in the United Nations'. *Asian Survey*, 17 (9), Sept.

Feldbrugge, F. J. M. (ed.), 1973, *Encyclopedia of Soviet Law*, Vols. I and II. Sitjhoff/Leiden/New York: Oceana Publications.

Feuer, L.S., 1982, 'The Social Role of the Frankfurt Marxists'. *Survey*, 26 (2), Spring.

Fletcher, R. A., 1981, 'Revisionism and Empire: A Study of the Views of Eduard Bernstein, Joseph Bloch and the "Sozialistische Monatshefte" on Germany's Place in the World Community, 1900–1914'. Brisbane, University of Queensland, unpublished Ph.D. thesis.

Foster-Carter, A., 1973, 'Neo-Marxist Approaches to Development and Underdevelpment'. *Journal of Contemporary Asia*, 4.

—— 1976, 'From Rostow to Gunder Frank: Conflicting Paradigms in the Analysis of Underdevelopment'. *World Development*, 4 (3), Mar.

—— 1978, 'The Modes of Production Controversy'. *New Left Review*, No. 107, Jan.–Feb.

Frank, A. G., 1969, *Capitalism and Underdevelopment in Latin America: Historical Studies of Chile and Brazil*. New York and London: Monthly Review Press, 2nd edn.

—— 1969, *Latin America: Underdevelopment or Revolution: Essays on the Development of Underdevelopment and the Immediate Enemy*. New York and London: Monthly Review Press.

—— 1977, 'Dependence is Dead, Long Live Dependence and the Class Struggle: An Answer to Critics'. *World Development*, 5 (4).

—— 1980, *Crisis in the World Economy*. London: Heinemann.

—— 1981, *Crisis in the Third World*. New York and London: Holmes and Meier.

Frank, P., 1979, *The Fourth International: The Long March of the Trotskyists*. London: Ink Links.

Franklin, B. (ed.), 1972, *The Essential Stalin: Major Theoretical Writings 1905–1952*, New York, Anchor Books, Doubleday.

Fraser, A., 1978, 'The Legal Theory We Need Now'. *Socialist Review*, 8 (4–5), July-Oct.

Friedman, E., 1979, 'On Maoist Conceptualizations of the Capitalist World System'. *China Quarterly*, No. 80, Dec.

Fuandez, J., 1980, 'The Sea-bed Negotiations: Third World Choices'. *Third World Quarterly*, 2 (3), July.

Furtado, C., 1970, *Economic Development of Latin America: A Survey from Colonial Times to the Cuban Revolution*. Cambridge: CUP.

—— 1977, 'Development'. *International Social Science Journal*, XXX (4).

Gallie, W. B., 1978, *Philosophers of Peace and War: Kant, Clausewitz, Marx, Engels and Tolstoy*. Cambridge: CUP.

Galtung, J., 1964, 'A Structural Theory of Aggression'. *Journal of Peace Research*, No. 2.

—— 1971, 'A Structural Theory of Imperialism'. *Journal of Peace Research*, No. 2.

Gantman, V., 1969, 'Class Nature of Present-Day International Relations'. *International Affairs* (Moscow), No. 9.

Garaudy, R., 1970, *Marxism in the 20th Century*. London: Collins.

Gati, T. T., 1980, 'The Soviet Union and the North-South Dialogue'. *Orbis*, 24, Summer.

Genovese, E. D., 1969, *The World the Slaveholders Made*. New York: Pantheon.

—— 1974, *Roll, Jordan Roll: The World the Slaves Made*. New York: Pantheon.

Gilpin, R., 1975, *U.S. Power and the Multinational Corporation: The Political Economy of Foreign Direct Investment*. New York: Basic Books.

Girvan, N., 1973, 'The Development of Dependency Economics in the Caribbean and Latin America: Review and Comparison'. *Social and Economic Studies*, 22 (1).

Godelier, M., 1977, *Perspectives in Marxist Anthropology*. Cambridge: CUP.

Goodman, E. R., 1960, *The Soviet Design for a World State*. New York: Columbia University Press.

Gramsci, A., 1971, *Selections from the Prison Notebooks of Antonio Gramsci*. London: Lawrence and Wishart.

Granov, V., 1975, 'The Struggle of Ideologies and Cooperation Between States'. *International Affairs* (Moscow), No. 1.

Gray, L., 1979, 'Eurocommunism: a Brief Political-Historical Portrait'. *Res publica*, 21 (1).

Greig, I., 1977, *The Communist Challenge to Africa: An Analysis of Contemporary Soviet, Chinese and Cuban Policies*. Richmond, Surrey: Foreign Affairs Publishers.

Griffith, W. E., 1978, 'The Diplomacy of Eurocommunism', in Tökés, R. L. (ed.), *Eurocommunism and Détente*. New York: New York University Press.

Groom, A. J. R., and Mitchell, C. R., 1978, *International Relations Theory. A Bibliography*. London: Frances Pinter.

Grzybowski, K., 1970, *Soviet Public International Law: Doctrines and Diplomatic Practice*. Leyden: A. W. Sitjhoff.

Gülalp, H., 1981 'Frank and Wallerstein Revisited: A Contribution to Brenner's Critique'. *Journal of Contemporary Asia*, 11 (2).

Gutkind, P., and Wallerstein, I. (eds.), 1976, *The Political Economy of Contemporary Africa*. Beverly Hills: Sage.

Habermas, J., 1971, *Knowledge and Human Interests*. Boston: Beacon Press.

—— 1973, *Legitimation Crisis*. Boston: Beacon Press.

Halliday, F., 1976, 'Marxist Analysis and Post-Revolutionary China'. *New Left Review*, No. 100 Nov.–Jan.

—— 1983, *The Making of the Second Cold War*. London: Verso.

Hammond, R., 1968, 'Ho Chi Minh: Fifty Years of Revolution'. *Comparative Communism*, 1 (1 and 2), July–Oct.

Hanson, P., 1980–1, 'Economic Constraints on Soviet Policies in the 1980s'. *International Affairs*, 57 (1), Winter.

Hayter, T., 1971, *Aid as Imperialism*. Harmondsworth: Penguin.

Hazard, J. N., 1938, 'Cleansing Soviet International Law of anti-Marxist Theories'. *American Journal of International Law*, 32.

—— 1957, 'Legal Research on "Peaceful Co-existence" ' (Editorial Comment). *American Journal of International Law*, 51.

—— 1957a, 'Pashukanis is no Traitor' (Editorial Comment). *The American Journal of International Law*, 51.

—— 1961, 'Codifying Peaceful Co-existence'. *The American Journal of International Law*, 55.

—— 1963, 'Co-existence Codification Reconsidered'. *The American Journal of International Law*, 57.

—— 1965, 'Co-existence Law Bows Out'. *The American Journal of International Law*, 59.

—— 1971, 'Renewed Emphasis upon a Socialist International Law'. *The American Journal of International Law*, 65.

—— 1979, 'International Law under Contemporary Pressures'. *Military Law Review*, 83, Winter.

Hechter, M., 1975, *Internal Colonialism: The Celtic Fringe in British Nationalist Development 1536–1966*. London: Routledge and Kegan Paul.

Higgott, R., 1978, 'Competing Theoretical Perspectives on Development and Underdevelopment: A Recent Intellectual History'. *Politics*, XIII (I), May.

Hilferding, R., 1910–55, *Finance Capital: a Study of the Most Recent Development of Capitalism*. First published Vienna 1910; further editions Moscow 1912, Berlin, 1947, 1955.

Hindess, B. and Hirst, P. Q., 1975, *Pre-Capitalist Modes of Production*. London: Routledge and Kegan Paul.

History of the CPSU: Short Course (1951). Moscow: Foreign Languages Publishing House.

Ho Chi Minh: Selected Writings, 1920–1969, 1973, Hanoi: Foreign Languages Publishing House.

Hobson, J. A., 1965, *Imperialism—a Study*. Ann Arbor, Mich: University of Michigan Press.

Hoffheimer, D. J., 1979, 'China and the International Legal Order'. *Case Western Reserve Journal of International Law*, 11 (2).

Hoffman, S., 1963, 'The Study of International Law and the Theory of International Relations'. *Proceedings of the American Society of International Law*, 57th Annual Meeting, The American Society of International Law, Washington D.C.

Hook, S., 1980, 'Spectral Marxism'. *American Scholar*, 49.

Horowitz, I., 1966, *Three Worlds of Development*. London: OUP.

Horwitz, D. (ed.), 1967, *Containment and Revolution: Western Policy towards Social Revolution 1917 to Vietnam*. London: Anthony Blond.

—— 1969, 'The Corporations and the Cold War'. *Monthly Review*, 21, Nov.

—— 1969, *Imperialism and Revolution*. Harmondsworth: Penguin.

Howard, M., 1977, 'Helsinki Reconsidered. East-West Relations five years after the "Final Act" '. *Round Table*, July.

Hsiung, J. C., 1972, *Law and Policy in China's Foreign Relations: A Study of Attitudes and Practice*. New York: Columbia University Press.

Hsüeh, Chün-tu, 1977, *Dimensions of China's Foreign Relations*. New York/London: Praeger.

Hymer, S., 1978, 'International Politics and International Economics: A Radical Approach'. *Monthly Review*, Mar.

Jacobson, H. K., 1963, *The USSR and the UN's Economic and Social Activities*. Notre Dame, Ind.: University of Notre Dame Press.

Jaffe, P. J., 1972, 'The Varga Controversy'. *Survey*, 18 (3), Summer.

—— 1973, 'The Cold War Revisionists and What They Omit'. *Survey*, 19 (4), Autumn.

Jalée, P., 1968, *Le Tiers monde dans l'economie mondiale: l'exploitation impérialiste*. Paris: Maspero.

—— 1969, *The Pillage of the Third World*. New York: Monthly Review Press.

—— 1970, *L'Impérialisme en 1970*. Paris: Maspero.

Janke, P., 1978, 'Marxist Statecraft in Africa: What Future?', *Conflict Studies*, 95, May.

Jashek, S., 1978, 'Die Chinesische Völkerrechtsdoctrin im Lichte der Drei-Welten Theorie'. *German Yearbook of International Law*, 21.

Jay, M., 1973, *The Dialectical Imagination*. Boston and Toronto: Little, Brown.

—— 1982, 'Misrepresentations of the Frankfurt School: A Reply to Lewis S. Feuer'. *Survey*, 26 (2), Spring.

Jenkins, R., 1970, *Exploitation: The World Power Structure and the Inequality of Nations*. London: MacGibbon and Kee.

Jenks, C. W., 1958, *The Common Law of Mankind*. London: Stevens and Sons.

—— 1971, *A New World of Law*. London: Longmans.

Jinadu, L. A., 1973, 'Some African Theorists of Culture and Modernization: Fanon, Cabral and Others'. *African Studies Review*, 21, Apr.

Kahn, M. E., 1980, 'Antonio Gramsci and Modern Marxism'. *Studies in Comparative Communism*, 13 (2 and 3), Summer–Autumn.

Kaldor, M., 1978, *The Disintegrating West*. Harmondsworth: Penguin.

—— 1981, *The Baroque Arsenal*. New York: Hill and Wang.

—— and Smith, D. (eds.), *Disarming Europe*. London: Merlin Press.

Kardelj, E., 1976, 'Historical Roots of Non-Alignment?', in *Yugoslavia in the Contemporary World*. Beograd: Federal Committee for Information.

Katz, M. N., 1982, *The Third World in Soviet Military Thought*. London and Canberra: Croom Helm.

Kautsky, J. H. (ed.), 1962, *Political Change in Underdeveloped Countries*. New York: John Wiley.

—— 1968, *Communism and the Politics of Development*. New York: John Wiley.

Kautsky, K., 1970, 'Ultra-imperialism'. *New Left Review*, 59, Jan.–Feb.

Kay, G., 1975, *Development and Underdevelopment: A Marxist Analysis*. London: Macmillan.

Kelsen, H., 1955, *The Communist Theory of Law*. New York: F. A. Praeger.

Kemp, T., 1967, *Theories of Imperialism*. London: Dobson Books.

Kennan, G. F., 1956, *Russia Leaves The War*, Princeton, Princeton University Press

Kidron, M., 1962, 'Imperialism, Last Stage But One'. *International Socialism*, 9, Summer.

—— 1970, *Western Capitalism Since the War*, revised edn. Harmondsworth: Penguin.

Kiernan, V. G., 1974, *Marxism and Imperialism*. London: Edward Arnold.

Kim, S. S., 1978, 'The People's Republic of China and the Charter-Based International Legal Order'. *American Journal of International Law*, 72.

—— 1979, *China, the UN and World Order*. Princeton, NJ: Princeton University Press.

—— 1981, 'Whither post-Mao Chinese Global Policy?' *International Organization*, 35 (3), Summer.

Kim, Y. M., 1981, 'The Role of Ideology in Chinese Foreign Policy: the Theory and Practice of the Three Worlds'. *Journal of East Asian Affairs*, 1.

Kindersley, R., 1978, 'Eurocommunism'. *Ditchley Journal*, 5 (2), Autumn.

Kinsey, R., 1978, 'Marxism and the Law: Preliminary Analyses'. *British Journal of Law and Society*, Winter.

Kiracofe, C. A. Jr., 1979, 'Marxist – Leninist Theory and the Third World'. *Journal of Social and Political Studies*, 4 (3), Fall.

Klinghoffer, A. J., 1969, *Soviet Perspectives on African Socialism*. Rutherford: Fairleigh Dickinson University Press.

Kohler, F. D., 1973, *Soviet Strategy for the Seventies; from Cold War to Peaceful Coexistence*. University of Miami Center for Advanced International Studies.

Kolakowski, L., 1981, *Main Currents of Marxism*, 3 vols. Oxford: Clarendon Press.

—— 1981a, 'Miliband's Anti-Kolakowski'. *Political Studies*, XXIX (1).

Kolko, G., 1968, *The Politics of War: The World and United States Foreign Policy, 1943–1945*. New York: Random House.

Kolko, J., 1974, *America and the Crisis of World Capitalism*. Boston: Beacon.

—— and Kolko, G., 1972, *The Limits of Power: The World and United States Foreign Policy, 1945–1954*. New York: Harper and Row.

Konstantinov, F., 1968, 'Internationalism and the World Socialist System'. *International Affairs* (Moscow), No. 7.

—— 1970, *Sociological Problems of International Relations*. Moscow: Izdatelstvo 'Nauka'.

Korovin, E. A., 1924, *International Law of the Transitional Period*. Moscow.

—— 1958; 'Proletarian Internationalism and International Law'. *Soviet Yearbook of International Law*, Moscow.

—— 1959, *Osnovnye problemy sovremennykh mezhdunarodnykh otnoshenii*. Moscow.

Korsch, K., 1970, *Marxism and Philosophy*, London, NLB.

Kovalev, S., 1969, 'Sovereignty and the Internationalist Obligations of Socialist Countries'. *The Current Digest of the Soviet Press*, XX (39).

Krippendorff, E., 1975, *Internationales System als Geschichte: Einführung in die Internationalen Beziehungen*, Frankfurt, Campus Verlag.

—— 1975a, 'Towards a Class Analysis of the International System', *Acta Politica*, Vol. 10, Jan., Part 1.

—— *International Relations as a Social Science*, Sussex, Harvester (translated from German *Internationales Beziehungen als Wissenschaft*, 1975, Frankfurt, Campus Verlag).

Kubálková, V. and Cruickshank, A. A., 1977, 'A Double Omission'. *British Journal of International Studies*, 3 (3).

—— 1980, *Marxism – Leninism and Theory of International Relations*. London: Routledge and Kegan Paul.

—— 1981, *International Inequality*. London: Croom Helm.

Kühne, K., 1979, *Economics and Marxism*. London: Macmillan.

Kulski, W. W., 1955, 'The Soviet Interpretation of International Law'. *American Journal of International Law*, 49.

Labedz, L., 1962, *Revisionism: Essays on the History of Marxist Ideas*. London: George Allen and Unwin.

Laclau, E., 1971, 'Feudalism and Capitalism in Latin America'. *New Left Review*, No. 67, May–June, 19–38, reprinted in Laclau (1977)

—— 1971a, 'Imperialism in Latin America'. *New Left Review*, 67, May–June.

—— 1977, *Politics and Ideology in Marxist Theory*, London, New Left Books.

Lall, S., 1975, 'Is "Dependence" a Useful Concept in Analysing Underdevelopment?' *World Development*, 3 (11–12).

Lapenna, I., 1975, 'The Soviet Concept of "Socialist" International Law'. *The Year Book of World Affairs*. New York: Praeger.

—— 1977, 'Human Rights: Soviet Theory and Practice'. *Conflict Studies*, No. 83, May.

Lavigne, M., 1983, 'The Soviet Union inside COMECOM'. *Soviet Studies*, XXXV (2), Apr.

Lenin, V. I., 1963, *Collected Works*. Moscow: Foreign Languages Publishing House, 45 vols.

—— 1966, *Against Imperialist War: Articles and Speeches*. Moscow: Progress Publishers.

—— 1967, *On Proletarian Internationalism*. Moscow: Progress Publishers.

—— 1968, *The State and Revolution: the Marxist Theory of the State and the Tasks of the Proletariat in the Revolution*. Moscow: Progress Publishers.

—— 1970, *On the Foreign Policy of the Soviet State*. Moscow: Progress Publishers.

—— 1971, *Selected Works in Three Volumes*. Moscow: Progress Publishers.

—— 1971a, *Speeches at the Eighth Party Congress*. Moscow: Progress Publishers.

—— n.d., *On the International Working-Class and Communist Movement*. Moscow: Foreign Languages Publishing House.

Leogrande, W. M., 1982, 'Foreign Policy: The Limits of Success', in Dominguez, J. I., (ed.), *Cuba: Internal and International Affairs*. Beverly Hills and London: Sage.

Levi, W., 1978, 'Are Developing States more Equal than Others?' *Year Book of World Affairs*, 32.

Lichtheim, G., 1964, *Marxism: a Historical and Critical Study*. London: Routledge and Kegan Paul.

—— 1971, *Imperialism*. Harmondsworth: Penguin.

Little, R., 1980, 'The Evolution of International Relations as a Social Science', in Kent, R. C. and Nielsson, G. P. (eds.), *The Study and Teaching of International Relations*. London: Frances Pinter.

Löwenthal, R., 1977, *Model or Ally? The Communist Powers and the Developing Countries*. New York: OUP.

Löwy, M., 1976, 'Marxists and the National Question'. *New Left Review*, No. 96, Mar.–Apr.

Lukács, G., 1971, *History and Class Consciousness: Studies in Marxist Dialectics*, London: Merlin.

Luxemburg, R., 1951, *The Accumulation of Capital*, London: Routledge.

—— and Bukharin, N., 1972, *Imperialism and the Accumulation of Capital*. London: Allen Lane. The Penguin Press.

McInness, N., 1972, *The Western Marxists*. London: Alcove Press.

MacLeod, A., 1980, 'The PCI's Relations with the PCF in the Age of Eurocommunism, May 1973–June 1979'. *Studies in Comparative Communism*, 13 (23), Summer–Autumn.

McNeal, R. H., 1967, *International Relations among Communists*. Englewood Cliffs, New Jersey: Prentice-Hall.

McWhinney, E., 1964, *Peaceful Coexistence and Soviet-Western International Law*. Leyden: Sijthoff.

—— 1967, *International Law and World Revolution*. Netherlands: Sijthoff.

—— 1971, 'Ideological Conflict and the Special Soviet Approach to International Law'. *University of Toledo Law Review*, Nos 1–2.

—— 1978, *The International Law of Detente*. Alphenaan den Rijn: Sijthoff.

—— 1979, *The World Court and the Contemporary International Law-making Process*. Alphenaan den Rijn: Sijthoff.

Magdoff, H., 1969, *The Age of Imperialism: The Economics of U.S. Foreign Policy*. New York: Monthly Review Press.

Maitan, L., 1976, *Party, Army and Masses in China*. London: New Left Books.

Mandel, E., 1970, *Europe versus America? Contradictions of Imperialism*. London: New Left Books.

—— 1970a, 'The Laws of Uneven Development'. *New Left Review*, No. 59, Jan.–Feb.

—— 1974, 'Ten Theses of the Social and Economic Laws governing the Society Transitional between Capitalism and Socialism'. *Critique*, No. 3.

—— 1975, *Late Capitalism*. London: New Left Books.

—— 1977, 'Peaceful Coexistence and World Revolution', in Blackburn, R. (ed.), *Revolution and Class Struggle: A Reader in Marxist Politics*, London, Fontana.

—— 1978, *From Stalinism to Eurocommunism*. London: New Left Books.

—— 1979, *Revolutionary Marxism Today*. London: New Left Books.

—— 1979a, *Trotsky: A Study in the Dynamic of his Thought*. London: New Left Books.

—— 1983, 'The Threat of War and the Struggle for Socialism', *New Left Review*, Number 141, Oct. 1983.

Marcuse, H., 1964, *One Dimensional Man: Studies in the Ideology of the Advanced Industrial Society*. London: Routledge and Kegan Paul.

—— 1971, *Soviet Marxism: A Critical Analysis*. Harmondsworth: Penguin.

Marx, K., 1901–1902, *Letters to Dr Kugelmann*, in *Die Neue Zeit*, II, No. 1; No. 2.

—— 1911, *Die Klassenkämpfe in Frankreich, 1948 bis 1850*. Berlin.

—— 1933, *Capital I, II, III, A Critique of Political Economy*, F. Engels (ed.). Chicago: Charles H. Kerr.

—— 1934, *Letters to Dr Kugelmann*. New York: International Publishers.

—— 1959, *Economic and Philosophic Manuscripts of 1844*. London: Lawrence and Wishart.

—— 1962, *Capital*, Vol. III. London: Lawrence and Wishart.

—— 1964, *Pre-Capitalist Economic Formations*, E. J. Hobsbawm (ed.). London: Lawrence and Wishart.

—— 1968, *On China* (1853–1860), London: Lawrence and Wishart (articles from the *New York Daily Tribune*, introduced by Dona Torr).

—— 1973, *Grundrisse: Foundations of the Critique of Political Economy (rough draft)*, trans. with a foreword by M. Nicolaus. Harmondsworth: Penguin.

—— n.d., *The Poverty of Philosophy*. London: Martin Lawrence.

—— and Engels, F., 1902, *Aus dem literarischen Nachlass von Karl Marx, Friedrich Engels*, F. Mehring (ed.), Stuttgart.

—— 1913, *Der Briefwechsel zwischen Friedrich Engels und Karl Marx, 1844 bis 1883*, A. Bebel, B. Bernstein, 4 vols. Stuttgart.

—— 1934, *Correspondence 1846–1895: A Selection with Commentary and Notes*. London: Martin Lawrence.

—— 1956, *The Holy Family*. Moscow.

—— 1960, *On Colonialism*. London: Lawrence and Wishart.

—— 1962, *Selected Works in Two Volumes*. Moscow.

—— 1965, *German Ideology*. London: Lawrence and Wishart.

—— 1968, *Selected Works in One Volume*. London: Lawrence and Wishart.

—— 1969, *Letters to Americans 1848–1895: a Selection*. New York: International Publishers.

—— 1969a, *Manifesto of the Communist Party*. Moscow: Progress Publishers.

278   Bibliography

—— 1972, *The Marx-Engels Reader*, R. C. Tucker (ed.). New York: Norton.

—— n.d., *The Civil War in the U.S.* London: Lawrence and Wishart.

—— n.d., *On Colonialism*. Moscow: Foreign Languages Publishing House.

Mazrui, A. A., 1972, 'Africa in the 1970s'. *Survey*, 18 (2), Spring.

Mehrish, B. N., 1979, 'The Role of the Third World in the Law of the Sea Negotiations'. *Foreign Affairs Report*, 28 (3), Mar.

Meisner, M., 1973, *Li Ta-chao and the Origins of Chinese Marxism*. New York: Atheneum.

Melotti, U., 1977, *Marx and the Third World*. London: Macmillan.

Mezhdunarodnye otnoshenia: bibliograficheskii sparavochnik, 1945–1960. Moscow, 1961.

Michalet, C.-A., 1976, *Le Capitalisme Mondial*. Paris: Presses Universitaires de France.

Mickiewicz, E. and Kolkowicz, R. (eds.) 1983, *The Soviet Calculus of Nuclear War, Soviet Union/Union Sovietique*, Special Issue, vol. 10, Parts 2–3.

Miliband, R., 1969, *The State in Capitalist Society*. London: Weidenfeld and Nicolson.

—— 1981, *Marxism and Politics*. London: OUP.

—— 1981a, 'Kolakowski's Anti-Marx'. *Political Studies*, XXIX (1).

Miroshchenko, B., 1966, 'Socialist Internationalism and Soviet Foreign Policy'. *International Affairs*, No. 3.

Mitchell, R. J., 1972, 'The Brezhnev Doctrine and Communist Ideology'. *Review of Politics*, 34 (2).

Modrzhinskaya, E. D. and Stepanian, C. A. (eds.), 1971, *Budushchee Chelovecheskogo obshchestva*. Moscow: 'Mysl'.

Morgenthau, Hans J., 1967 *Politics among Nations*. New York, Alfred A. Knopf

Mouffe, C. (ed.), 1979, *Gramsci and Marxist Theory*. London: Routledge and Kegan Paul.

Mrázek, J., 1976, 'A Code of Socialist International Law'. *Nová Mysl*, No. 2, Feb.

Nairn, T., 1975, 'Marxism and the Modern Janus'. *New Left Review*, 94, Nov–Dec.

—— 1977, *The Break-up of Britain: Crisis of Neo-nationalism*. London: New Left Books.

Nash, J., 1981, 'Ethnographic Aspects of the World Capitalist System'. *Annual Review of Anthropology*, 10.

Nicolaus, M. 1970, 'U.S.A.: The Universal Contradiction', in *New Left Review*, 59

Nkrumah, K., 1966, *Neo-Colonialism: the last stage of Imperialism*. New York: International Publishers.

Nove, A., 1973, 'On Reading Andre Gunder Frank'. *Journal of Developmental Studies*, 10, (3–4).

O'Brien, P., n.d., 'A Critique of Latin American Theories of Dependency'. *Occasional Papers*, No. 12, University of Glasgow.

Ogden, S., 1976, 'China and International Law: Implications for Foreign Policy'. *Pacific Affairs*, 49 (1), Spring.

—— 1977, 'The Approach of the Chinese Communists to the Study of International Law, State Sovereignty and the International System'. *China Quarterly*, 70.

Olesczuk, T., 1982, 'Dissident Marxism in Eastern Europe', *World Politics*, Vol. XXXIV (4), July.

Orridge, A. W., 1981, 'Uneven Development and Nationalism: 2'. *Political Studies*, XXIX (2).

Osakwe, C., 1972, 'Socialist International Law Revisited'. *American Journal of International Law*, 66.

—— 1974, *The Soviet Union and the Law of International Organisations*. University of Illinois at Urbana-Champaign.

Ottaway, M., 1978, 'Soviet Marxism and African Socialism'. *Journal of Modern African Studies*, 16 (3), September.

Owen, R. and Sutcliffe, B., 1972, *Studies in the Theory of Imperialism*. London: Longman.

Pashukanis, 1980, *Selected Writings on International Marxism and Law*, Beirne and Sharlett (eds.). London: Academic Press.

Petras, J. F., 1976, 'Class and Politics in the Periphery and the Transition to Socialism'. *Review of Radical Political Economics*, 8 (2).

—— and Selden, M., 1981, 'Social Classes, the State and the World System in the Transition to Socialism'. *Journal of Contemporary Asia*, 11, 189–207.

Pettman, R., 1979, *State and Class: A Sociology of International Affairs*. London: Croom Helm.

Poulantzas, N., 1973, *Political Power and Social Classes*. London: New Left Books.

—— 1975, *Classes in Contemporary Capitalism*. London: New Left Books.

—— 1976, 'The Capitalist State: A Reply to Miliband and Laclau', *New Left Review*, No. 95, Jan.–Feb.

Primakov, E. M., 1980–1, 'The USSR and the Developing Countries'. *Journal of International Affairs*, 34 (2), Fall-Winter.

Purdy, D., 1973, 'The Theory of the Permanent Arms Economy—A Critique and an Alternative'. *Bulletin of the Conference of Socialist Economy*, Spring.

Radice, H., 1975, *International Firms and Modern Imperialism: Selected Readings*. Harmondsworth: Penguin.

Rakovski, M., 1978, *Towards an East European Marxism*. London: Allison and Busby.

Ramet, P., 1982, 'Soviet-Yugoslav Relations Since 1976'. *Survey*, 26 (2), Spring.

Ramondo, B. A., 1967, *Peaceful Coexistence: International Law in the Building of Communism*. Baltimore: Johns Hopkins.

Rees, D., 1977, 'The New Vietnam: Hanoi's Revolutionary Strategy'. *Conflict Studies*, No. 89 (Special Report), Nov.

Reisner, W. (ed.), 1973, *Documents of the Fourth International*. New York: Pathfinder.

Rey, P. P., 1971, *Colonialisme, neo-colonialisme et transition au capitalisme*. Paris: Maspero.

—— 1973, *Les Alliances de Classes*. Paris: Maspero.

—— *The Road to Communism. Documents of the 22nd Congress of the CPSU*, 17–31 Oct., 1961. Moscow: Foreign Languages Publishing House.

Roberts, J. W., 1977, 'Lenin's Theory of Imperialism in Soviet Usage'. *Soviet Studies*, XXIX (3), July.

Rodney, W., 1969, *The Groundings with my Brothers*. London: Bogle-L'Overture.

—— 1973, *How Europe Underdeveloped Africa*. London: Bogle-L'Overture.

Rolph, H., 1968, 'Ho Chi Minh: Fifty Years of Revolution'. *Studies in Comparative Communism*, 1 (1–2), July-Oct.

Rosenstock, R., 1971, 'Declaration of Principles of International Law concerning Friendly Relations: a Survey'. *American Journal of International Law*, 65.

Rothenberg, M., 1980, *The USSR and Africa: New Dimensions of Soviet Global Power*. Miami: Advanced International Studies Institute in association with the University of Miami.

Roxborough, I., 1979, *Theories of Underdevelopment*. Atlantic Highlands, NJ: Humanity Press.

Rubinstein, A. Z., 1964, *The Soviets in International Organizations*. Princeton, NJ: Princeton University Press.

Sartre, J.-P., 1976–7, 'Socialism in One Country'. *New Left Review*, No. 100, Nov.–Jan.

Satyamurthy, T. V., 1978, 'Role of China in International Relations'. *Economic and Political Weekly*, 13 (45), November 11; 13 (46); November 18; 13 (47), November 25.

Shapiro, L., 1978, 'The Soviet Union and "Eurocommunism" '. *Conflict Studies*, 99, Sept.

—— 1979, 'The Move to Rehabilitate Bukharin'. *The World Today*, 35 (4), Apr.

Schlesinger, R., 1945, *Soviet Legal Theory*. London: Kegan Paul.

Schram, S. R., 1969, *The Political Thought of Mao Tse-tung*.

Harmondsworth: Penguin.

Scott, G. L., 1975, *Chinese Treaties. The Post-revolutionary Restoration of International Law and Order*. New York: Oceana Publications Leiden: A. W. Sijthoff.

Seddon, D. (ed.), 1978, *Relations of Production: Marxist Approaches to Economic Anthropology*. London: Frank Cass.

Shipley, P., 1977, 'Trotskyism: ''Entryism'' and Permanent Revolution'. *Conflict Studies*, No. 81, Mar.

Sigmund, P. E., 1980, 'Marxism in Latin America', in Elliott, C. F. and Linden, C. A. (eds.), *Marxism in the Contemporary West*. Boulder, Col.: Westview.

Sivachev, N. V. and Yakovlev, N. N., 1979, *Russia and the United States*. Chicago: Univerity of Chicago Press.

Sklar, R., 1976, 'Postimperialism: A Class Analysis of Multinational Corporate Expansion'. *Comparative Politics*, 9 (1), Oct.

Skocpol, T., 1976, 'France, Russia, China: A Structural Analysis of Social Revolutions'. *Comparative Studies in Society and History: An International Quarterly*, 18, 175–210.

—— 1976a, 'Old Regime Legacies and Communist Revolutions in Russia and China'. *Social Forces*, 55 (2), Dec.

—— 1977, 'Wallerstein's World Capitalist System: A Theoretical and Historical Critique'. *American Journal of Sociology*, 82, Mar.

—— 1979, 'State and Revolution: Old Regimes and Revolutionary Crises in France, Russia and China'. *Theory and Society*, 7.

Smith, T., 1977, 'Changing Configurations of Power in North-South Relations since 1945'. *International Organization*, 31 (1), Winter.

—— 1979, 'The Underdevelopment of Development Literature: The Case of Dependency Theory'. *World Politics*, XXXI (2), Jan.

—— 1981, 'The Logic of Dependency Theory Revisited'. *International Organization*, 35 (4), Autumn.

Sokolovsky, M.V.D., 1976, *Soviet Military Strategy*, London: MacDonald and James.

Staar, R. F., 1979, 'The Bear versus the Dragon in the Third World'. *Policy Review*, Winter.

—— 1982, 'Checklist of Communist Parties and Fronts', *Problems of Communism*, Mar.–Apr., Vol. XXXI

Stalin, J. V., 1946–51, *Sochinenia*, 16 vols. Moscow.

—— 1972, *The Essential Stalin: Major Theoretical Writings*, B. Franklin (ed.). New York: Anchor.

Steinkühler, M., 1982, 'Eurocommunism after the Polish Repression'. *Aussen Politik*, 33 (4).

Stojanovic, R., 1983, *Conflicts Between Socialist Countries—a Marxist View*. Paper delivered on 28 Apr. at A.N.U., Research School of Pacific Studies, Department of International Relations.

Sumner, C., 1979, *Reading Ideologies: an Investigation into the Marxist Theory of Ideology and Law*. New York: Academic Press.

Sweezy, P. M., 1968, *The Theory of Capitalist Development. Principles of Marxian Political Economy*. New York and London: Modern Reader

—— 1979, 'On the New Global Disorder'. *Monthly Reveiw*, 30 (11), Apr.

—— 1980, *Post Revolutionary Society*. New York and London: Monthly Review.

—— and Bettelheim, C., 1971, *On the Transition to Socialism*. 1st edn. New York.

Szawlowski, R., 1976, *The System of the International Organisations of the Communist Countries*. Netherlands: A. W. Sijthoff-Leyden.

Szymanski, A., 1979, *Is the Red Flag Flying? The Political Economy of the Soviet Union Today*. London: Zed Press.

—— 1981, *The Logic of Imperialism*. New York: Praeger.

Taracouzio, T. A., 1935, *The Soviet Union and International Law*. New York: The Macmillan Co.

Tarbuck, K. J., 1972, *Imperialism and the Accumulation of Capital: Rosa Luxemburg and Nikolai Bukharin*. London: Allen Lane.

Taylor, J. G., 1972, 'Marxism and Anthropology'. *Economy and Society*, 1 (3).

—— 1974, 'Neo-Marxism and Underdevelopment: A Sociological Phantasy'. *Journal of Contemporary Asia*, IV (1).

—— 1979, *From Modernization to Modes of Production*. London: Macmillan.

Thompson, E. P., 1980, 'Notes on Exterminism, the Last Stage of Civilization' *New Left Review*, Number 121, May–June.

—— *et al.*, 1982, *Exterminism and Cold War*, London: Verso.

Thorndike, T., 1978, 'The Revolutionary approach: the Marxist perspective', in Taylor, T. (ed.), *Approaches and Theory in International Relations*. Longman: London.

Ticktin, H., 1973, 'Towards a political economy of the USSR,' *Critique 1*

—— 1975, 'The Capitalist Crisis and Current Trends in the U.S.S.R.'. *Critique*, 4.

—— 1976, 'The Contradictions of Soviet Society and Professor Bettelheim', *Critique*, 6.

—— 1976–7, 'The U.S.S.R.; the beginning of the end'. *Critique*, No. 7.

—— 1979–1980, 'The Afghan War: The Crisis in the USSR'. *Critique*, No. 12.

Tökés, R. L. (ed.), 1979, *Eurocommunism and Détente*. USA: New York University Press.

Tomlinson, J., 1977, 'Hillel Ticktin and Professor Bettelheim: A Reply'. *Critique*, No. 8.

Trofimenko, H., 1981, 'The 3rd World of the U.S.-Soviet Competition: A Soviet View'. *Foreign Affairs*, 59, Summer.

Trotnow, H., 1975, 'The Misunderstood Karl Liebknecht'. *European Studies Review*, 5 (2).

Trotsky, L. 1924, *Piat' let Kominterna*. Moscow.

—— 1928, *The Real Situation in Russia*. New York.

—— 1931, *My Life*. New York.

—— 1936, *The Third International After Lenin*. New York.

—— 1941. *Stalin*. New York.

—— 1945. *The Revolution Betrayed*. New York.

—— 1947, *The Permanent Revolution*. Calcutta.

—— 1951, *Europe and America*. Colombo.

—— 1970, 'Not a Workers' and Not a Bourgeois State', in *Writings, 1937–38*. New York. Pathfinder.

Tsien, T., 1976, 'Conception et pratique du droit international public en République populaire de Chine'. *Journal du Droit International*, 103 (4), Oct.-Nov.-Dec.

Tunkin, G. E., 1962, *Voprosy Teorii Mezhdunarodnovo Prava*. Moscow: State Publishing House of Legal Literature.

—— 1974, *Theory of International Law*. London: George Allen and Unwin.

Turley, W. S. (ed.), 1980, *Vietnamese Communism in Comparative Perspective*. Boulder, Col.: Westview Press.

Ulam, A. B., 1974, *Expansion and Coexistence: Soviet Foreign Policy 1917–73*, 2nd edn. New York: Praeger.

—— 1980, 'The Soviet Union and the Rules of the International Game', in London, K. (ed.), *The Soviet Union in World Politics*. London: Croom Helm.

Valenta, J., 1981, 'The Soviet-Cuban Alliance in Africa and the Caribbean'. *The World Today*, 37 (2), Feb.

Valentinov, A., 1976, 'One Year after Helsinki'. *International Affairs*, No. 9, Sept.

Valkenier, E. K., 1968, 'Recent Trends in Soviet Research on the Developing Countries'. *World Politics*, XX, July.

—— 1973, 'The USSR and the Third World'. *Survey*, 19 (3), Summer, 41–9.

Varga, E., 1968, 'The Problem of inter-imperialist Contradictions and War', in *Politico-Economic Problems of Capitalism*. Moscow: Progress Publishers.

—— and Mendelsohn, L. (eds.), 1939, *New Data for V.I. Lenin's 'Imperialism, the Highest Stage of Capitalism'*. London: Lawrence and Wishart, New York: International Publishers.

Vernon, G. D., 1979, 'Controlled Conflict: Soviet Perceptions of Peaceful Co-existence'. *Orbis*, 23 (2), Summer.

284   Bibliography

Vigor, P. H., 1976, *The Soviet View of War, Peace and Neutrality*. London: Routledge.

Vyshinskii, A. I., 1948, *The Law of the Soviet State*. New York: Macmillan.

—— and Lozovskii, S. A. (eds.), 1948–50, *Diplomatic Dictionary*, 2 vols. Moscow.

Wallerstein, I., 1972, 'Social Conflict in Post-Independence Black Africa: The Concepts of Race and Status-Group Reconsidered', in Campbell, E. Q. (ed.), *Racial Tensions and National Identity*. Nashville.

—— 1973, 'Africa in a Capitalist World'. *A Quarterly Journal of Africanist Opinion*, II (3), Fall.

—— 1974, 'Dependence in an Interdependent World: The Limited Possibilities of Transformation within the Capitalist World Economy'. *African Studies Review*, XVII (1), Apr.

—— 1974a, *The Modern World-System*. New York: Academic Press.

—— 1974b, 'The Rise and Future Demise of the World Capitalist System: Concepts for Comparative Analysis'. *Comparative Studies in Society and History*, Vol. 16.

—— 1975, 'Africa, the United States, and the World Economy: the Historical Bases of American Policy', in Arkhurst, F. S. (ed.), *U.S. Policy Toward Africa*. Praeger.

—— 1975a, 'Class and Class Conflict in Africa'. *Monthly Review*, 26 (9), February.

—— 1975b, 'Class-Formation in the Capitalist World-Economy'. *Politics and Society*, Vol. 5.

—— 1975, 'The Present State of the Debate on World Inequality', in Wallerstein, I. (ed.), *World Inequality*. Montreal: Black Rose Books.

—— 1976, 'Semi-Peripheral Countries and the Contemporary World Crisis'. *Theory and Society*, 3 (4), Winter.

—— 1976a, 'A World-System Perspective on the Social Sciences'. *British Journal of Sociology*, 27 (3).

—— 1977, 'Rural Economy in Modern World-Society'. *Studies in Comparative International Development*, 12 (1).

—— 1980, *The Modern World-System II: Mercantilism and the Consolidation of the European World-Economy, 1600–1750*. New York, London: Academic Press.

—— 1980a, 'The Withering Away of the States', *International Journal of the Sociology of Law*, 8.

—— 1981, 'On How Accumulation Works'. *Contemporary Sociology*, 10.

Warren, W., 1973, 'Imperialism and Capitalist Industrialization'. *New Left Review*, No. 81, Sept.-Oct.

Wesson, R., 1983 'Checklist of Communist Parties, 1982: *Problems of Communism*, Mar-Apr., Vol. XXXII

Wight, M., 1966, 'Why is There no International Theory?', in Butter-field, H. and Wight, M. (eds.), *Diplomatic Investigations*. London: George Allen and Unwin.

—— 1977, *Systems of States*, Leicester University Press.

—— *Power Politics*, Harmondsworth: Penguin.

Wiles, P. (ed.), 1982, *The New Communist Third World: An Essay in Political Economy*. London and Canberra: Croom Helm.

Willetts, P., 1979, *The Non-Aligned Movement: The Origins of a Third World Alliance*. London: Frances Pinter.

Williams, R., 1977, *Marxism and Literature*. London: OUP.

Williams, W. A., 1959, *The Tragedy of American Diplomacy*. London: New Left Books.

Willmott, W. E., 1971, 'Thoughts on Ho Chi Minh'. *Pacific Affairs*, 44 (4), Winter.

Winslow, E. M., 1931, 'Marxian, Liberal and Sociological Theories of Imperialism'. *Journal of Political Economy*, Vol. 39.

Wolfers, A., 1962, *Discord and Collaboration*. Baltimore: Johns Hopkins Press.

Wright, E. O., 1978, *Class, Crisis and the State*. London: New Left Books.

Yahuda, M. B., 1978, *China's Role in World Affairs*. London: Croom Helm.

Yermolenko, D., 1967, 'Sociology and International Relations'. *International Affairs* (Moscow), No. 1.

Yin, C., 1983, 'Peiping's Foreign Policy after the 12th CCP National Congress: Its Continuity and Changes'. *Issues and Studies*, XIX (1), Jan.

Young, S. B., 1979, 'Vietnamese Marxism: Transition in Élite Ideology'. *Asian Survey* 19 (8), Aug.

Zadorozhnyi, G. B., 1965, *Mirnoe Sosushchestvovanie i Mezhdun-arodnoe Pravo*. Moscow: Foreign Languages Publishing House.

Zagladin, V. V. (ed.), 1973, *The World Communist Movement: Outline of Strategy and Tactics*. Moscow: Progress Publishers.

Zimmerman, W., 1969, *Soviet Perspectives on International Relations 1956–1967*. Princeton, NJ: Princeton University Press.

Bibliographical Supplement

Alker, H. E., 1981, 'Dialectical Foundations of Global Disparities'. *International Studies Quarterly*, Vol. 25, No. 1, Mar.

—— and T. J. Biersteker, 1984, 'The Dialectics of World Order: Notes for a Future Archeologist of International Savoir Faire'. *International Studies Quarterly*, Vol. 28.

Ashley, R. K., 1980, *The Political Economy of War and Peace: The Sino-Soviet Triangle and the Modern Security Problematique*. London: Frances Pinter.

—— 1981, 'Political Realism and Human Interests'. *International Studies Quarterly*, Vol. 25, No. 2.

—— 1983a, 'The Eye of Power: The Politics of World Modelling'. *International Organization*, Vol. 37, No. 3.

—— 1983b, 'Three Modes of Economism'. *International Studies Quarterly*, Vol. 27.

—— 1984, 'The poverty of neorealism'. *International Organization*. Vol. 38, No. 2.

Cox, R. W., 1981, 'Social Forces, States and World Orders: Beyond International Relations Theory'. *Millenium*, Vol. 10, No. 2.

—— 1983, 'Hegemony in International Relations: An Essay in Method'. *Millenium*, Vol. 12, No. 2.

—— 1987, *Production, Power, and World Order: Social Forces in the Making of History*. New York: Columbia University Press.

Gorbachev, M. S., 1986, *Political Report of the Central Committee to the 27th Congress of the CPSU*. Feb. 25, Novosti Press Agency.

—— 1987, *Perestroika: New Thinking for Our Country and the World*, New York: Harper and Row.

Gromyko, A. and Hellman, M. (eds.), 1988, *Breakthrough/Proryv: Emerging New Thinking: Soviet and Western Scholars Issue Challenge to build a World beyond War*. New York: Walker.

Hoffman, M., 1987, 'Critical Theory and Inter-Paradigm Debate'. *Millenium*, Vol. 16.

Huan Hiang, 1988, 'World Prospects for the Years Ahead'. *Beijing Review*, 18–24 Jan..

Keohane, R. (ed.), 1986, *Neorealism and its Critics*. New York: Columbia University Press.

Kubálková, V. and Cruickshank, A., 1986, 'The ''New Cold War'' in ''critical'' International Relations Studies'. *Review of International Studies*, Vol. 12, No. 3.

—— 'A Rambo Come to Judgement: Marxism, International

Relations and Fred Halliday'. *Review of International Studies*, Vol. 15, No. 1.

Linklater, A., 'Realism, Marxism and Critical International Theory'. *Review of International Studies*, Vol. 12, No. 4.

Maclean, J., 1981a, 'Marxist Epistemology, Explanations of "Change" and the Study of International Relations', in B. Buzan *et al.* (eds.), *Change and the Study of International Relations*. London: Frances Pinter.

—— 1981b, 'Political Theory, International Theory, and Problems of Ideology'. *Millenium*, Vol. 10, No. 2.

—— 'Interdependence—An ideological intervention in International Relations', in R. J. Barry Jones and P. Willetts (eds.), *Interdependence on Trial: Studies in the Theory and Reality of Contemporary Interdependence*. London: Frances Pinter.

Primakov, E., 1987, 'Novaia filosofiia vneshnei politiki'. *Pravda*, 10 July.

Shakhnazarov, G., 1988, 'Governability of the World'. *International Affairs* (Moscow), 3.

Name Index

Adelman, I. and Morris, C. T. 141
Adler, A. 46
Adorno, T. 206, 254–5
Alavi, H. 205
Alker, H. E. 249, 251, 257
Althusser, L. 8, 22, 208, 211, 224, 254–6
Amin, S. 97, 99, 106, 205, 209, 212, 216–18, 220–3, 225, 229, 248
Anderson, P. vii, 4, 197, 199, 224–6, 246, 254–6
Aron, R. 119
Arrighi, G. 205, 217, 224
Ashley, R. K. vii, 250–1, 253, 256–8

Bahro, R. 128–9, 237
Balibar, E. 211, 224–5
Baran, P. A. and Sweezy, P. M. 135, 205, 254–5; see also Sweezy, P. M.
Bauer, O. 46, 60–2, 111, 236–7
Bellis, P. 237
Bello, E. G. 186
Berki, R. N. 2, 40–1, 214–15
Bernstein, E. 42, 63–4, 126, 204, 235
Bettelheim, C. 205, 237, 240–1
Binns, P. 237, 241
Bloom, S. F. 30
Bobbio, N. 210
Bondarevsky, G. and Sofinsky, V. 145
Bottomore, T. 10, 12, 60, 247
Bourdieu, P. 251, 254–6
Boutros-Ghali, 163
Brenner, R. 225
Brewer, A. 28, 37
Brezhnev, L. 76, 89 95–6; 'Brezhnev doctrine' 89, 95, 190
Brinkley, G. A. 95–6
Brucan, S. 19, 23, 214
Bukharin, N. 20, 45, 48–53, 59, 126, 232, 234, 246, 260
Bull, H. 1, 13
Burawoy, M. vii, 211, 256
Burke, W. S. and Brokaw, F. S. 186

Cabral, A. 126–7, 183
Caporaso, J. A. 11
Cardoso, F. H. and Faletto, E. 216
Carillo, S. 126
Carlo, A. 237, 239–40
Carr, E. H. 208
Castro, F. 205
Chase-Dunn, C. K. 236, 243–4
Ch'iao, K.-h. 98
Chiu, H. 176
Ch'iu, J.-c. 176
Chou, F.-l. 176–7
Claudin, F. 205
Clausewitz, K. von 32, 52, 260
Cliff, T. 241
Colletti, L. 208
Cox, R. W. vii, 253, 257–8

Davis, H. B. 182
Debray, R. 151, 205
Dej, G. 127
d'Encausse, H. C. and Schram, S. R. 112
Deng 99, 249–50
Deutsch, K. 250–1, 254–5
Dimitrov, G. 122
Duiker, W. J. 153

Einstein, A. 258
Emmanuel, A. 205, 216, 220–1
Engels, F. 1, 3, 31–3, 36, 39, 43–4, 207, 245, 254–5, 257
Evriviades, E. L. 181

Falk, R. A. 186, 254–5, 259
Fanon, F. 135, 205
Feuer, L. S. 207
Foster-Carter, A. 205, 224
Foucault, M. 251, 254–6, 258
Frank, A. G. 136, 205, 213, 216–18, 220, 230, 244
Furtado, C. 216

Gallie, W. B. 31–2, 35
Gantman, V. 90
Garaudy, R. 208

290   Name Index

Genovese, E. D. 197, 212
Gilpin, R. 64–5
Gorbachev, M. S. 249, 252, 259
Gramsci, A. vii, 22, 126, 139, 195–206, 210–11, 234, 254–8, 260
Granov, V. 90
Grünberg, C. 46, 206
Grzybowski, K. 159, 174
Guevara, C. 151, 205

Habermas, J. 254–8
Halliday, F. 251, 258
Hanson, P. 244
Haya de la Torre, V. R. 150–1
Hazard, J. N. 129, 159–60, 182, 191
Hegel, G. W. F. 252, 254
Hilferding, R. 45, 47–8, 58–60
Hindess, B. 241
Hindess, B. and Hirst P. Q. 225
Ho, Chi Minh 122, 140, 149–50, 153–7, 205
Hobbes, T. 35, 83, 113; see also international relations: Hobbesian tradition
Hobson, J. A. 47–8, 53
Hoffman, M. 249
Hoffman, S. 158
Horkheimer, M. 206, 254–5
Horowitz, D. 205, 235

Jalée, P. 205, 232
Jashek, S. 97
Jay, M. 206–7
Jenkins, R. 205, 213–14
Jenks, C. W. 186

Kant, I. 14–15, 254; see also International relations: Kantian tradition
Kapchenko, N. 146
Kardelj, E. 130–1
Kautsky, K. 15, 46, 52, 107, 126, 234, 254–5
Kelsen, H. 159
Kennan, G. F. 78
Khruschev, N. 76, 87, 95–6, 132
Kidron, M. 233
Kiernan, V. G. 39
Kim, I. S. 205
Kim, S. S. 100, 106, 113
Kim, Y.-s. 148
Kolakowski, L. 3
Kolko, G. 235, 254–5

Kolko, J. 229
Kolkowicz, R. 93
Korovin, E. A. 19, 165–9, 172–3
Korsch, K. 195–6, 205–6, 210, 256
Kozhevnikov, S. B. 19, 171–3
Krippendorff, E. 12, 212, 215, 225 229
Krylov, F. I. 171
Kubálková, V. and Cruickshank, A A. 31, 85, 103, 216, 251–2
Kun, B. 122

Labriola, A. 46
Laclau, E. 213, 233–4
Lapenna, I. 159
Lavigne, M. 129, 190, 243
Lenin, V. I. 3, 15–16, 30, 44–6, 52–3 57, 74, 76–9, 83–4, 101, 113, 126 140, 144, 154, 164, 182–3, 196–8 205, 232, 234, 253–5, 257, 260
Leogrande, W. M. 150
Li Ta-chao 4, 22, 100, 108–11, 113 126, 140
Liang, C.-c. 108
Liebknecht, K. 44, 55–6, 242
Lin, H. 176–7
Lin, P. 135
Linklater, A. 249, 253, 261
Little, R. 10–11
Löwy, M. 57
Lukács, G. 8, 22, 195–7, 205–6 210–11, 236, 254–6
Luporini, C. 30
Luxemburg, R. 45, 54–7, 106, 126 139, 182–3, 196, 242, 254–5

Maclean, J. vii, 249, 253, 257, 259
MacLeod, A. 121
MacNeal, R. H. 120
Machiavelli, N. 35, 83
Magdoff, H. 205, 232
Maitan, L. 135
Mandel, E. 135, 212, 217, 225, 233 239, 244–5, 248, 254–5
Mao 3–4, 97, 99, 112–15, 122, 140 153–4, 205
Marcuse, H. 87, 135, 206, 254–5
Mariategui, J. G. 150
Marx, K. vii, 1, 13, 19, 27–30, 33–5 38–9, 43–4, 60, 63, 74–6, 139–40 167, 196–7, 207–8, 214, 216, 221 245, 252–5, 257 and Engels, F. 31 36, 40; see also Engels, F.

Subject Index

'accumulation on the world scale' 220; see also Amin, S.
'actual socialism' 69, 118, 209, 243–5
Albania 148; and China 105
alienation 3, 6, 70, 248
anthropologists, French 225
anticolonialism 91
anticommunism 91
antimilitarism 55–6; see also Liebknecht, K; peace; peace movement
anti-hegemony see hegemony
arms race 101, 209, 247
Asiatic mode of production 37–8, 221–2
Austromarxists 42, 46, 57, 59–64, 206

'backwardness' 113
balance of power 27, 63, 169, 188, 249
'balance of interests' 249
Bolsheviks 77–9, 195, 199; Decree on Peace 78; foreign policy 78–9
bourgeoisie: national 51, 104
Brest-Litovsk, Treaty of 164

capital 221; centralization of 47; concentration of 47; export of 44, 76, 78; finance 47–8, 58–9, 63; industrial 37; internationalization of 48; merchant 37; nationalization of 48; organic composition 47
capitalism 28, 54, 81, 140, 208, 212, 219–20, 226; as mode of exchange 212; as mode of production 212–13, 224; general crisis 70, 87–8; progressive nature of 37–8, 212; self-destruction 54–5; state monopoly capitalism 233, 240
'catastrophes' 55, 107, 242, see also Luxemburg, R.
Centre and Periphery 22, 54, 77, 139, 217–23, 231, 233–4, 243; division of labour 220; semi-periphery 220

China 96–116, 122, 210, 237; and Albania 105; contradictions 22, 97, 99–100, 112–16; 'four modernizations' 98, 100; and Soviet Union 97–8, 101–4, 124, 146 [see also Sino-Soviet split]; state-centric approach 106; theory 21–2; and Third World 99–103, 105–6, 145–6; three worlds theory vii, 22, 97–112, 116, 178, 243
class: conflict 17, 20, 71, 73, 85, 88; external class struggle 6, 93; global classes 103–4, 247; struggle 8, 15, 28–9, 34, 85, 92–3, 126, 166, 168, 208, 222, 257, 260–1
class determination of international relations see foreign policy, class determination of
'classical international politics' 27
'classical Marxism' see Marx, K.
coexistence, peaceful of socio-economic systems 20–1, 32, 36, 39, 71, 77, 86–8, 92–4, 118, 125, 132, 156, 165, 173–5, 184, 188, 249; Chinese Version 106, 178; codification attempts 181; impossibility of 36, 52, 118; Yugoslav version 36, 118
Cold War 63, 94, 130–2, 172, 217, 229, 231, 235–7; 'new' 91, 93, 209; revisionist historians 235–6, 254–5, 258
collective security 82, 163
colonialism 6, 44, 63, 154, 188, 209; Marx's view 38–9, 63
Comecon (CMEA) 123, 127, 130, 147–8, 190, 244
Cominform (Communist Information Bureau) 123
Comintern 77–8, 80–3, 87, 121–3, 134, 140, 147, 153, 155, 183–4, 198
commodity exchange theory of law 167, 169–70; see also Pashukanis, E. B.
'common heritage of mankind 138–9, 188